101
PEOPLE
WHO ARE
REALLY
SCREWING
AMERICA

(AND BERNARD GOLDBERG IS ONLY #73)

ALSO BY JACK HUBERMAN

The Bush Hater's Handbook: A Guide to the Most Appalling
Presidency of the Past 100 Years
and
Bushit!: An A–Z Guide to the Bush Attack on Truth,
Justice, Equality, and the American Way

101
PEOPLE
WHO ARE
REALLY
SCREWING
AMERICA

(AND BERNARD GOLDBERG IS ONLY #73)

JACK HUBERMAN

BESTSELLING AUTHOR OF
THE BUSH HATER'S HANDBOOK AND *BUSHIT!*

Nation Books • New York

101 PEOPLE WHO ARE REALLY SCREWING AMERICA:
(AND BERNARD GOLDBERG IS ONLY #73)

Published by
Nation Books
An Imprint of Avalon Publishing Group
245 West 17th Street, 11th Floor
New York, NY 10011

AVALON
publishing group incorporated

Copyright © 2006 Jack Huberman

Nation Books is a co-publishing venture of the Nation Institute and Avalon Publishing Group Incorporated.

Library of Congress Cataloging-in-Publication Data

ISBN-10: 1-56025-875-6
ISBN-13: 978-1-56025-875-9

9 8 7 6 5 4 3 2 1

Book design by Maria E. Torres
Printed in the United States of America
Distributed by Publishers Group West

CONTENTS

Introduction | ix

INTRODUCTION

L ike many readers of a peculiar book called *100 People Who Are Screwing Up America (and Al Franken Is #37)* (awful title!), I concluded that its author, **Bernard Goldberg**, must be a secret liberal agent who was merely playing conservative devil's advocate to set the stage for a book about people who are *really* screwing up America. I took my cue. Enter, stage left,[1] *this* book.

But it seems I was mistaken. Strong evidence suggests Goldberg meant his *100 People* to be taken seriously.

I had forgotten that in his earlier book, *Bias: A CBS Insider Exposes How the Media Distort the News*, Goldberg (see #73), a former CBS reporter, argued that the media are pervaded by liberal bias, when of course it is *conservative* bias that prevails. The

---

1 I know, I know—I mean stage right, which to the audience is left.

right *alleges* liberal bias to help disguise the conservative bias and to pressure the media to lean even further rightward. So Goldberg is seriously wrong about *that*.

He is, however, very well qualified to write a book called *Bias*. Or one called *81 Liberals, 7 Conservatives, and 12 Others, of Whom Maybe 5 Altogether Are Really Screwing Up America*, which would be a more accurate title for his *100 People*.

Four or five of Goldberg's people could in fact have made my list. Fully thirty more might have made my Screwing Up America 500 index—but not the more prestigious, large-cap SUA 100. But Goldberg's omission of so much as a **Tom DeLay** (my #6) or **Ralph Reed** (#56) or Jack Abramoff, let alone a **Karl Rove** or **Donald Rumsfeld** or indeed *any* **Bush** administration member— and his inclusion of so many absurdly minor liberal villains— suggest that his dastardly purpose was to deflect attention from America's real screwer-uppers.

This fairly typical remark, for example, did not earn **Pat Robertson** (#55) a Bernie: "Just like what Nazi Germany did to the Jews, so liberal America is now doing to the evangelical Christians. It's no different. . . . It is the Democratic Congress, the liberal-based media and the homosexuals who want to destroy the Christians. . . . More terrible than anything suffered by any minority in history." African slavery, extermination of Native Americans—nothing compares to the way Christians are being forced to occupy the White House, Congress, the courts, and scores of powerful organizations—often under appalling conditions.

Goldberg's #3 villain? Senator Ted Kennedy, who, Goldberg charges, opposed **Clarence Thomas** (#11)'s appointment to the Supreme Court because Thomas is a *black* conservative (a standard right-wing slander and inversion: the racists are in the "Democrat" Party). Goldberg's evidence? None, of course.

Regarding Kennedy's opposition to the invasion of Iraq, Goldberg writes: "I doubt that the women and girls who were raped during Saddam's reign of terror would agree." Perhaps not . . . but it is a well-documented fact that rapes—some of them committed by U.S. troops—increased so much in post-invasion Iraq that women disappeared from the streets. The rapes have triggered an increase in "honor killings," in which male relatives murder rape survivors because the attack has "shamed" the family, a human rights group reported. "Extremists hostile to women's rights have filled the power vacuum. . . . In many areas Islamic militants now patrol the streets, beating and harassing women who are not 'properly' dressed or behaved."

So Kennedy's on Goldberg's list—but not one Bushie responsible for Mess-o-potamia, nor one GOP member of Congress. No Senator **Rick Santorum** (#23), who compares homosexuality to incest and bestiality and is a top enforcer in the DeLay-GOP-corporate corruption racket known as the K Street Project. No Senator **James Inhofe** (#33), who called global warming "the second-largest hoax ever played on the American people, after the separation of church and state," and likened the Environmental Protection Agency and the Occupational Safety and Health Administration to the "Gestapo." No Senator **Tom Coburn** (#58), who called "the gay agenda" "the greatest threat to our freedom that we face today" and said after the Columbine school shootings, "If I wanted to buy a bazooka . . . to do something, I ought to be able to do that."

And these guys—unlike Kennedy and company—are *in power*. (Or still were as of early 2006.)

Goldberg begins his book by suggesting that liberals are to blame for the increasing popularity of the f-word—but quickly excuses **Dick Cheney** for telling Democrat Patrick Leahy, on the Senate floor, to "f**k yourself" (which, Goldberg writes, "struck me as a very good and long-overdue suggestion"). The provocation? Leahy had criticized the administration's awarding of huge no-bid contracts for work in Iraq to Cheney's firm **Halliburton** (#72), which then proceeded to rob U.S. taxpayers blind by overcharging for goods and services provided (and *not* provided). Talk about *screwing* America.

But Goldberg never mentions that. He's more exercised by rap lyrics and by ribald jokes on *Will & Grace*. But not, apparently by any of the trash and porn put out by right-wing tycoon **Rupert Murdoch** (#14)'s media empire, including books like *How to Make Love Like a Porn Star* and *How to Have a XXX Sex Life* (as well as one called *100 People Who Are Screwing in America*, I mean, *Screwing UP America*, by B. Goldberg)—all well promoted on Murdoch's **Fox News** network (#28).

If Goldberg is as troubled as he says by the increasing rudeness and incivility of our public life, where in his list is Fox News host **Bill O'Reilly** (#29)? Where is **Sean Hannity** (#30), author of *Deliver Us from Evil: Defeating Terrorism, Despotism, and Liberalism*? (Yes, terrorism and liberalism. Like Astaire and Rogers, or **George W. Bush** and Saudi crown prince Abdullah.) Where is **Ann Coulter**, who told the *New York Observer* "it would be fun to nuke North Korea" and that she was "fed up with hearing about . . . civilian casualties in Iraq"? She's in *here*, disgracing position #32. (If you can't do position #32 properly, I say, don't do it at all.)

The media flap surrounding a CBS *60 Minutes* report, based on a phony memo, that Bush dodged his National Guard service—which happens to be true—earned no less than three separate entries in Goldberg's book. Need I tell you how many mentions he gave to the *utterly* bogus, infinitely sleazier, but richly financed, far more publicized, far more damaging, GOP-backed Swift Boat Veterans for Truth smear of John Kerry's distinguished Vietnam War record? Zero. Zip. Nada.

Regarding "Memogate," Goldberg quotes a former colleague of *60 Minutes* producer Mary Mapes as follows: "If you're as liberal and activist as Mary and work on the news rather than the opinion side, it creates problems." If you're *liberal* and activist. Not, evidently, if you're "former" GOP operative **Roger Ailes** (#28), CEO of Fox News, where, according to the liberal media watchdog group FAIR, conservative and Republican guests outnumber liberals and Democrats eight to one on *news* programs. No, to Goldberg, "bias" means *liberal* bias.

Where in Goldberg's book are the legions of rabid bigots, homophobes, and nut jobs who dominate the conservative movement? Where are the Jerry Falwells and **Pat Robertsons** (#55), the **James Dobsons** (#15), the **Paul Weyriches** (#9) and **Tim LaHayes** (#66) and **Laura Schlessingers** (#68) and **Bill Donohues** (#80)? Well, down at his #70, Goldberg offers one quote from a Jimmy Swaggart church sermon—"If one [gay man] ever looks at me like that [amorously], I'm gonna kill him and tell God he died" (ah, yes, Christian love)—and spends the rest of the section talking about how liberals "see 'intolerance' everywhere," including "where it is not." End of story—an awful but thankfully isolated instance of right-wing intolerance in America.

Meanwhile, way up at #7, Goldberg spends more than three pages hyperventilating over Margaret Marshall, chief justice of the Massachusetts Supreme Court, who authored the four-to-three decision legalizing gay marriage in the state in 2003. According to Goldberg, this means Marshall "feels free to dictate to everyone else what kind of America they should live in." ("What happens, for instance, if a gay couple, married in Massachusetts, moves to Georgia?" Goldberg worries. I guess the water becomes unsafe to drink. By the way, no big-time polluters or their political enablers on Goldberg's list.) "According to every survey," Goldberg writes, "an overwhelming majority of Americans oppose this dramatic change [gay marriage] in the culture." Actually, a large majority supports gay civil unions, if not marriages. In any case, as the Founding Fathers decreed, there *are* rights that even an overwhelming majority has no right to deny to even a minority of one. Could Goldberg possibly not see that it is the minority who seek to make America a "Christian nation"—one in which consenting adults could be arrested for what they do in their bedrooms—who are trying "to dictate to everyone else what kind of America they should live in"?

Goldberg is in similar denial about white supremacists, which he reduces to/quarantines as former Klansman and Republican candidate David Duke, thus whitewashing, as it were, "mainstream" Republicans and their organizations. But see, for example, #7, #54, #71, and #81. No, not in *81 Liberals*—here.

Goldberg does include a "liberal" college professor who was convicted for insurance fraud after faking a racist and anti-Semitic vandalism attack on her own car. The main cause of Goldberg's rage? The whole campus was initially "seized by righteous indignation" over the apparent hate crime. The unforgivable "political correctness" of those who *protest* hate—*that's* Goldberg's idea of what's screwing up America.

It is (weirdly) consistent, then, for Goldberg to praise the American Civil Liberties Union's defense of Nazis' right to march through Skokie, Illinois, yet make ACLU director Anthony Romero his #5 villain for the organization's zealous defense of church-state separation and of the civil liberties of Muslims after 9/11.

Goldberg says his book exposes not just "the usual suspects, the big-name windbags" but also "people who operate away from the limelight and behind the curtain." But don't look in his book for billionaire tycoons like **Richard Scaife** (#21), the **Coors** family (#53), or His Supreme Messianic Holiness **Sun Myung Moon** (#54), who all fund right-wing causes. Don't look for **James Baker** (#60), who, while representing the U.S. government in persuading foreign countries to *forgive* Iraqi debt, serves as senior counsel at a company seeking to profit by *collecting* Iraqi debt. Don't look for **Arthur Finkelstein** (#82), a political consultant described as "so secretive that some doubted whether he really existed," yet who helped elect George W. Bush, George Pataki, Senator Jesse Helms, and Israel's Benjamin Netanyahu.

No, Goldberg of course means financier-philanthropist George Soros, who had the effrontery to support Kerry and fund an anti-Bush organization in 2004—and help black students attend university in apartheid South Africa, and promote democracy in

Eastern Europe. And Goldberg means Susan Beresford, whose focus as president of the Ford Foundation is on, in her words, "racism, sexism, the environment, peace and justice." Horrors!

The right's "few rotten apples" line on the religious bigots and white supremacists in its midst also applies, of course, to corporate malefactors. Goldberg exposes Enron's Ken Lay and tsk-tsks at a few other already-busted CEOs. No mention of corporate America's successful campaign post-Enron, WorldCom, et al. to block tougher oversight of corporate accounting. No mention of the decades of successful lobbying against higher fuel economy standards by the U.S. auto industry (#16) or **ExxonMobil** (#12)'s funding of "research" to challenge the reality of global warming and its connection to fossil fuel use.

Goldberg writes that his book is "about a country where as long as *anything* goes . . . sooner or later *everything* will go." But he does not mean the Republicans' "anything goes" for HMOs, whom they have shielded from lawsuits brought by those denied treatment; for drug companies to gouge and to advertise dubious claims; for industries to spew whatever they want into the air and water; or for corporations to export jobs, evade taxes by exploiting Caribbean tax havens, and own half of Congress courtesy of DeLay-Abramoff Inc. and opponents of campaign finance reform like #47 and #79. No, Goldberg's "anything" means foul language and the Howard Stern show.

I wholeheartedly agree with Goldberg's inclusion of Paul Eibeler, the CEO of Take-Two Interactive Software, which publishes the cop-killing video game *Grand Theft Auto*. And I wholeheartedly urge Goldberg to apologize for *omitting* the **National Rifle Association** (#22), which opposes gun control laws supported by every police organization in America—but has most of the Republicans in Congress in its pocket.

Who earns three full pages' worth of Bernie's wrath at #34 (compared to Ken Lay's third of a page at #45)? Bill Moyers, whose PBS broadcasts "on war and disease and poverty and [and, you know, all that liberal crap] . . . *and, over and over and over, corporate greed* [emphasis added] have won him fans among like-minded souls everywhere, writes Goldberg, from Beverly Hills to New York's Upper West Side; from Malibu to Martha's Vineyard."

These are Goldberg's favorite villains of all: upscale liberals, especially the rich and famous, who nonetheless champion the poor and downtrodden, the environment, and all that liberal crap—and who, worst of all, *think they're right.* (Unlike conservatives.) The reason there are so many liberals on his list, Goldberg explains, is:

> their *eagerness* . . . to live up to the most embarrassing stereotypes many of us hold about today's cultural-elite liberals: that they're snooty, snobby know-it-alls . . . who think they're not only smarter, but also *better* than everyone else, especially everyone who lives in a "Red State"—a population they see as hopelessly dumb and pathetically religious. . . . this elitist condescension—this smug attitude that Middle America is the land of right-wing yahoos who are so damn unenlightened that they probably don't even know where the Hamptons are.

(Sigh.) Where to begin? (a) Your average liberal is still a very average Joe or Jane, not Goldberg's "Malibu to Martha's Vineyard" stereotype, while it was the wealthy vote that probably clinched the '04 election for Bush. (b) What could be more self-righteous and snootier than believing, like the religious right, that you and your kind alone possess the Truth and everyone else is so *literally* "damned unenlightened" that they probably don't even know where *Heaven* is? If that's not thinking you're "*better* than everyone," what is? (c) Those "right-wing yahoos" seem pretty eager to live up to the "embarrassing stereotypes" many hold about *them.* To judge by test scores, IQ scores, and surveys of public beliefs about everything from current events to the existence of angels, demons, and honest Republican leaders, millions of Americans *are* cognitively challenged—and they *are* found in higher concentrations in the red states and *do* tend to vote Republican. (As John Stuart Mill said, "Conservatives are not necessarily stupid, but most stupid people are conservative.") Funny how conservatives, who have been those most inclined to bewail the lowering of educational standards and the decline of Western civilization, are equally inclined to turn around and scream "elitist" at any liberal who points out how astoundingly ignorant so many **Americans** (#57) are. I guess it all depends. If they vote R, well then, hurray for dumbocracy.

After all, it's been a winning strategy. For decades, wrote author Thomas Frank, conservative populists have cast "the average American, humble, long-suffering, working hard, and paying his taxes" against "the liberal elite, the know-it-alls of Manhattan and Malibu, sipping their lattes as they lord it over the peasantry with their fancy college degrees and their friends in the judiciary." Conservatives "regard class as an unacceptable topic when the subject is economics—trade, deregulation, shifting the tax burden." But from George Wallace to George W. Bush, "a class-based backlash against the perceived arrogance of liberalism has been one of their most powerful weapons"—a backlash that is "workerist in its rhetoric but royalist in its economic effects," that poses as "an uprising of the little people even when its leaders . . . cut taxes on stock dividends and turn the screws on the bankrupt" (see #86).[2]

But I say, *let* Goldberg attack Barbra Streisand and Harry Belafonte. Americans are far more liberal on most issues than is supposed—and they are, I believe, increasingly aware that the real elitism in America is the government's care and feeding of the corporate and economic elite, the Republicans' *real* base.

2 Thomas Frank, "What's the Matter with Liberals?" *New York Review of Books,* May 12, 2005.

Authors of *100 People* books must perforce be elitists, too, and ignore the demands of the *demos*. I was pressed from all sides with names of merely annoying and overhyped celebs to include. I resisted heroically. The general rule was: screw up America big-time or find yourself a Bernard Goldberg book to be in.

(I will, however—with more sorrow and remorse than you can know—apologize for omitting Senators Bill Frist, Pat Roberts, Orrin Hatch, and Saxby "turn the sheriff loose and arrest every Muslim that crosses the state line" Chambliss, Rep. Bill Thomas, Katie Couric, Larry King, Wolf Blitzer, Larry Kudlow, John Gibson, David Brooks, Michelle Malkin, Bob Novak, Jerry Falwell, Pat Buchanan, Frank Luntz, Louis Farrakhan, Jessica Simpson, Tyra "I'm going to finally reveal the truth about my breasts" Banks, Christian Reconstructionist Gary North (liberals "never ask the pertinent question: Was the advent of the European in North America a righteous historical judgment of God against the Indians?"), Jeb Bush, Newt Gingrich, Billy "OxyClean" Mays, Milton Friedman, my cable TV company, Leo Strauss, Richard Perle, Brent Bozell, Karen Hughes, George Lucas, Jerry Bruckheimer, Steve Forbes, Jonah Goldberg, and Michael Medved, among many others.)

It follows that many of my names will seem awfully usual-suspect-ish. But leave out DeLay? Reed? O'Reilly? Cheney? Rove? I couldn't. I won't, I tell you.

It also follows that I made little room for liberals and lefties. Some, of course, *have* made important contributions—but mainly to the lesser screwups of bygone decades, which in their day generated innumerable critiques, of which Goldberg's *100 People* book is but a belated, outdated example: complaints about *The Culture(s) of Complaint* and *Narcissism* and victimhood; about the policing of language and behavior for "political correctness"; about support for any self-styled Third World "liberation movement," however brutal, bigoted, or misogynist; about the *Decline* of this, the *Death* of that, the *End* of the other.

But the liberal idiocies and excesses weren't as malignant nor as rampant in high places as those of the right-wing backlash we suffer through today. Yet Goldberg continues to cry "liberal domination." Where? In the **so-called liberal media** (#13)? In academia? While a majority of professors (or, as Goldberg says, "intellectual thugs") may lean left, they no longer set the agenda on campuses (see #31). As for Hollywood actors and entertainers— upon whom Goldberg lavishes so much good old-fashioned McCarthyist attention—what cabinet departments or federal agencies do they control? Where are *their* think tanks and *their* cable news network? Where is their counterpart to the vast Republican machine that includes most of the corporate lobbying community and takes in the lion's share of political donations? Is Goldberg serious? Only about stamping out all traces of liberalism in America.

This book may not change the minds of those who believe liberalism is evil, abortion is simply wrong, homosexuality is depravity, life did not evolve, Iraq was involved in 9/11, **God** (#77) chose George W. Bush to be president, and country music (#97) is good. But if this book fails to persuade even them that most of the *people* it describes are scumbags or idiots, then either I have failed or else those readers are hopelessly stranded on an ice floe of faith that, thanks to Bush and global warming, has broken off from the continent of reason—and not even photographs of Bush signing his soul over to Satan or accepting bribes from the American Petroleum Institute will change their minds. (After all, those liberal Photoshop experts can do anything these days—and will stop at nothing.)

#101: THE OBNOXIOUSLY LOUD AND CONSTANT CELL PHONE USER

The restaurant, of course, was an early casualty. And the culprit isn't necessarily at the *next* table but may be sitting across from you at your own. And it's often not just the cell phone but also the Blackberry—phone calls *and* text messages *and* e-mails. All wonderful aids to conversation—just not for the people you're actually *with*. On second thought, not for anyone.

Even worse is how the invasion of the cell phones has given public outdoor places of relaxation and beauty, like the park or the beach, the *un*relaxing, *un*beautiful atmosphere of the office. Take it outside, I say. I mean, inside.

No doubt the curmudgeons of the day grumbled likewise when the telephone was invented—but has there really been a doubling over the past decade in the need to communicate, or just in (a) fear of being alone with one's thoughts, or lack thereof; (b) the desire to appear important or popular; (c) the even more profound psychological need to ruin the lunch, journey, conversation, and/or thought process of everyone around?

Whatever the causes of OLCCPUD (Obnoxiously Loud and Constant Cell Phone Use Disorder), it's got to stop. And it will, I promise you.

#100: THE MYSTERIOUS SMILE
OF DAN (*DA VINCI*) BROWN

You don't read airport novels or thrillers. But your view is, as long as they stay on their side of the literature/mass-market-fiction border and don't bother you, you don't bother them. You may even like to know they're there should you ever need them. (Like that street you drive down to every so often.) But if they begin to stray off the reservation, raid across the border, adopt high-culture airs in an attempt at what Britain's *Observer* called the "trick of intellectual flattery" (see *Flaubert's Parrot, Galileo's Daughter, Wittgenstein's Mistress, Newton's Manicurist*, etc.) and make not just literary but grand historical and conspiratorial claims that billions of readers take seriously—if they become the best-selling hardback adult novel of all time and make their maker so rich that you sit around all day mumbling, "Why didn't *I* think of that plot"—then it's time to get the women and children into the fort and mount a punitive expedition in the *New York Review of Books* or someplace. You know—really spoil it for the author as he's gazing across his vineyards at the Mediterranean from the terrace of his château in Provence or New Hampshire.

As of October 2005, Dan Brown's *Da Vinci Code* (despite some critics deriding it as "Umberto Eco–lite," and "nothing more than a James Bond–style romp cloaked by a veneer of erudition") had been on the *New York Times* hardcover best-seller list for 135 weeks. More than 25 million copies sold. Forty-two foreign translations. Lavish movie version coming out. "In danger of becoming better known than Leonardo himself," one newspaper remarked. There was even a Da Vinci Diet. (Help yourself to bread as though it's your last supper.) One shudders to think of the thousands of would-be Browns even now foraging for wild historical speculations upon which to weave the next blockbuster novel. After all, Brown has told the press it all began when, while working as an English teacher, he finished reading a Sidney Sheldon thriller "and thought, 'Hey, I can do that.'" (Brown's own sequel tackles the Freemasons. Hey, I know—how about *The Protocols of the Elders of the Rococo*?)

The Da Vinci Code dares to ask: What if Christianity was founded not on solid, scientifically and historically proven fact but on a myth? According to *Code*, Jesus Christ did not die on the Cross; he and his *wife*, Mary Magdalene, moved to France, bought a house, and raised a family whose descendants became the Merovingian line of French kings. (Most of this is drawn from the 1982 "nonfiction" best-seller *Holy Blood, Holy Grail*. Perhaps Brown read the *Newsweek* review: "The plot has all the elements of an international thriller.") The Christ family's descendants survive to this day; they and their secret are guarded by a secret society whose past members included Leonardo da Vinci and Sandro Botticelli, who left clues about the whole story in their paintings. *Code* opens with the murder of a contemporary member, the curator of the Louvre, by an agent of the (real) Roman Catholic Church organization Opus Dei.

Brown begins by professing to tell the truth, and many readers take him at his word: On "Grail Trail" tours of Europe, tourists retracing his characters' steps have reportedly asked bewildered Louvre staff, "Is this the room where the curator was murdered?" Opus Dei was deluged with e-mails asking why it is hiding the truth about the Holy Grail.

The novel may not do Roman Catholicism any favors, but it does encourage New Age nonsense by portraying Mr. and Mrs. Christ as having cultivated pagan practices of ritual sex (the French influence?) and worship of "the sacred feminine." According to *Code*, the figure to Jesus' right in Leonardo's *Last Supper* is really Mary Magdalene. Her and Jesus' A-shaped figures together form a giant M. The V-shaped space between them refers to Magdalene's womb—the real Holy Grail. You get the picture. Or rather, you don't. Reviewing *Code*, the art historian and classicist Ingrid Rowland worried that readers may come away believing they have learned something about

Leonardo and his art. Adam Gopnik wrote in the *New Yorker*: "A cultural anthropologist, a hundred years from now, will doubtless find, in the unprecedented success of *The Da Vinci Code* during the time of a supposed religious revival, some clear sign that, in the Elvis mode, what a lot of Americans mean by spirituality is simply an immense openness to occult superstitions of all kinds."

Both critics also point out embarrassing anachronisms. Part of the novel hinges on decoding the original meaning of "Mona Lisa"—a name not used for the picture until the nineteenth century. And "Da Vinci," Rowland notes, is the one thing Leonardo would never have been called in his lifetime, "any more than 'Of Arc' was Joan's surname."

I leave up to the reader what to make of the fact that Brown's villains are devoutly Catholic as well as *gay*.

"In a world where a rich turbaned sheik takes aim at skyscrapers, discotheques, and train stations in the name of holy war," writes Rowland, *Code* satisfies readers' thirst for black-and-white certainties and for confirmation "that the West has contributed something more to humanity than McDonald's, cowboy presidents, and the stock market"—something like, for example, the Italian Renaissance, and what it stands for: civilization.

But this novel's conservatism goes a lot farther. True, it makes heroes out of humanists and villains out of churchmen, but it also peddles nostalgia for divinely ordained and sired monarchs. Outside of Republican politics, you can't get much more reactionary than that.

Rowland contrasts *Code* with another recent novel set in the Renaissance Europe, *Q*, which, unlike *Code*, suggests "that there is no secret code to make everything right" but "the secret of our own nature"—that "the answers to our woes lie plain before us, accessible to all, as they have always been: the arts of coexistence

[and] a citizen's constant vigilance, laced with a Good Samaritan's instinctive compassion."

Brown's first book was *187 Men to Avoid: A Guide for the Romantically Frustrated Woman*. From there to *The Da Vinci Code*—or, as it should have been titled instead, *187 Convoluted Absurdities to Overlook: A Guide for the Historically Credulous*—is perhaps not so great a leap. Men to avoid? Start here.

#99: BILL AND BRIAN FRANCE AND NASCAR: TANK UP!

"What's the appeal of watching . . . traffic?" wrote one commentator on National Association for Stock Car Auto Racing (NASCAR). That's pretty much how I always felt about auto racing. But in the Bush era, that prejudice has deepened and ripened, gaining complexity, roundness, and a nice finish with brisk acidity and notes of Quaker State. My sentiments were well summarized by Jonathan Miles, writing in the *New York Times*. Noting that "NASCAR dads now get to pick our presidents," Miles observed:

> For a certain segment of the population, NASCAR's raid on American culture . . . triggers the kind of fearful trembling the citizens of Gaul felt as the Huns came thundering over the hills. To these people, stock-car racing represents all that's unsavory about red-state America: fossil-fuel bingeing; lust for violence; racial segregation; run-away Republicanism; anti-intellectualism (how much brain matter is required to go fast and turn left, ad infinitum?); the corn-pone memes of God and guns and guts; crass corporatization; **Toby Keith** [#98] anthems; and, of course, exquisitely bad

fashion sense. . . . [They are] repulsed by the deep-fried spectacle of a NASCAR event, with its schizo mix of beery loutishness and Promise Keeper piety.[3]

Lest the America-hating liberal media elite have the last word, the conservative-elite *National Review* dispatched columnist John Derbyshire to put on his pith helmet and make "One journalist's journey of discovery" to "NASCAR Nation," where he discovered a "noisy and beery" crowd sporting "a lot of tattoos and a lot of Confederate flags"—in short, "a sport in which physical courage is admired, family bonds are treasured, the nation's flag [*which one?*] is honored."

What's beyond debate is NASCAR's phenomenal growth. From its rural Southern roots, NASCAR has become the fastest-growing "sport" in America. It estimates it has 75 million U.S. fans. Its TV deals are worth at least $2.8 billion; product licensing brings in $2 billion a year. "Its logo festoons everything from cell phones to honey jars to post office walls to panties," wrote Miles. "Race coverage, it can seem, has bumped everything else off television. . . . It's as if *Hee Haw* reruns were dominating prime time."

Blame it all on Bill France, Sr., who founded NASCAR in 1948. Or visit the sins of the father upon the son, Bill France, Jr., who took over as chairman and CEO in 1972—or upon *his* son, Brian France, who took the wheel in 2003. (Family dynasties are stock-car-racing's stock-in-trade.)

If, as Miles noted, NASCAR racing is "no different, fundamentally, from Friday afternoons on the West Side Highway," this, "paradoxically, makes up a major chunk of its appeal." The cars are souped-up versions of ordinary sedans—"not so different from the cars NASCAR fans use daily to pick up their groceries, shuttle their kids and get themselves to work." If NASCAR fans identify

3 Jonathan Miles, "NASCAR Nation," *New York Times Book Review*, May 22, 2005.

with their heroes more intensely than fans of other sports (PBS interviewed one who had the face of champion driver Dale Earnhardt, Jr., tattooed on his arm), it is partly, wrote Miles, because they "understand, with sharp precision, what their heroes do. Every time they drive to the 7-Eleven . . . they do the same thing."

Not always at the same speeds—although it is perhaps no coincidence that rural Americans, NASCAR's base, are statistically the most likely to be killed in traffic accidents. At any rate, fans can, uh, appreciate NASCAR drivers' risk of getting killed. Fans, suggests Miles, see their own lives *and* their potential deaths mirrored on the track, where, to date, thirty-two drivers have died in crashes. But no one denies that, as *The Wildest Ride: A History of NASCAR* observed, "without the ever-looming specter of wrecks . . . the sport would lose much of its appeal."

Whether or not the "sport" encourages DUIN (driving under the influence of NASCAR), it isn't doing much to improve America's traffic accident statistics. NASCAR is almost as much about booze and beer as it is about speed. It's a sport that traces its history back to moonshine-runners-turned-champion-drivers like Junior Johnson. Beer brands like Bush—I mean, Busch—are chief sponsors.

In 2004, despite the well-publicized DUI arrest of driver Scott Wimmer, NASCAR lifted a long-standing ban on hard-liquor advertising. NASCAR did not suspend Wimmer but did sign up Jack Daniel's, Jim Beam, and Crown Royal whisky as sponsors. As part of his endorsement deal with Crown Royal, champion driver Kurt Busch (no relation to the brewers) preached a message of responsibility. In 2005, Busch failed a roadside sobriety test (beer in his bloodlines after all?), received a citation for reckless driving, and was suspended for the remainder of the season. In 2006, however, Busch would be back—racing for the Miller Beer team. NASCAR, meanwhile, made clear it would stand by liquor sponsorship. Well, provided the ads say, "Drink responsibly and stop being a redneck, know-nothing Republican voter," maybe it's okay.

#98: TOBY KEITH AND THE BOMB-AST OF BUSH-COUNTRY MUSIC

I was ashamed of Peter Jennings in 2002 when my fellow former Canadian, who was hosting a July Fourth ABC special, asked country music star Toby Keith either to soften the lyrics of *Courtesy of the Red, White and Blue (The Angry American)*—Keith's smash-hit-bomb-and-strafe response to 9/11—or else to choose a different song to perform. Like, you invited him on, let him perform his song with his words.

And let us deplore them. *And,* briefly, country music itself, with its lyrical *and* musical cornball sentimentality and stultifying conservatism, its sheer musical *poverty,* and, more often than not, its glorification of redneck values and politics—a genre that has nonetheless invaded and occupied all of America like some political plague out of Texas. You might think of contemporary country music as basically what rural and southern whites were left with after blacks got all the *good* music. Many whites have embraced it *as* "white music." ("It is awful, but dagnabbit, it's ours.") Where there is country, can the Confederate flag be far away?

Of course there are noble exceptions to the caricature—notably, the Dixie Chicks, whose Texas-born lead singer, Natalie Maines, got her band banned from country stations owned by the **Clear Channel** (#50) radio chain and boycotted by some fans for telling a London audience in March 2003, on the eve of the Iraq invasion, that the band was "ashamed the president of the United States is from Texas."

The Chicks weren't the only victims of the backlash. As the Associated Press reported in 2004: "While Toby Keith gets airtime, Emmylou Harris [a Bush critic] gets ignored. . . . Country music artists are hardly united in their support of the war in Iraq," the story continued, "but you'd never know it from listening to the radio. While Keith, Darryl Worley and Charlie Daniels have scored hits with patriotic, war-themed songs, others such as Willie

Nelson, Merle Haggard and Nanci Griffith released anti-war, or at least questioning, songs that went nowhere." No country music radio stations would even test them, a Nashville-based market researcher said: "I've been in country music since 1972. . . . Every time we bomb somebody it's 'Hell yeah!' Let's kick their. . . .' That's where country music is coming from."

The Chicks, who won three Grammys in 2003, were shunned at the Academy of Country Music awards—which named as entertainer of the year (the envelope, please) . . . *Toby Keith*—who had said of Natalie Maines, "I'll bury her. She has never written anything that's been a hit." Granted, Maines had first said of Keith's *Courtesy* that it was "ignorant, and it makes country music sound ignorant." Well, let's see:

Now this nation that I love
Has fallen under attack. . . .
Justice will be served
And the battle will rage. . . .
And you'll be sorry that you messed with
The U.S. of A.
'Cause we'll put a boot in your ass
It's the American way.

Following an event like 9/11, *my* American way would be to quietly determine who did it and quietly determine to do what was necessary to ensure no one ever did it again—provided the remedy and punishment were proportional to the crime and did not merely make matters worse. The invasion of Iraq—which Keith, who endorsed **Bush** in 2004, supported—made matters worse. So did the mindless mass flag-waving and jingoistic braying that followed 9/11. What did pride have to do with anything? Is it only because we're so *great* that we didn't deserve the attack? Too much crowing "proud to be American" only makes one *ashamed* to be American. Individual or nation, a braggart is a braggart. But I'm Canadian, eh? What do I know?

Courtesy continues (referring to the U.S. invasion of Afghanistan):

> Man, we lit up your world
> Like the 4th of July. . . .
> Man, it's gonna be hell
> When you hear Mother Freedom
> Start ringin' her bell
> And it feels like the whole wide world is raining down on you
> Brought to you Courtesy of the Red White and Blue.

This isn't quiet steel—it isn't even *anger*: we're enjoying the fireworks, havin' a barbecue.

It's also Miller time after the violence in *Beer for My Horses*, Keith's ode to vigilantism and lynching. At first I thought he was joking. After a litany of the crime stories on the 6 o'clock news, he sings:

> Grandpappy told my pappy, back in my day, son
> A man had to answer for the wicked that he done
> Take all the rope in Texas
> Find a tall oak tree, round up all of them bad boys
> Hang them high in the street for all the people to see. . . .
> You got to saddle up your boys
> You got to draw a hard line
> When the gun smoke settles we'll sing a victory tune
> We'll all meet back at the local saloon
> We'll raise up our glasses against evil forces
> Singing whiskey for my men, beer for my horses.
> We got too many gangsters doing dirty deeds . . .

too much crime in the streets . . .
put a few more in the ground.

By 2004, patriotic, prowar country songs were on the wane, partly
because of disenchantment about Iraq. So will Nashville *think* a
little next time before cheerleading for an immediate, indiscrimi-
nate ass-kicking? Or would that just not be the American way?

#97: JOE FRANCIS, *GIRLS GONE WILD*, AND AMERICA GONE DUMB

The left has long been inclined to condemn sexploitation and
pornography, whether on feminist grounds or out of the old-left
view of eroticism as bourgeois and decadent, or out of neo-
Marxist, Frankfurt School–style hostility toward capitalism's com-
mercialization and cheapening of everything good in life,
including sex. (Don't worry, we *will* make it from Marcuse and
Fromm to *Girls Gone Wild*.)

But with the religious right in America seeking, as self-
appointed "decency" police, to impose its values on the media and
the culture, liberals may feel more inclined to *defend* raunch as
the lesser evil. This, frankly, explains why Howard Stern is not
in this book.

But there is raunch and there is raunch. And *Girls Gone Wild*
(GGW), the hugely successful video series of which I admit I have
seen only the inescapable (and censored) TV commercials, makes
Stern's TV show (which typically features some porn star or stripper
removing her clothes in the studio while Stern makes lewd to her)
look like a Shakespeare festival, vis-à-vis relative quantities of
brains, boobs, buns, and, well, bimbos. (Unless there are some
Shakespeare plays I should really bone up on.)

California-based Mantra Films, which produces GGW, sends its camera crews to popular spring-break destinations, where they invite coeds to "parties" at bars and clubs, supply them with free drinks, then get them to lift their T-shirts and display their breasts or bend and display most of their behinds—with lots of wiggling and jiggling and sometimes girl-on-girl smooching and simulated sex. Perhaps most unbearably dumb of all are the accompanying whoops and screams by all concerned. (The inventor or popularizer of the modern American whoop—part of the disastrous Southernization of America—deserves inclusion on this list.)

The "girls" are overwhelmingly white, blond, and scantily dressed (I mean to *begin* with). Most manage to look stunningly unbeautiful, thanks of course to being in GGW and to an invariable look of mindless conformity and appalling stupidity.

The mantra is that "[t]hese are just regular girls," as a male aficionado told the *Palm Beach Post*. But when they "see the camera guys in those *Girls Gone Wild* T-shirts, they just take it off. . . . The guys don't have to tell them what to do. They just do it." A woman bartender raised in supposedly licentious, godless France said: "You'd have trouble finding girls in France to do what they did last night for a video. . . . They're educated, university students, showing their breasts. I don't know. I'm 29 and I don't understand it."

Of course, the motives of Mantra Entertainment CEO Joe Francis pose no such difficulty. GGW made him a multimillionaire by the age of twenty-eight. He's sold over $100-million-worth of GGW videos and DVDs with titles like *Dormroom Fantasies*, *Wild Island Orgy*, and *Daddy's Little Girls*. Mantra has expanded the GGW line into pay-per-view specials, a feature film, and a line of clothing and other gear bearing the GGW logo.

The *Palm Beach Post* described Francis's start: He "was working on the TV show *Real TV* in 1997 and noticed that gruesome video was routinely cut. He spliced those edits—including a shotgun suicide and a woman being hit by a train—into a video called *Banned from Television* that took in $10 million in a year."

Although it has drawn fire from conservative groups, GGW seems quite well suited for the conservative Bush era, and not only in its sheer idiocy. This, after all, is R-rated porn—which is the secret of its success: It can be advertised on TV. As a hardcore magazine publisher told the *Post*, "it's a stroke of genius because it's not sex, it's girls taking their tops off." GGW's Web site boasts that it does not feature "used up porn hags" but "real college girls." Good, wholesome, all-American porn.

Francis told *Los Angeles* magazine that "feminists love us, because girls are doing what they want to do. It's like girls burning their bras in the '70s, you know?"

No it's not. It's like the opposite.

In *Macleans* magazine, Judith Timson described a group of college girls: "She and her friends talk about it constantly: How to go out and have a great time. How to make their way through a sexual landscape that somehow has upped the ante in racy behaviour . . . how not to feel like a misfit." Discussing the book *Female Chauvinist Pigs: Women and the Rise of Raunch Culture*, Timson wrote that author Ariel Levy "sees the relentless pressure women place on themselves to look a certain way as evidence of a return to 'plasticity,' a mass conforming to a Hooters ideal of what a woman should look like." Levy observed high school girls everywhere trying to "look as slutty, willing and wanton" as they could. "Hot," wrote Timson, has replaced "beautiful" as the ultimate compliment. "Snapping their thongs and baring their cleavages, these girls had astoundingly gone any sexist male one step better: they were treating themselves and each other like pieces of meat." And they made it clear it was *all about getting the guy*. As Levy said, "raunchiness and liberation are not synonymous."

And of course, it's not just high school and college girls. "I believe there is a porno-ization of the culture," said publisher Judith Regan. Throughout the popular culture, "you will see females scantily clad, implanted, dressed up like hookers, porn stars and so on, and . . . this is very acceptable." That must be why her firm—an imprint of **Rupert Murdoch** (#14)'s HarperCollins (**Bernard Goldberg**'s publisher) and a frequent publisher of conservatives like **Sean Hannity** (#30)—published porn actress Jenna Jameson's 2004 bestseller, *How to Make Love Like a Porn Star*. And why Murdoch's **Fox News** (#28) promoted it on the air.

Thank God there are still a few liberals and leftists around to defend family values.

#96: J. K. ROWLING, DIRTY *HARRY POTTER*, AND THE GOBLETYGOOK OF GOLD

They said I was mad. Attack the *Harry Potter* books, which have kids surrendering their Game Boys en masse to *read*? Which are full of whimsy and cute, funny names yet are "dark" and "morally complex"? Which the religious right wanted to ban for being "the work of the devil," for helping "disciple children into the darkest aspects of black magic," according to a video promoted by **Tim LaHaye** (#66)—a recommendation of the highest order, surely?

Why am I growling at Rowling?

For starters, the sheer scale of her success is unforgivable—not only because she's sold over 300 million books in this galaxy alone (as Charles Taylor wrote in *Salon*, "When a book sells 5 million hardcover copies in its first day, it's inevitable that there's going to be someone who slams it"), but because—well, I've never wanted to be reading what everyone else is reading. I want to read a book, not take part in a cult phenom, or what Gregg Easterbrook called "Harry Potter and the Global Marketing Campaign of Doom." (Ordered your Apple iPod engraved with the Hogwarts logo yet?)

I further confess a prejudice against the fantasy/sword-and-sorcery genres, which have conquered all before them and now threaten the very gates of . . . whatever. The *Lord of the Rings* "saga" may be forty-three volumes or sixty-six hours long and cost $300 trillion to make (grandiosity and profitability alike dictate multiple Roman-numeraled sequels; the very word "trilogy" seems to thrill the young male mind)—but it's still basically a *comic book*. And what comic books threaten, when consumed in such quantities, is our national grip on reality.

Rowling's grip on reality—if that means existing literary formulas—is firm enough. *Potter* has been compared with an earlier Japanese comic book about a boy wizard from Wales and another about three children who study in an academy of magic and battle a dark lord who killed the hero's parents—as well as with at least four earlier children's novels or series about child wizards and wizardry academies, and the 1985 film *Young Sherlock Holmes*, scripted by the director of the first two *Harry Potter* movies.

Not to mention many much earlier antecedents/models. The *Potter* theme of the orphaned/exiled child-hero who, haunted by memories of his parents and their killer, struggles to discover his true identity and mission, then takes up battle with his cosmic enemy, echoes not only Moses, Oedipus, and Hamlet but also Spiderman, Batman, and Superman. The unloved child whose mean stepparents/aunts/uncles make him/her sleep behind the stove or, in Harry's case, in a closet is standard fairy-tale fare. Been there, done that—well, read that—perhaps too often.

Potter shares with sword-and-sorcery not only the sorcery and the Teuto-Celto-medievalesque trappings—names like Voldemort (compare "Mordor") and Gryffindor—but also the hokey, comic-book spirituality. Who here hasn't *had it* with Forces of fucking Good and Evil? Anyone? I suspect **George W. Bush**'s theology—not just his ABM missile policy—was inspired by *Star Wars*. He's so convinced the Force is with him, he's convinced half the United States of it. Both Georges, Lucas and Bush, must be stopped! For the force of *Star Wars* has filled the universe of children's books and films. Harry Potter, for example, sees some of the evil wizard Voldemort in himself. Will

Voldemort, Harry's father, and Darth Vader turn out to be one and the same? That would be, like, *so cool.*

As Steven Waldman observed in *Slate,* the Potter books and LaHaye's *Left Behind* books have more in common than fans of either would like to think. Both center on conflicts between good and evil, believers and nonbelievers. Minor yet remarkable similarities: Both series involve a "tribulation" period lasting seven years. Voldemort takes the form of a lizard, LaHaye's Antichrist, that of a snake—and Harry taps into the evil world by speaking snake. In both, the good guys bear a special, protective mark on their foreheads.

Despite certain liberal themes (how badly, really, do kids still need lessons in the toleration of diversity—the Potter books' principle claim to moral and social value?), *Potter* is packed with morals, character, and, if you scrape a bit, political lessons on which George Dumbledore Bush would gladly stamp his great seal of presidential approval. Potter and his classmates constantly disobey the rules and get in trouble but in the end are winked at or praised by their professors and Headmaster Dumbledore precisely for ignoring all those *regulations* and the stuffy, broomstick-in-the-mud authorities who try to enforce them, and for using their own, well, entrepreneurial initiative to save the day. In *The Order of the Phoenix,* Harry spends as much time battling the Ministry of Magic as he does Voldemort. Newt Gingrich would have that ministry shut down before you could say abracadabra. Perhaps the only way to reform this bloated bureaucracy is through privatization, beginning with individual, tax-sheltered magic accounts.

In short, if kids really need more role models for contempt toward rules and regs (see every movie hero from Sam Spade to *Dirty* Harry to #70, *Ahnuld*)—and by extension, toward government, the Constitution, and international law—can't we just direct their attention to the Bush administration?

Meanwhile, kids are growing up deeply literate in the details of mythologies like *Lord of the Rings* and *Harry Potter* but not so well informed about the basic facts of history, geography, science. The only thing Rowling teaches kids about the world, in this hopelessly material sense, is that there's an invisible barrier in London's King's Cross Station, behind which lies a magical world. . . .

Sounds rather like . . . TV. On a recent night—granted, it was the Christmas season—the choice of movies on my rather basic cable package included *Miracle, Miracle on 34th Street, A Season for Miracles, Unlikely Angel* ("Dead country singer turns holiday helper"), *Three Days* ("Angel helps literary agent whose wife died"), and *A Christmas Carol* (ghosts), plus, for a bit of realism, *The Wizard of Oz* and *Lord of the Rings*. Over the past decade, TV has been haunted by ghosts, *Touched* by angels, *Charmed* by witches, *Buffy'*d by vampires. . . . The fall 2005 season introduced such series as *Invasion*, a prime-time drama about aliens visiting Earth; *Supernatural; Threshold; Ghost Whisperer;* and *Medium,* a drama about a psychic. ABC broadcast a "news" special that made a case for UFOs. Movie releases in 2005 included *Birth,* about the possibility of life after death, a *Bewitched* remake, and Steven Spielberg's *War of the Worlds*. "So," wrote TV critic Lee Siegel, "thanks a lot, Al Qaeda. . . . We now share with Islamic fanatics an all-consuming desire to escape into fantastical imaginings of the Beyond."

Indeed, a 2004 Gallup poll showed that 78 percent of Americans believe in angels, a large increase over ten years earlier. Only 40 percent, another poll found, believed in evolution (see #75 and #34), and most of those took it with lots of milk and sugar—that is, **God** (#77) and creationism. (God takes His black.)

"Narr" is German for "fool." Well, welcome to Narrnia.

I know, I know—the Potter books are *children's* books. And I'm not saying "no more fantasy, magic, or make-believe." But jeez Louise, we're drowning in the stuff. All I'm suggesting is a fifty- to seventy-five-year moratorium (or Mordoratorium, or Voldemoratorium) on ghosts, angels, hobbits, witches, wizards, and, while we're at it, lizards. Eventually, we may even be able to distinguish *political* fact from fiction again.

#94 & #95: MARC CHERRY, CANDACE BUSHNELL, AND DESPERATE SEX IN THE CITY AND SUBURBS

As per #97: I don't object to raunch per se on TV—especially in times like these. I say, if it upsets the right-wing morality police, great.

But my ultrasensitive detector of hazardous conservatism crackles in response to ABC's seemingly liberal, screamingly salacious, hit Sunday-night soap series *Desperate Housewives*.

Within two months of its premiere in October 2004, *Housewives* was the top-rated show on TV. The media, wrote Richard Goldstein in *The Nation*, were "galvanized by its success at a time when red-state reverence is seeping into everything." Most remarkably, *Housewives* was a hit both among bicoastal urbanites, gay men, and feminists—"the *Sex and the City* set," Goldstein noted—and, "despite its gleeful attitude toward fornication," in Bush country. "It even grabs men who never watch such sudsy stuff," Goldstein observed. "One reason is its subject: babes behaving badly. These sexy suburban sisters don't have faggot friends—or careers, like most women in sitcoms today. And this trad but funky set-up suits the *Monday Night Football* crowd just fine."

Indeed, in a "controversial" cross-promotional opening to an ABC *Monday Night Football* broadcast, *Housewives* star Nicollette Sheridan appeared in the Philadelphia Eagles' locker room dressed in a towel, dropped it, and jumped into Eagles star Terrell Owens's arms. The Federal Communications Commission (FCC) said it received 50,000 complaints, although it isn't known how many were duplicates from conservative "e-mail factories" like the Parents Television Council—which did not, as it happens, mobilize in this instance. Or how many were prompted by the fact that Sheridan is white and Owens black. (**Rush Limbaugh**, #27, said the scene reminded *him* of the Kobe Bryant case, in which the African-American basketball star was charged with sexually assaulting a white woman! Odd—I thought I saw

Sheridan jump on *Owens*. One of us must have had his TiVo set on "ass-backwards.") At any rate, the Republican-dominated FCC declined to take action against Disney-owned ABC. The usual Bushist priorities—corporate interests first, the religious right's second—prevailed (while the conservative-bred "controversy" must have done wonders for *Housewives'* ratings).

These facts perhaps hint that, despite its raunchiness and con-servatives' complaints, *Housewives* is a Trojan® horse (just a little product placement) for subversive Bushist values. The fact that the show's creator, Marc Cherry, calls himself a Republican is perhaps another.

I had a similar love-hate relationship with *Sex. And the City*, I mean. Based on a book by Candace Bushnell, that show—which is in reruns for the remainder of the twenty-first century—is a crime not against decency but against *sex*, which it succeeds, through its very matter-of-factness, in thoroughly de-eroticizing. The sex in *Sex*—instead of quietly generating the electricity for other goings-on, and instead of being a wonderful, once-in-a-life-time experience—is just another everyday event, about as sexy as that ubiquitous clinical expression, "having sex." It isn't inci-dental that the show features four supposedly smart, sophisti-cated, liberated, glamorously employed New York women who talk about virtually *nothing but* men and "relationships." Their jobs themselves seem like mere fashion accessories—part of their man-catching kits. In fact—except with regard to the terminally libidinous Samantha character—the show is fraudulently adver-tised: it would more accurately have been titled *Trying to Meet Mr. Right, Get Married, and Live Happily Ever After—Not Nec-essarily in the City*. But as they say, *Sex* sells.

Housewives is even more deceptive—and exploitative. As Goldstein writes:

The show features more unhappy couples than a **Doctor Phil** [#91] special. With a knowing smirk, it showcases infidelity, treachery and outright schadenfreude. If that sounds like a scathing indictment of Bush time, it also plays as a critique of Godless narcissism. This two-edged tenor is what allows the show to cross over from red to blue. *Housewives* is liberal on the surface but conservative at the core. . . . [A] sense of imminent retribution hovers over Wisteria Lane [*Housewives'* suburban setting]. . . . Religious conservatives are perfectly willing to be entertained by immorality; they only require that it be punished, at least eventually. . . . [Meanwhile] The right can view the show's sexual politics—women competing for men, men struggling for dominance over their wives—as fidelity to the patriarchal code. . . . What's more, a babe is a babe, a hunk is a hunk, and the joys of watching their unseemly meeting cross party lines.[4]

"In these shows," wrote *New Republic* TV critic and *Housewives* enthusiast Lee Siegel (who was also discussing two CBS TV movies), "the marital crisis is no longer caused by a society that represses women's instincts and keeps them confined in punishing unions. Rather, it's the result of a society that tells women to go out and seek their hearts' desire." For all their desperation, *Housewives'* wives—in particular, the Lynette (Felicity Huffman) character, who is struggling to transition from powerful executive to stay-at-home mom—serve as guides to help women, well, stay at home and deal with similar domestic desperations. These, however, wrote Michelle Cottle, are "cheesed- and sexed-up for melodramatic purposes"—while, presumably for male-audience purposes, "the homebound hotties parade around in tight, skimpy outfits." A little something for everybody.

4 Richard Goldstein, "Red Sluts, Blue Sluts," *Nation*, January 3, 2005.

Shows like *Housewives*, writes Siegel, "portray the dark side of feminism, implying as they do that the idea of a mutually supportive sisterhood of women free from old-boy networks and demeaning male quid pro quos is as chimerical as the classless society. They suggest that woman is as much a wolf to woman as man has always been to man—maybe even more so." All of which accords, if not with reality, at least with conservative thought: Wolf eat wolf; every she-wolf for herself. It's an ugly message *Housewives* conveys. That it does it so entertainingly (at least in the opinion of millions) only makes it worse.

#93: TUCKER CARLSON: "AS LOW AS YOU CAN GO"

Carlson—host of MSNBC's *The Situation with Tucker Carlson*, former host of PBS's *Tucker Carlson: Unfiltered* and cohost of CNN's *Crossfire*, and a contributor to the conservative *Weekly Standard* and the fashionist *Esquire*—has always been the conservative pundit I've most wanted to meet in a bar and invite outside. I guess that makes it formal and official.

It's the snide, smarmy, supercilious, smart-ass, East-Coast elitist 'tude, for one thing (Carlson on Hillary Clinton: "Every time I see her I think I could, you know, help. . . . She seems tense"), and the Young Republican look—all neatly and punchably summed up by the bow tie. And, for that matter, the name. Tucker Swanson McNear Carlson, I'm not at all surprised to learn, attended St. George's prep school in Newport, Rhode Island, and didn't bother finishing college. Sons of former chairmen of the Corporation for Public Broadcasting and stepsons of heiresses to the Swanson frozen-food fortune perhaps don't need to worry about college degrees.

Carlson claims to care about conservative ideas but not about parties. He has, in fact, pissed off Republicans more than once, such as when, after visiting Iraq in 2004 to report for *Esquire*, he reversed his support for the war and told the *New York Observer* it was "a total nightmare and disaster, and I'm ashamed that I went against my own instincts in supporting it."

Carlson, on *Crossfire*, on the *same day*: "Kerry did vote for [the war], but then he opposed it. . . . What does John Kerry think about Iraq? Who knows. Who cares."

What does Tucker Carlson think about *anything*? Who knows? The problem is his habitual . . . well, "falsehoods and misrepresentations," as MediaMatters.org put it. And his raving partisanship. And, of course, the snide, snot-nose O'Carlson factor:

- September 2002: Carlson accuses Rep. Bob Filner (D-CA) of being a liar and of committing "slander on the United States" for saying the U.S. had sold biological weapons to Iraq. *Newsweek*, that same week: "According to confidential Commerce Department export-control documents," there were "numerous shipments of 'bacteria/fungi/protozoa' to the [Iraq Atomic Energy Commission]. According to former officials, the bacteria cultures could be used to make biological weapons, including anthrax." A few months later, *Crossfire* guest Kenneth Pollack of the Brookings Institution—a supporter of the Iraq invasion—told Carlson: "Well, we sold Saddam the anthrax and we kind of looked the other way." (Carlson: "Have we done that?")
- October 2002: Carlson says the memorial service for the passionately liberal senator Paul Wellstone (D-MN), who had died in a plane crash, was "hijacked by partisan zealots and turned into a political rally. Republican friends of Senator Wellstone were booed and shouted down as they tried to speak." A "nauseating display." "Revolting." "It makes me sick." Carlson repeatedly and incorrectly referred to the service

as a "funeral"—for, as he later admitted, he hadn't actually watched it. And, as it happened, what he described *hadn't* happened. "To politicize a man's tragic death is about as low as you can go, isn't it?" said Tucker. Indeed.

- May 2003: Carlson falsely denies that any Homeland Security Department resources were used to track the plane of Texas Democrats who left the state in order to thwart a quorum on **Tom DeLay** (#6)'s scandalous redistricting plan.

- March 2004: **Halliburton** (#72) "is actually losing money on its Iraqi contracts." Not even Halliburton claimed that.

- May 2004, after the Associated Press reported that fifteen *state* Democratic parties were "determined to ensure that gays and lesbians are part of their convention ranks": "*The Democratic Party* has announced a new affirmative action plan for gays, lesbians, and cross-dressers." Previously, Carlson referred to "cross-dressing and abortion" as "two great Democratic values that go great together." Perhaps he would know.

Carlson seems to feel a special need to mock gays and show how virile and into women he is. (As blogger Daily Howler wrote: "Carlson runs with a tough, rude crowd, and occasionally wants to be one of the boys.") Also how un-uptight, un-PC he is—unlike "humorless Democrats." Thus: "One area of liberal phenomenon [*sic*] I support is female bi-sexuality—this apparent increased willingness of girls to bring along a friend. That's a pretty good thing." And, when asked which woman he would most like to be: "Elizabeth Birch of the Human Rights Campaign, because you'd be presiding over an organization of thousands of lesbians, some of them quite good-looking." And: "You will admit that at least 40 percent of any vote in a Democratic race is humorless feminists." And: Women "want to be listened to, protected and amused. And they want to be spanked vigorously every once in a while." Come on . . . *you* don't, Tucker?

- June 2004: "I must say, though, that most of the hate I run across these days seems to be coming from the left. Check out MoveOn.org sometime if you don't believe me." Check out #9, #15, #20, #22, #23, #24, #27, #30, #31, #32, #33, #53, #58, #65, #66, #71, #80, #81, and #84 if you *do* believe him.
- "I think Michael Moore is loathsome . . . not because he dislikes Bush, but because he seems to dislike America." That's true—*if* you equate corporate greed, political incompetence, hypocrisy, cronyism, fraudulently advertised wars, and weak gun laws with *America.*
- July 2004: "That's a total lie. . . . Nobody prevented anyone from voting" in Florida in 2000. Thousands of voters were purged from Florida's voter lists, said Carlson, because "they were convicted felons." In its 2001 report, the U.S. Commission on Civil Rights said "Florida's reliance on a flawed voter exclusion list had the result of denying African Americans the right to vote." *Orlando Sentinel*: "[Katherine] Harris's office . . . mistakenly [sic] purged thousands of voters who did not have criminal records. A disproportionate number of them were black." Salon.com: "A close examination suggests thousands of voters may have lost their right to vote . . . with as many as 15 percent of names incorrectly identified as felons." Governor Jeb Bush: "These are issues that must be addressed."
- August 2003: "I draw the line at honesty. . . . I try to tell the truth." Tucker, anything you put your mind to . . .

#92: LONNIE "BO" PILGRIM: PRIDE, POULTRY, PREACHING, PREJUDICE, AND 31 BILLION POUNDS OF CHICKEN SHIT

The septuagenarian chairman and principal owner of Pilgrim's Pride Corp. of Pittsburgh, Texas, America's second-largest poultry producer, is a Texas legend. The legend was described in a *Philanthropy World* profile in 2003:

> Lonnie Pilgrim . . . stands for something profoundly grand. "Bo" . . . is a gentleman of impeccable character, a generous spirit, and a crusader for Christ. . . . Along the path of taking a small farm supply store to a $2.5 billion company, Bo . . . kept honesty and integrity at the forefront. . . . [H]e is on a first-name basis with many employees. He refers to them as "partners," and he takes an interest in their needs—ensuring that troubled employees receive counseling and an opportunity to know Jesus. . . . "He is respected by all who know him because of his high ethical standards."

After suffering a heart attack in 1982, the profile continues, "Bo turned his attention to developing a more nutritious product," and introduced "the world's first fresh boneless chicken . . . followed by the first lean chicken with less fat and cholesterol and fewer calories [and] nutritionally enhanced EggsPlus with Omega 3, Omega 6 fatty acids, and vitamin E."

But Bo's "greatest joy comes from witnessing and introducing the plan of salvation to as many people as he possibly can." That refers to a pamphlet Bo published which he hands out everywhere he goes, inviting readers to receive Jesus as their Savior. "Inside the back cover is a crisp $20 bill, which he says encourages people to hold on to it."

That kind of generosity seems to be a Bo habit. In 1989, he handed out $10,000 checks on the Texas Senate floor during debate on a bill he supported to gut state workers' compensation laws. (Meatpacking is one of the most dangerous jobs.) Bo left the "payee" line of the checks blank for lawmakers to fill in themselves, presumably to avoid any appearance of, like, bribery or anything like that. The episode prompted the next legislative session to pass ethics reforms. Getting Texas politicians to pass ethics reforms *is* the stuff legends are made of.

From 1980 to 1995, Pilgrim's paid Texas's notoriously lax environmental regulators a record $825,000 in fines for pollution, improper wastewater discharges, and "nuisance odors." We're talking chicken carcasses and vast amounts of shit, containing arsenic and bacteria such as salmonella and E. coli that make their way into surrounding streams and wells. Exceptionally high rates of bacterial meningitis and other diseases caused by fecal contamination were found in areas surrounding poultry plants in East Texas and Arkansas and had claimed at least thirteen lives, according to a 1996 exposé by Mark O'Connor in *Touchstone* magazine.

Bo (is "Lonnie" too formal? too polysyllabic?) meanwhile sponsored "scientific research" claiming, contrary to numerous studies, that his industry does *not* cause environmental problems. That sponsorship, wrote O'Connor, "completely corrupted" Texas's leading agricultural research centers, which delivered "watered down, misleading, pseudoscientific research in order to protect [Lonnie Pilgrim's] interests."

By this time, perhaps not coincidentally, **George W. Bush** was governor of Texas. Bo was one of Bush's biggest gubernatorial and, later, presidential campaign contributors. By 2002, Pilgrim's Pride was the tenth largest recipient of federal agricultural subsidies and that year received U.S. Department of Agriculture (USDA) meat marketing contracts worth more than $12 million.

But as it is written: To him that buyeth influence and preacheth salvation, but scrubbeth not, shall come affliction. In 2002, in the wake of an outbreak across the Northeast of a bacterial infection called listeria that killed eight people, hospitalized dozens, and caused three miscarriages, listeria was discovered at a Pilgrim's plant in Pennsylvania, leading to the largest recall of meat in U.S. history. "A federal meat inspector said his USDA superiors previously overruled inspector recommendations to close the plant, which had mold and algae growing on its walls and ducts that dripped on processing tables," Texans for Public Justice reported. Inspectors also complained that Pilgrim's often cleaned up the plant prior to inspections because the USDA gave it a week's notice before it showed up. On top of it all, USDA failed to close the plant until six weeks after the outbreak.

New regulations requiring tougher inspections for listeria had been proposed by the Clinton administration in 2000, but the Bushies, at the meat industry's wish, had failed to adopt them, insisting that existing rules were adequate.

Another illness Bo has helped spread is hate. From 2000 to 2002, he was the second largest contributor to a group called the Free Enterprise PAC, which in 2002 targeted for defeat six moderate Republican Texas legislators that it deemed too tolerant of gays, abortion, and assisted suicide; the group attacked the six in mailings that included photos of "suicide doctor" Jack Kevorkian and of two men kissing. The PAC's largest contributor also gave to the political campaign of former KKK Grand Wizard David Duke.

In 2004, People for the Ethical Treatment of Animals (PETA) released a video showing workers at a Pilgrim's plant in West Virginia "stomping on chickens, kicking them, and violently slamming them against floors and walls. Workers also ripped the animals' beaks off, twisted their heads off, spat tobacco into their eyes and mouths, spray-painted their faces, and squeezed their bodies so hard that the birds expelled feces—all while the chickens were still alive."[5] The plant had been named a KFC Supplier of the Year. It also seems to have been the one where former Army reservist Lynndie England worked before going to work torturing featherless bipeds at Abu Ghraib prison in Iraq. Maybe Bo also had a Pentagon contract to train reservists for duty in the war on terrorism.

---

5 "Cruelty in the KFC Slaughterhouse," PETA.org.

By the way, Bernard Goldberg preferred to include PETA's president, Ingrid Newkirk, on his list. Can't entirely blame him. Newkirk, 1983: "Six million Jews died in concentration camps, but six billion broiler chickens will die this year in slaughterhouses."

#91: PHIL "DR. PHIL" MCGRAW: FOUR MORE LIVES WHIPPED INTO SHAPE— RIGHT AFTER THESE MESSAGES

In his book *SHAM: How the Self-Help Movement Made America Helpless*, author Steve Salerno notes that the most likely customer for a self-help book is someone who bought a similar book in the past eighteen months. (Which it's probably too late to return.) As Salerno says of the "self-help and actualization movement," or "SHAM": In no other phenomenon have American consumers "invested so much . . . based on so little proof of efficacy."

Of course, it depends on what's meant by self-help. The number of Americans who seek happiness through cosmetic surgery (nearly 12 million procedures were performed in 2004) is gaining on the number that turn to psychotherapy. But these two seemingly divergent consumer choices have much in common. In an economy "that grows ever more ruthless and competitive," wrote Laura Miller in *Salon:*

> "constant self-improvement" is presented to us as "the only reliable insurance against economic insecurity." The result is what [Micki] McGee [author of *Self-Help, Inc.: Makeover Culture in American Life*] calls "the belabored self," the personality as a perpetual renovation project, driven by the fear that . . . "it is no longer sufficient to be married or employed." When your spouse might leave you or your

boss might fire you at any moment, you have to be ready to hit the market again at any time; "it is imperative that one remains marriageable and employable."

For McGee, the problem is that instead of leading toward political activism, self-help "deceives us into thinking that we can function in complete independence, that every problem in our lives can be addressed as a purely individual challenge."

Some who "crave a counterforce to the brutality of the marketplace," notes Miller, "seek it in church and a retreat to 'traditional values.'" Others, however, "look at the ever-widening gap between rich and poor in this country" and bet on a "success" guru in "the giddy hope . . . of achieving Life Mastery, of becoming highly effective and having it all."

Phil McGraw, aka "Dr. Phil"—the hugely popular psychologist whose syndicated *Dr. Phil Show* debuted in 2002—shares with other SHAM artists the neat packaging of simple instructions for success. His books, for example, reveal "The seven keys to weight loss freedom," "The five-step action plan," and "Your step-by-step plan for creating a phenomenal family." They are packed with numbered lists, bullet points, charts, and sidebars—"like little flowcharts to happiness," as the *New Republic*'s Michelle Cottle put it.

McGraw's real genius, however, was to grasp that the touchy-feely, victimhood-embracing 1970s are long gone—that in the **Bush** era, the treatment people crave, for foreign and domestic problems alike, is, as #98 put it so daintily, "a boot in your ass." On his show, on speaking tours, in his column in mentor Oprah Winfrey's *O* magazine, and in his books—at least five of which have hit number one on the *New York Times* best-seller list—Dr. Phil, a big, bald Texan and self-described "country boy," dispenses a manly, no-nonsense, stop-sniveling, straighten-up-and-fly-right, that's-a-direct-order brand of frontier justice—I mean, self-help—befitting the oh-oh (00) decade.

At the same time, McGraw, shrewd showman that he is, knows what his estimated 6.6 million voyeurs—I mean, viewers—want: shameless self-exposure of the sordid details of his guests' lives. Wrote Cottle:

> [McGraw] relies on much the same exploitative freak-show format as Jerry Springer or Jenny Jones, with everyone from drug-addicted housewives to love-starved transsexuals spinning their tales of woe for a salivating audience. But to help himself—and his audience—feel less icky about their voyeurism, Dr. Phil exposes America's dark side under the guise of inspiring hope and change. In Dr. Phil's formulation, cheating couples who air every nauseating detail of their sex lives on national television aren't shameless media whores, they are troubled souls courageous enough to seek help.

How relevant to most viewers, at the end of the day, is a case such as parents struggling with a child exhibiting homicidal tendencies? Dr. Phil "reassures us that the publicity is beneficial to other families because . . . a six-year-old with low-grade behavior problems today could, if left unchecked, turn out to be a serial killer down the road."

Indeed, McGraw's tendency to drag children into the cesspool of daytime television is particularly disturbing, Cottle observed: "Despite his oft-professed obsession with protecting kids from adult realities, McGraw is constantly spotlighting the little darlings on his very adult show." Bad enough that they and their friends, classmates, and teachers will see or hear about "their disgusting, pathetic parents on national television, talking about, for instance, how [dad] liked to do it with his mistress on his and [mom's] bed when poor [mom] was off tending to her dying father"; kids themselves are interviewed about all the things that go on at home. We see a wife and her philandering husband screaming at each other in front of their three kids. We hear a recorded phone conversation between a fourteen-year-old—who is in the studio—and a twenty-eight-year-old pedophile.

The show's pornographic aspect hasn't prevented conservatives from applauding McGraw for his willingness to pass moral judgment and denounce idiocy and irresponsibility. *Newsweek* cheered his assault on "the culture of victimology." **Myron Magnet** (#39)'s *City Journal* pointed to McGraw's popularity as proof of Americans' "growing thirst for moral direction," praising him for "doing exactly what the elite media has attacked George W. Bush for doing."

But some people *do* need to learn to love themselves, not just to be dressed down. Many *are* victims. McGraw merely replaces the old clichés and oversimplifications with their opposites. Regardless of your background or circumstances, your problems are evidently all your own fault: "You create your own experience," McGraw writes; "There is no reality, only perception." Written like an evolution-denying, Iraq-war-promoting Bushite. ("We create our own reality," said the Bush aide who first termed non-Bushies "the reality-based community.")

Yet in "telling it like it is," as McGraw boasts, the apostle of personal responsibility takes the "self" part out of self-help. Dr. Phil's core message, wrote Cottle, is: " 'If you know what's good for you, you'll listen to me.' " While McGraw may insist that "I don't expect you to substitute my judgment for yours," that is precisely what he expects. It's the premise of his entire show:

> [McGraw] has a blueprint for how to overcome virtually every life challenge. . . . For a nervous, insecure nation, nothing is more seductive than a stern yet benevolent father figure offering to lift the burden of decision-making from our shoulders. . . . (Think of him as the George W. of daytime television.) . . . Forget personal responsibility, what McGraw is promoting is sweet submission to his

authority. And, as his popularity grows, so do his ego and his ambitions, to the point where it is increasingly hard to tell if Dr. Phil sees himself more as America's daddy or its messiah.[6]

And you can call me narrow-minded, but I'm not worshipping any savior named Phil.

#90: THE UNREAL MARK BURNETT

"Reality" television (RTV) is, of course, an escape into fantasy—and that's all very well. But when fantasy labeled "reality" becomes a cultural phenomenon of the magnitude of RTV, we'd better at least consider what other specific and pernicious false-hoods are being sold.

So much ink has been spilled, so many high brows furrowed over the menace of RTV since it invaded our shores from Europe around 2000, when the mother of all RTV shows, CBS's *Survivor*, debuted. On the other hand, most critics are so loathe to look stuffy and unhip about pop culture that many have cheered RTV, or at least its better products, such as *Survivor* and NBC's *The Apprentice*—both produced by RTV pioneer/genius Mark Burnett, a British-born former paratrooper and T-shirt salesman.

There *have* been more grossly objectionable reality shows—above, or rather, below all, *Extreme Makeover* and *The Swan*, in which women happily undergo surgery to make themselves more marketable. But highbrow celebrations of RTV make it all the more incumbent upon us, standing here today, to *take* a crotchety stand, especially vis-à-vis the "better" shows.

---

6 Michelle Cottle, "Daddy Knows: The Bad Doctor," *New Republic*, December 27, 2004.

"People are missing the real life in their lives," wrote a culture editor in Germany (which exported *Fear Factor* to the United States around the time *Survivor* debuted) to explain RTV's huge success. In other words, having to get your kids to school, suck up to your boss, and put up with your mother-in-law is *not* "real," but a show about being part of a warring tribe on a desert island, eating worms, backstabbing your way to a job with Donald Trump, or winning $1 million by "surviving"—a show highly structured and heavily edited "so as to give everyday life the scripted and directed structure of film," as critic Lee Siegel wrote—is. Give me a commercial break. It'll be much more real.

Like all commercial TV, only more so, *The Swan* and its illk are at bottom commercials for consumerism. They sell the repugnant proposition that not only can and should you radically alter your face and body to better compete socially, sexually, and professionally — not only should you submit to and embrace appearance-based discrimination—but more broadly, that whatever your problem (real or imaginary), there's something you can and should *buy* to remedy it. The answer is not in your inner resources, meager as they are, but in your pocketbook.

The same, it would seem, could hardly be said of *Survivor* or *The Apprentice*, whose contestants rely on native wit, cunning, brains, and balls. And of course, boobs, buns, pecs, abs, and winning smiles: even while replacing actors with less "perfect" (and much cheaper) "real" people—even while exploiting viewers' satisfaction in watching contestants be rejected and humiliated (as viewers themselves often are in *their* lives)—Burnett is not *too* wedded to "reality" or to character to cast hunks and babes in his shows. Or for that matter, beer, car, and snack-food brands: *Survivor* is a pioneer not just of RTV but of ZP (zap-proof) TV; it is filled with product placements—stealth advertising—to foil viewers who use their TiVo-type video recorders to "zap" out commercials.

But it is what the stories themselves sell that should cause you to join me in walking around mumbling about the end of civilization.

The product is not, in the end, physical perfection; your diet and exercise program alone isn't going to cut it in the wilderness of modern life. You'd better perfect your psychological and political skills as well. RTV is there to help you learn. Whether on Manhattan Island or one of the Marquesas, civilization is far away, and it is your scheming, backstabbing fellow "contestants" that are the wildlife, red in tooth and claw, over which you must prevail. That life is a Hobbesian war of all against all, that alliances and friendships are merely means to individual victory and its rewards ($1 million, to be precise, on *Survivor*)—and that you're either a winner or a loser— is a given, indeed, the whole premise of a show like *Survivor*. Admittedly, it wouldn't be much of a *game* show otherwise. Still, call me a communist, but it's not a very idealistic outlook. And you know what? *Anti*utopianism is not only a lot uglier than utopianism but just as false. Life isn't much like *Survivor*. Whether life will increasingly *imitate* the art of Mark Burnett is another matter.

#89: STEVEN ROSEN
AND THE AMERICA-ISRAEL
POLITICAL ACTION COMMITTEE (AIPAC)

AIPAC is a Washington-based organization that lobbies the U.S. government on behalf of Israeli interests as it sees them. The trouble is with the "as it sees them" part—and the small matter of U.S. interests.

As a lover and supporter of Israel—one who believes (a) that the injustice done to Arab Palestinians by the creation of Israel is outweighed by the justice of giving the world's most long-persecuted people a haven and national homeland in their original homeland—that indeed, the world, including the Arab-Muslim world, which is responsible for its share of that persecution, *owed* it to the Jews; (b) that the "Israeli-Palestinian conflict" is not in the end about the Palestinians (whose Turkish, Egyptian, and Jordanian Muslim rulers for eight hundred years never dreamed of granting Palestinian independence—not that there was any Palestinian nationalist movement or indeed "Palestinians" until Zionism inspired them) but about the determination of Israel's enemies to wipe the Jewish state off the map and re-Islamize "Muslim land"; (c) that after the 1967 war, Israel should have withdrawn immediately from most of the conquered territories, less for moral reasons (Israel didn't instigate the war;[7] Israel from the start welcomed a two-state solution—none of its enemies did), much less because it would buy Israel peace, than because the territories would prove more trouble to Israel than they were worth—I question whether, on the whole, AIPAC's influence has been in the best interests of either the United States or Israel.

Israel is unfairly singled out for criticism. It's also singled out by the U.S. as by far the largest recipient of foreign aid. Surely that entitles Americans to criticize Israeli policies if they feel they're not in America's best interests as *they* see them—and to question a lobby for *any* other country's interests having the kind of influence in Washington that AIPAC has, especially if that "influence" extends to helping a foreign government illegally obtain classified U.S. national security information.

It doesn't help at all that AIPAC's support for Israel has tended to mean support for the policies of Ariel Sharon's (former) Likud Party, that AIPAC supported the war in Iraq, and that it appears to support U.S. military action against Iran and Syria.

While AIPAC's sixty-to-a-hundred-thousand-strong membership is *babkes* compared to, say, the **NRA** (#22)'s 4 million-plus, AIPAC is "unique in the top tier of lobbies," wrote Michael Massing in *The Nation*, because its concerns are for the well-being of a foreign nation. AIPAC "is widely regarded as the most

7 "Our basic objective will be the destruction of Israel. The Arab people want to fight."—Egyptian President Nasser, one week before it began.

powerful foreign-policy lobby in Washington." Its members "shower millions of dollars on hundreds of members of Congress on both sides of the aisle." Its main goal "is making sure there is 'no daylight' between the policies of Israel and of the United States." The *New York Times* in 1987 described AIPAC as "a major force in shaping [U.S.] policy in the Middle East." AIPAC "has gained power to influence a presidential candidate"s choice of staff . . . and to serve as a catalyst for intimate military relations between the Pentagon and the Israeli army. Its leading officials are consulted by State Department and White House policy makers, by senators and generals." "You are the most effective general interest group . . . across the entire planet," Newt Gingrich once told an AIPAC gathering.

U.S. policy in the Israeli-Arab conflict is far from one-sided. We sell plenty of weapons to Arab states, and it isn't Israel that has the oil. Still, AIPAC's clout has yielded overwhelming congressional votes expressing unqualified support for Israeli policies—and arrogance and excess on AIPAC's part.

According to Jeffrey Goldberg in the *New Yorker*, it was Steven Rosen, then AIPAC's director of foreign-policy issues, who in the early 1980s introduced the idea that AIPAC could influence policy not only in Congress but within the Pentagon, the State Department, and the National Security Council.

In 1992, AIPAC president David Steiner was caught on tape boasting that he had "cut a deal" with the Bush I administration to give more aid to Israel and was "negotiating" with the incoming Clinton administration to appoint a pro-Israel secretary of state. "We have a dozen people in [Clinton's] headquarters, and they are all going to get big jobs," Steiner said.

In May 2005, following an investigation that begun in 2002, the FBI arrested Larry Franklin, a senior Pentagon analyst on Iran with close ties to Deputy Defense Secretary Paul Wolfowitz and Undersecretary of Defense Douglas Feith, on suspicions of espionage. Franklin—who was allegedly found in possession of eighty-three classified documents and who wanted the U.S. to undertake "regime change" in Iran—was charged with providing "highly classified" information about U.S. strategy regarding Iran and about potential attacks on U.S. forces in Iraq to AIPAC's Steven Rosen and a junior colleague. (Rosen had told Jeffrey Goldberg that his main role at AIPAC was to collect evidence of "Iranian perfidy.") The two were fired by AIPAC and, in August 2005, indicted for passing the information on to the Israeli government. (Rosen's lawyer, Abbe Lowell, also represented GOP lobbyist-criminal Jack Abramoff.)

According to Robert Dreyfuss in *The Nation*, the FBI investigation was also "looking at a group of neoconservatives who have occupied senior posts at the White House, the Pentagon and in Vice President **Cheney**'s office . . . to ascertain whether Sharon recruited or helped place in office people who knowingly, and secretly, worked with him to affect the direction of U.S. policy in the Middle East"—that is, "the possibility that U.S. officials . . . are working on Sharon's behalf." The most likely targets were Feith and Harold Rhode of the Office of Net Assessment, the Pentagon's in-house think tank. In 2002, Feith and Rhode had formed the Pentagon's Office of Special Plans (OSP), which reportedly fabricated exaggerated intelligence reports on the threat from Iraq. Along with **Michael Ledeen** (#26) of the **American Enterprise Institute** (#7), the two had also taken part in a rogue Pentagon initiative to discuss regime change in Iran and Syria.

You see, it's not good, this secret scheming to spread war. Nor is breaking the laws of the country that provides Israel with tens of billions of dollars in aid and military technology every year—if that is what was done. It is foolish for purported friends of Israel and America to take America's support so for granted and repay it with such insults.

#88: RICHARD WILKINS AND THE MORMON-EVANGELICAL-ISLAMO-FASCIST AXIS OF EXTREME EVIL

Richard Wilkins was the mayor of Sunnydale in the television series *Buffy the Vampire Slayer*, who sold his soul to demons in return for never aging. But the Richard Wilkins we're concerned with is a law professor at Brigham Young University (BYU) in Utah who has literally made a pact with different demons.

In recent years, while leaders of the Christian right have made a habit of attacking Islam with some of most lively and colorful vilification in the history of American religious bigotry (Jerry Falwell: Muhammad was "a demon possessed-pedophile" and "a terrorist"; also see #9, #55, and #84), some, recognizing the affinities between Christian and Muslim fundamentalism, have forged ties even with Islamic clerics and governments that endorse jihad against America—all for the greater good of attacking homosexuality, women's rights, and the rest of the moral corruption for which Western societies must and will be destroyed by the hand of God.

Wilkins heads the World Family Policy Center (WFPC) at BYU, which is owned and operated by the Church of Jesus Christ of Latter-Day Saints, aka the Mormons. He also runs the Web site DefendMarriage.org, which, along with the WFPC, is devoted to "defending the family," meaning, above all, fighting gay marriage —and attacking homosexuality itself, abortion rights, birth control, condom use, sex education, secularism, women having careers, women going outside with their faces uncovered . . . (you'll see—one step at a time). In November 2004, Wilkins and the WFPC helped organize a conference in Doha, Qatar, that brought together the Mormons, Cardinal Alfonso Trujillo, who campaigns against condoms on behalf of the Catholic Church, and Mahathir Mohamad, the former Malaysian prime minister who jailed his deputy for alleged homosexuality. Mohamad has also suggested that those killed on 9/11 were, like civilians killed in Iraq and Afghanistan, just "collaterals whose deaths are necessary for operations to succeed," and that "the Jews rule the world by proxy" and "get others to fight and die for them." (But, he added, "1.3 billion people [Muslims] cannot be simply wiped out," as the Jews evidently intend.)

Dominating the Doha conference was Sheikh Yusuf al-Qaradawi, dean of Qatar's College of Shariah and Islamic Studies. Regarded by some as the world's foremost Islamic scholar, Qaradawi approves of wife-beating and the death penalty for sodomy and believes that "resisting the invaders" of Iraq is a religious duty. He has been accused of supporting suicide bombers and has been banned from the United States since 1999 for advocating violence and for spelling his name with a Q rather than an identical-sounding K. Qaradawi is famous throughout the Arab world for his appearances on Qatar-based al-Jazeera television and in 2001 visited the Vatican as a guest of the Pope. He also supervises IslamOnline.net, where, as Brian Whitaker reported in the *Guardian*, he describes homosexuality as an abominable, depraved, foul, and illicit practice that is punished by eternity in the fires and reality shows of Hell, and oral sex as a disgusting Western practice resulting from Westerners' habit of "stripping naked during sexual intercourse" (see diagram, p. 483). IslamOnline provides links to and "scientific" information from U.S. Christian groups like United Families International, which blames condoms and sex education for the spread of HIV, and the National Association for Research and Therapy of Homosexuality (NARTH), which promotes "sexual reorientation therapy" to "cure" gays. NARTH, whose views are rejected by all the main professional bodies in the U.S., Whitaker notes, "reciprocates by welcoming IslamOnline's 'very useful contribution to the ongoing dialogue.'"

The Qatar government—which sponsored the conference and assigned Wilkins and the WFPC to arrange preliminary meetings in other countries—"rejects basic family rights legislation such as the international Convention for the Elimination of Discrimination Against Women . . . using 'religious precepts' as an excuse," Whitaker noted. (Qatar also owns al-Jazeera, whose views are perhaps reflected by the Al Qaeda tapes it broadcasts.) The Doha conference was officially held to "celebrate the 10th anniversary of the UN's Year of the Family," but "in reality, it brought together some of the world's most socially conservative religious forces" to " 'defend the family' and fight progressive social policies" at the UN.[8]

A week after the conference, Wilkins's lobbying efforts somehow got a Qatar-sponsored, "profamily," anti–women's rights resolution approved by the UN General Assembly—without a vote. "For the first time at the UN, we had the anti-family powers scrambling by surprising them," boasted the Mormon magazine *Meridian*.

But it wasn't the first time these seemingly disparate forces of darkness had joined forces to fight social progress. In 1996, at the UN's Habitat 2 conference in Istanbul, where delegates sought recognition of the fact that "various forms of the family exist" and are perhaps entitled to "legal support," Wilkins gave a speech challenging this. It won him a warm embrace by the Saudi ambassador and persuaded the Arab delegations not to sign the Habitat agenda unless it was altered to define "marriage" as a relationship between "husband and wife" and to delete all references to abortion. And so it came to pass. The event is known to "profamily" activists as the Istanbul Miracle.

The Christian and Muslim far right got even cozier in 2000 at the UN's Beijing+5 conference to promote "gender equality in the twenty-first century," where they banded together to keep out of the agreement language that could be construed as condoning abortion or suggesting that women should have the right to work outside the home. Joining in this holy alliance were the Vatican and

8 Brian Whitaker, "Fundamental Union," *Guardian Unlimited*, January 25, 2005.

countries like Iran, Algeria, Syria, Libya, and Pakistan. At the time, as Michael Lind noted in the *Observer,* "the Taliban in Afghanistan were banning women from working and forcing them to wear the veil" while "the Southern Baptist Convention urged wives to 'submit graciously to the servant leadership of their husbands.' "

But the logic of a Christian-Islamist axis could be discerned years earlier. In 1989, the conservative Catholic pundit/politician Pat Buchanan—a frequent critic of Israel who has defended accused Nazi war criminals and praised Hitler and Francisco Franco—denounced Salman Rushdie for writing "a defamatory novel [*The Satanic Verses*], a blasphemous assault on the faith of hundreds of millions." When a caller to the *Larry King Live* show asked conservative moralist William Bennett, then the U.S. drug czar, "Why build prisons? Get tough like Arabia. Behead the damned drug dealers," Bennett replied, "morally, I don't have any problem with that at all," and went on to call for more executions in the U.S.

This axis, like others we've known and loved, is actually a tri-angle, its third corner made up of neofascist European politicians such as France's Jean-Marie Le Pen, Austria's Jörg Haider, and Russia's Vladimir Zhirinovsky who whip up hatred of Muslim immigrants and other minorities yet have found common cause with Islamists and/or with the U.S. religious right in opposing women's rights and vilifying Jews. (Hitler himself was a total "traditional family values" guy who wanted women to focus on having babies *fur das Vaterland* and declared, in signing the Nazi-Vatican Concordat, that "secular schools can never be tolerated.")

But more than any other Western country, on social issues it is the U.S., "with a president who sounds increasingly like an old-fashioned imam," wrote Whitaker, that "now sits in the religious camp alongside the Islamic regimes."

America's Christian right shares one especially noteworthy belief with the radical Islamists: that America brought September 11 upon itself. As Jerry Falwell said (and #55, **Pat Robertson** amened) shortly after 9/11: "[T]he pagans, and the abortionists, and the feminists, and the gays and lesbians . . . the ACLU, People for the American Way—all of them who have tried to secularize America—I point the finger in their face and say, 'You helped this happen' . . . [God] allow[ed] the enemies of America to give us probably what we deserve."

"The murders of abortion providers [see #69] show what such zeal can lead to," wrote conservative gay Catholic journalist (I hope I have that in the right order) Andrew Sullivan:

> If people truly believe that abortion is the same as mass murder, then you can see the awful logic of the terrorism it has spawned. This is the same logic as bin Laden's. . . . If you believe that women should be consigned to polyga- mous, concealed servitude, then Manhattan must appear like Gomorrah. If you believe that homosexuality is a crime punishable by death, as both fundamentalist Islam and the Bible dictate, then a world of same-sex marriage is surely Sodom. It is not a big step to argue that such centers of evil should be destroyed or undermined, as bin Laden does.[9]

By the way, in February 2005, a Utah judge was found to have three wives. The state and the Mormon Church banned polygamy in 1890, but as the judge's attorney pointed out, the statute is rarely enforced. In Utah, at least—home to the biggest Bush majority of any state and to about thirty thousand polygamists— *really* traditional family values live!

9 Andrew Sullivan, "This Is a Religious War," *New York Times Magazine*, October 7, 2001.

#87: LINDA "LABOR'S WORST NIGHTMARE" CHAVEZ

It is a standard right-wing insinuation that liberals are racists who deny freedom of opinion to minorities: "Liberals believe they own the franchise on minorities and can't stand any Hispanic or black who breaks rank," says Linda Chavez, a conservative Hispanic political activist, commentator, and nationally syndicated columnist who has broken rank with Hispanics, most loudly on bilingualism and affirmative action, which she loudly opposes.

You might say that kind of rank-breaking takes guts. You might also say it guarantees adulation in the conservative world—which Chavez, a regular **Fox News** (#28) contributor, certainly receives. (You might also ask how much Chavez—the product of a father with roots in Spain and a mother of English-Irish ancestry—has in common with the Latin-American immigrants and descendants from whom she has "broken" yet for whom she has spoken. Well, she's certainly Hispanic enough for the right's purposes.)

The break goes back to Chavez's opposition to major civil rights policy as head of the U.S. Commission on Civil Rights under Reagan. After that she served as a Reagan White House aide and as president of U.S. English, which lobbies to make English the official national language. Since 1985, she's headed the Center for Equal Opportunity, an outfit that opposes affirmative action and has published a guide for parents to "learn how to remove their children from harmful [bilingual education] programs." Along with former judge Robert Bork, **Kenneth Tomlinson** (#48), and Reagan attorney general Ed Meese, Chavez serves on the board of the American Civil *Rights* Union, which defines itself as an anti-ACLU, supports gun "rights" and the death penalty, and opposes affirmative action, environmental laws, and church-state separation. She was also a signatory to the Project for a New American Century, the neocon group behind **George W. Bush**'s foreign policy and the push for war in Iraq.

Where Chavez *would* seem to be in accord with most Hispanics is on keeping America's borders wide open to immigration—correction: to cheap labor for business. "Make no mistake," she wrote in 2001: "U.S. employers in many industries are desperate for Mexican and other foreign labor." Chavez would know. She serves on the board of directors of ABM Industries, Inc., a large janitorial services firm. That's an industry that depends almost entirely on cheap labor.

So: Let in a flood not of *immigrants* but of *labor* (Chavez, like Bush, calls for a temporary guest-worker program)—and above all, *don't let them join unions!* There is no cause to which Chavez is more dedicated than crushing organized labor. While noting (gleefully) that overall, only 12 percent of all American workers belong to a union—down from about one third in the 1950s—Chavez heads a group called Stop Union Political Abuse (SUPA or STUPA), which is dedicated to the proposition that unions—whose political donations are around one ninth the amount corporations give—have too much voice and power in politics and the workplace.

Chavez's love for organized labor made her Bush's *first* pick for labor secretary (before **Elaine Chao**, #46) in 2001. Business groups, naturally, praised the selection. AFL-CIO president John Sweeney called it "an insult to American working men and women to put an avowed opponent of the most basic workers' rights" in charge of enforcing labor laws, and noted that Chavez would be responsible for the largest anti-discrimination and affirmative-action program in the country, covering 26 million employees of federal contractors. Those are functions Chavez "has been hostile to," said a spokeswoman for the National Council of La Raza, the nation's largest Latino civil rights organization.

No, of course *that* wasn't why the nomination was withdrawn. It came out that Chavez had employed an illegal immigrant from Guatemala in her home. Or rather, as Chavez insisted, *provided money* to the woman while *allowing her to live* in her home.

Chavez, on CNN, shortly afterwards: "I think organized labor, I think quite mistakenly, somehow thought that I was going to be their worst nemesis. . . . I think I would have actually been very helpful in trying to bridge a gap . . . between the Republican Party and organized labor. . . . I had a very nice talk with John Sweeney this morning, by the way."

Chavez two years later, in a fund-raising letter for STUPA: "[T]he media were calling me 'Big Labor's Worst Nightmare.' . . . *And they were right!*" (her emphasis). She went on to call her good friend John Sweeney a "socialist" and say, "he's put BIL-LIONS into pushing the socialist agenda." And: "We can cripple liberal politics in this country by passing the Workers' Freedom of Choice Act"—a Republican bill attacking labor's right to contribute to political causes. (*Business* should have the exclusive right to buy elections.) And: "If we stop now, the terrorists win"! (Remember: Unions = Terrorism.)

As a guest on CNBC's *Dennis Miller* in June 2004, Chavez, whose book *Betrayal: How Union Bosses Shake Down Their Members and Corrupt American Politics* had just come out, stated her opposition to raising the minimum wage, saying it would hurt *workers* ("blacks and Latinos the most") by reducing job creation—the standard argument from those right-wing defenders of the working class. A report released the month before by the Economic Policy Institute "failed to find any systematic, significant job loss" associated with past minimum wage increases, and said: "A disproportionate share of minorities would benefit from a minimum wage increase." [10]

So anyway, Miller asks Chavez what the minimum wage currently is. Chavez: "You know, I don't know what it is, it's $5-something, $5.65, something like that." Try $5.15, Ms. Almost-Secretary of Labor. (That's $10,712 a year for a full-time worker.) Same dangerously high level it had stood at for seven years. (Notice any

10 "No Longer Getting By," Economic Policy Institute, May 11, 2004.

price increases in that time, Ms. Someone-from-Guatemala-probably-does-all-your-grocery-shopping-for-you?)

In May 2004, Fox News host Mike Jerrick felt compelled to ask Chavez whether it wasn't "too strong to call [John Kerry] a communist apologist" in her nationally syndicated column a few days earlier. "Well, I didn't call him that actually," Chavez lied. In fact, her column did so twice. She later admitted she "misspoke" in denying it. Why not? The damage was done. GOP Smear Tactics 101. Chavez also gave airtime on her radio program to a leader of the Swift Boat Veterans to Smear Hero John Kerry's Vietnam Record.

Speaking of war heroes, Chavez has suggested that "the presence of women in the unit" encouraged prisoner abuse at Abu Ghraib and said the prisoners at Guantánamo "are members of an international terrorist organization that has killed thousands of innocent civilians." Not one has been charged—but, hey, guilty until proven innocent. Bet every one of those prisoners is a card-carrying union member, too. No trials—just a simple firing squad.

#86: CHARLES CAWLEY AND SUCCESSORS AT MBNA: MORAL BANKRUPTCY WHERE CREDIT IS DUE (FREE BONUS VILLAIN: REP. JAMES SENSENBRENNER!)

George W. Bush promised to usher in an era of personal responsibility. Perhaps his most notable success in this area—second only to his administration's gift of proud self-reliance to the people of New Orleans in the wake of Hurricane Katrina—was the bankruptcy bill he signed into law in March 2005. (As we shall see, the two achievements are linked.) The bill—which Clinton had vetoed—makes it harder and more expensive for poor and moderate-income families to use bankruptcy protection, while exempting schemes used by wealthy families and corrupt corporations to shelter assets from creditors and doing nothing about predatory lending practices. (Oh, you're looking for *corporate* responsibility? Down the hall, next administration on your left.) The bill was a reward to and, indeed, largely written *by* the banking and credit card industries, which were Bush's largest campaign contributors in 2004 and had spent eight years and $40 million lobbying for the legislation. Its critics, by definition, had limited lobbying resources.

Leading the lobbying campaign—and heading the list of Bush's largest contributors in 2000 and 2004—was MBNA Corp., the largest independent credit card issuer, which stood to increase its annual profits by $75 million under the new law. Throughout the 1990s, MBNA CEO Charles Cawley stepped up the company's political activities. Company memos advised MBNA executives on what to donate to which candidates—Bush's gubernatorial campaigns were major beneficiaries—and asked them to send photocopies of their checks to MBNA's general counsel. In 1999, Cawley, who sits on the board of the George Bush Presidential Library Foundation and is close to the Bush family, was a Bush Pioneer, or $100,000-plus fund-raiser, and in 2004 was a $200,000-plus Bush Ranger—as were Lance Weaver, MBNA's chief administrative officer, and James Hance, Jr., vice chairman and chief financial officer of Bank of America, which in late 2005 was in the process of acquiring MBNA.

Cawley retired as CEO in December 2003—and why not? That year, his pay package was $45.5 million—the largest of seventy CEO pay packages in a survey of the largest U.S. firms. (CEO salaries at the two hundred largest U.S. companies rose 8.7 percent in 2003 while employees' average pay rose 1.5 percent and the economy lost 410,000 jobs.)[11]

The Bush-MBNA bankruptcy bill forces many debtors to file for bankruptcy under Chapter 13, which requires continued payments to the credit card companies, instead of Chapter 7. But

---

11 Mark Jaffe, "CEO Pay Eclipses Stock Gains," Bloomberg News, April 25, 2004.

according to the American Bankruptcy Institute, 96 percent of people who file Chapter 7 can't afford to pay anything more. The rise in bankruptcy filings was due not to irresponsibility, extravagance, and abuse of the laws, as the industry and its GOP shills charged: nine out of ten bankruptcies are triggered by job loss, divorce, and/or medical bills—which alone account for half of all bankruptcy filings. A Harvard study found that in the two years before filing for bankruptcy, 19 percent of families went without food, 40 percent had their phone service shut off, and 53 percent went without important medical care. In fact, the bankruptcy bill came at a moment when Bush was proposing cuts in Medicaid and when many Americans were losing part or all of their health insurance coverage.

Also to blame were the industry's heavy promotion of credit cards and loans, its onerous rates, and hidden fees. Typically luring in consumers in with low introductory rates, which the lenders are then free to change at will—at times to 30 percent or more—credit card companies (which netted $30 billion in 2004) aggressively target people they know can't afford to pay off their balances, such as college students, low-wage workers, and people already drowning in debt—which helped the industry collect *$11.7 billion* in penalty fees in 2004. Bush's laughably titled "Bankruptcy Abuse Prevention and *Consumer Protection* Act of 2005" did nothing to address these practices—yet, as columnist Robert Scheer observed, was backed by the party whose politicians "love to quote Scripture, [where] such outrageous usury was explicitly condemned."

Like other credit card banks, MBNA is based in Delaware because, unlike other states, Delaware has no usury laws—it in effect allows companies to charge as much interest as they want; and federal law allows corporations to "import" these laws from their home state. MBNA is a member of the so-called Partnership to Protect Consumer Credit, which lobbies to make the federal rules permanently override any state protections for borrowers.

Critics—including more than a hundred bankruptcy law professors—said the Bush-MBNA bill would primarily hit young, middle-income, and poor families, women, and the elderly, and would turn the bankruptcy courts into collection agencies for companies like MBNA. The Republicans defeated Democrat-sponsored amendments "to curb abusive bankruptcy practices by wealthy families, who can create special trusts to shelter their assets, and by corrupt companies like Enron and WorldCom, which were able [through bankruptcy] to deprive many of their employees and retired employees of benefits," the *New York Times* reported. The GOP also defeated amendments exempting those facing bankruptcy primarily for medical reasons and men and women in military service. Whom *did* these patriots exempt? Violent protesters at abortion clinics, like those of **Operation Rescue** (#69)! An amendment preventing them from using the bankruptcy laws to shield themselves from civil damages was shot down by the Republicans.

In September 2005, after Hurricane Katrina, Rep. James Sensenbrenner (R-WI), chairman of the House Judiciary Committee, refused even to hold hearings into the possibility of granting hurricane victims exemptions from the new bankruptcy law. The new requirements for bankruptcy filing, the Consumer Federation of America noted, "are difficult for the most organized person to meet, never mind someone who has had his or her home destroyed by Katrina." Sensenbrenner was also one of eleven Republicans who voted against a relief package for Katrina victims. My sense is that Sensenbrenner will be a *brenner* (German for *burner*) in the GOP-dominated Ninth Circle of Hell, and perhaps will be worked on with *sensen* (scythes) as well.

#85: L. RON HUBBARD AND SCIENTOLOGY: "CLOSER THAN YOU THINK"

Objective one—place Scientology at the absolute center of society. Objective two—eliminate psychiatry in all its forms.

—Church of Scientology leader David Miscavige

Hubbard, the science-fiction writer and Scientology founder, is, as of this writing, the only "dead" person included in this book. This unique honor is being accorded because (a) a discussion of the Church of Scientology (COS) without its founder would be like Christianity without Paul of Tarsus, UFOlogy without Erich von Daniken, Tae Bo without Billy Banks; (b) as Scientology teaches, our bodies may die, our movies may die at the box office or go straight to DVD, but *we* don't die. Those who suggest that L. Ron "died" in 1986 are strongly advised to decease and desist. (COS is famous for its extreme litigiousness against critics, which evidently stems from a confusion of the words "litigation" and "liturgy.")

Scientology, which grew out of Hubbard's 1950 book *Dianetics*, offers an "applied religious philosophy" and, as an alternative to psychiatry, purports to help cure depression, drug addiction, dyslexia, and other diseases starting with D. Calling psychiatrists "terrorists," Hubbard wrote that the psychiatrist "kidnaps, tortures and murders without any slightest police interference or action by western security forces." (True—still not a single raid on their training camps in Afghanistan.) COS claims 9 million members globally, 3 million in the United States.

Hubbard's teaching—or "technology," or "tech"—includes everything from the Way to Happiness to the nature or Dynamics of life. You will be pleased to learn that you are an immortal spiritual being or "thetan" who has lived through many past lives. (While describing Buddhism, along with Christianity and the rest, as a "dead end," Hubbard referred to himself as a reincarnation of Buddha.) Through Scientology, you may gain control over matter, energy, space, time, thoughts, form, life, scripts, residuals, even the choice of director: you may become an Operating Thetan (OT). Or an Operating Cretin (OC).

Of the "auditing," the "ARC Triangle," the "tone scale," and the rest of it, the less said, the better. But no ridicule of Scientology is complete without the story of Xenu. According to an advanced teaching reportedly imparted to those who reach OT level III, Xenu is:

> the galactic tyrant who first kidnapped . . . and loaded individuals into space planes for transport to the site of extermination, the planet of Teegeeack (Earth). . . . [Xenu] then stacked hundreds of billions of these frozen victims around Earth's volcanoes 75 million years ago before blowing them up with hydrogen bombs and brainwashing them with a "three-D, super colossal motion picture" for 36 days. . . . [They then occupied human bodies] as invisible spiritual parasites . . . that can only be removed using advanced Scientology techniques. Xenu is allegedly imprisoned in a mountain by a force field powered by an eternal battery.[12]

(An eternal battery! So it *is* possible.) Jesus, by the way, never existed but was implanted in humanity's collective memory by Xenu; Christianity is an "entheta [evil] operation" mounted by the Targs.

Hubbard's book *Have You Lived Before This Life* documented past lives described by Scientologists during "auditing" sessions, which included memories of "being run over by a Martian bishop driving a steamroller [and] being transformed into an intergalactic walrus that perished after falling out of a flying saucer."[13] The

12 "Scientology," Wikipedia.org.
13 Ibid.

intergalactic walrus is a feature common to many religions. No—
I've just double-checked—only Scientology.

Back on Planet Earth, according to at least eight witnesses,
Hubbard on at least five separate occasions said some variation
of: "The way to make a million dollars is to start a religion." And
lo, COS was incorporated in 1953. And L. Ron saw that it was
good. And there were drug treatment centers, criminal rehab programs, the World Institute of Scientology Enterprises, which
teaches Scientology management techniques to businesses, a consulting firm, a publishing company. Today, says Wikipedia, COS
"forms the center of a complex worldwide network of corporations" dedicated to the promotion of Scientology.

The Targs notwithstanding, recruits are taught that Scientology is fully compatible with all existing major religions. However, in its application for tax-exempt status, COS stated that
Scientologists "are required to look only to Scientology Scriptures
for the answers." Members are encouraged to cut off all contact
with friends or family members critical of the "Church."

Many governments have the idea that Scientology is a commercial business and/or a potentially dangerous, antidemocratic
cult. Allegations against the Church and its officials have included
sexual abuse, harassment of critics, deaths of Scientologists due
to mistreatment by other members, use of brainwashing and mind
control, use of high-pressure tactics to obtain money from members, and criminal activities for personal gain or on behalf of the
Church. At least two cases have led to criminal convictions of
COS officials:

- Operation Snow White, the internal COS name for a domestic
  espionage program, the largest in U.S. history, in which COS
  operatives infiltrated, wiretapped, and stole documents from
  the Internal Revenue Service and other U.S. government
  offices. Eleven Church executives, including Mary Sue Hubbard, L. Ron's wife and second in command, pleaded guilty or

were convicted in 1979. COS was also criminally convicted in Canada for a conspiracy to break into government offices.

- Operation Freakout, also in the 1970s, which attempted to frame the New York–based author of a book critical of Scientology, Paulette Cooper, for a series of bomb threats, and in Hubbard's words, get her "incarcerated in a mental institution or jail."

Hubbard termed anyone who criticized or was merely unindoctrinated into Scientology as "aberrated," and undeserving of civil rights. In a 1965 policy letter, he formulated what he called "The Fair Game Law," declaring that "Suppressive Persons"—those whose actions "suppress or damage Scientology or a Scientologist"—"may be deprived of property or injured by any means . . . tricked, sued or lied to or destroyed." While COS claims the policy was rescinded in 1968, the evidence suggests otherwise.

In 1993, after refusing for twenty-five years to recognize Scientology as a church and grant it tax exemption—refusals that were upheld in every court—the IRS suddenly and suspiciously reversed course. COS had, among other tactics, "hired private investigators to dig into the private lives of IRS officials and to conduct surveillance operations to uncover potential vulnerabilities, according to interviews and documents."[14] One PI said he interviewed tenants in buildings owned by three IRS officials, looking for housing code violations.

Scientologists call psychiatry a "pseudoscience" and mental illness a "fraud." "There is no such thing as a chemical imbalance," Scientologist actor Tom Cruise rants suggestively. Hubbard believed psychiatrists were behind a conspiracy to create a world government run by psychiatrists on behalf of Soviet Russia

14 "The Shadowy Story Behind Scientology's Tax-Exempt Status," *New York Times*, March 9, 1997.

and international financiers: "Our enemies are less than twelve men," he ranted suggestively. "They are members of the Bank of England and other higher financial circles." Psychiatrists assisted Xenu 75 million years ago! (Some *have* no doubt kept the same patients coming in twice a week for 75 million years.) COS blames psychiatry for the rise of Hitler and Stalin, all the wars of the past century, and 9/11. An exhibit in COS's Los Angeles head-quarters, "Psychiatry Kills," links psychiatry to Nazism, apartheid, and school violence—blaming the shooting spree at Columbine High School, for example, on "anger management" classes the shooters allegedly attended.

According to Scientologists, children suffering from attention-deficit disorders may only have a food allergy or need vitamins. In fact, there is abundant evidence that these and other psychiatric conditions are real and that medical treatment helps. "Physicians, psychiatrists and scientists have consistently said that Scien-tology's approaches to mental health have no basis in medical fact and can be dangerous to people [like Scientologists] who may need treatment," *Salon* noted.

But Scientology "is closer than you think to implanting its extreme beliefs in the nation's laws and schools." Scientologists have promoted and helped write legislation in several states that would limit any psychiatric treatment for common childhood psy-chiatric disorders and penalize, even criminalize, schoolteachers who recommended mental health treatments to students or parents.

The Scientology-backed drug-abuse program Narconon has "reached" over 1.7 million kids in schools around the country. Sci-entology's core treatment for drug abuse is to sweat out "toxins" and take vitamins. Fortunately, COS provides detoxification service "under expert supervision in Scientology organizations and missions around the world." "Their goal is to take over entirely the field of mental health," a recovering Scientologist told *Salon*.

Think they *can't* take over a field? Ask Tom Cruise, Katie Holmes, John Travolta, Patrick Swayze, Sharon Stone, Kirstie

Alley, Anne Archer, Jenna Elfman, Emilio Estevez, Juliette Lewis, Bernadette Peters, Peggy Lipton, Lisa Marie Presley, Priscilla Presley, Giovanni Ribisi, Mimi Rogers . . . .

#84: FRANKLIN "NOT OF THE SAME GOD" GRAHAM

Poverty-Stricken Africans To Receive Desperately Needed Bibles

—*The Onion,* March 16, 2006

Maybe it's too much to ask, but it would be nice if those engaged in the genuinely holy work of saving people's lives by feeding and caring for their bodies would allow them to keep possession of their souls—their own beliefs and heritage. And try not to embarrass and endanger America by enhancing its image as a land of ignorant, Bible-thumping, Muslim-hating redneck louts.

Reverend Franklin Graham is no ordinary, two-bit, sleazeball evangelical huckster. He's the eldest son of Billy Graham and, as president and CEO of the Billy Graham Evangelistic Association, heir to his evangelical empire. Franklin is also a friend and confidante of **George W. Bush,** who has credited Billy Graham with having turned him from booze to the opiate of the people. Graham the Younger gave the prayer at Bush the Younger's first inaugural.

As head of the Christian relief agency Samaritan's Purse, Franklin Graham:

> has earned international respect for supplying food, water, shelter, and medical care to regions where other angels fear to tread. Somalia, Rwanda, Bosnia, Kosovo, Afghanistan, southern Sudan—the more stricken and war torn the area,

the greater the opportunity to help, reasons Graham, who delights in personally piloting the group's small planes through airspace prone to artillery attacks and sniper fire.[15]

But why does he have to go and spoil it all by saying something stupid (on *NBC Nightly News*, right after 9/11) like: Islam is a "very wicked and evil religion," "wicked, violent, and not of the same God"; writing that Christianity and Islam are "as different as lightness and darkness"; and declaring, "The true **God** [#77] is the God of the Bible, not the Koran"?

And while it may be Graham's job as a Christian minister to *believe* this, was it wise, or good for America, for Graham to state at the Pentagon's Good Friday service in April, 2003, just a month into the war in Iraq, that "There's no other way to God except through Christ"? Or to announce that Samaritan's Purse, which mixes its humanitarian aid with a liberal dose of proselytizing, was heading to Iraq "to save [Iraqis] . . . in the name of Jesus Christ"—this at the very moment when America most needed to assure Iraqis and the Muslim world that we were *not* there on a religious crusade? (What ever gave them *that* idea—the fact that a Samaritan's Purse director said, "We are first a Christian organization and second an aid organization"? That Graham "asserts that the two religions are locked in an eternal struggle that will only end with the triumphant return of Christ"?[16] Where's these Muslims' sense of humor?)

You can't blame Graham alone. As the *New Republic*'s Michelle Cottle noted, "the Bush administration appears unwilling to ask Graham to tread lightly . . . **Karl Rove** [#3] would likely rather risk an international holy war than a drop in Bush's support among Christian conservatives."

15 Michelle Cottle, "Bible Brigade: Franklin Graham V. Iraq," *New Republic*, April 21, 2003.

16 Ibid.

But Graham showed reckless disregard for his country's, and others', welfare and rules long before Iraq. During the 1991 Gulf War, he had tens of thousands of Arabic-language New Testaments shipped to the troops in Saudi Arabia to be passed along to the locals—in direct violation of Saudi law and of the U.S. government's promise of no proselytizing. When General Norman Schwarzkopf tried to explain the problems he was causing, Graham replied, "Sir, I understand that, and I appreciate that, but I'm also under orders, and that's from the King of Kings and Lord of Lords." For the true believer, criticism only confirms the rightness of his cause.

While Samaritan's Purse, operating with a government grant from USAID, was helping with reconstruction of El Salvador following an earthquake in 1991, it turned out the group was "reconstructing" regular prayer services. (No tax dollars for proselytizing? The law of the land before the *Bible*? Toilets before tabernacles? Get real.)

At a prayer service following the 1999 Columbine massacre, Graham comforted the families and friends of those victims who may not have been Christian with the thought that only those who accepted Jesus Christ would enter Heaven. When George W. Bush told his mother the same thing in 1993, Billy Graham cautioned him: "Don't play God." But Bush is president now, and there's a new Graham in town.

#83: THE SNOWMOBILE, ATV, AND JET SKI INDUSTRIES AND THEIR BUSHITE FRIENDS, AKA THE YAHOO-INDUSTRIAL COMPLEX

America today is deeply divided. Blue America hikes, cross-country skis, and kayaks. Red America off-roads, snowmobiles, and jet skis.

The activities themselves reflect the politics of their adherents. As the saying goes: the recreational is political. The "conservative" "sports" (how totally inapt both words are) are unique in literally empowering a single person to disturb and harm hundreds or even thousands of others through noise, pollution, and the threat of decapitation. For some, I suspect that's part of the appeal. It's akin to that of monster **SUVs** (#67)—and indeed to Bush foreign policy: "Outta my way, here I come, and I'm *big and bad*." In short, your basic *asshole* appeal.

But even the average snowmobiler, "personal watercraft" user, and ATV-er (all-terrain vehicle) must simply *not care* that his wish to sit on his fat rump fulfilling the three basic requirements of American fun—moving fast, making a lot of noise, and consuming gasoline (and as often as not, beer)—robs others of their peace and quiet, their air and water quality, and their enjoyment of nature—not least, the way it sounds and smells. Personally, I don't understand the desire, after fighting traffic every day, to drive on the weekend to a place where you get into another vehicle and, well, drive some more. But that's just me. This isn't: The whole premise of these machines is that every last, quiet, unspoiled corner of the earth should be accessible to motorized vehicles.

We've already let roads, parking lots, and roadside commercial development become our dominant everyday landscape. We've created endless deserts of suburban ugliness. But the All-terrain, Sea, and Snow Harming Of Landscape and Environment (ASSHOLE) industry and its loyalists don't want to stop until there's no nature left at all. A single jet ski puts a large mosquito in the ear of everyone within a radius of up to twenty miles and can dump up to three gallons of oil and gasoline into the water per hour. They run over endangered manatees. They're driven by thrill-seeking, drunken yahoos. You may work for a year to buy a few days of winter beauty in the wild. You're lucky to enjoy even a moment of quiet. A snowmobile can also be heard up to twenty miles away. The noise screws up animals, too. Snowmobiles can emit one hundred times as much carbon monoxide and three hundred times as much hydrocarbons as cars. And they're driven by thrill-seeking, drunken yahoos. ATVs tear up land and disturb ecosystems. And they're driven by. . . . In fact, each of these "sports" features a high rate of alcohol-related accidents and fatalities. These industries and their loyalists purport to defend the "enjoyment" of our natural resources. (Hops, barley, rye . . .) But quiet is a natural resource. No form of enjoyment that destroys what it "enjoys" is legitimate.

Nonetheless, the **George W. Bush** administration, siding with the snowmobile industry, has scrapped a Clinton plan to phase out snowmobiles in Yellowstone National Park, and intends to allow as many as 720 a day. The National Park Service received more than 350,000 public comments—the highest number ever on any issue—and 80 percent favored a snowmobile ban. So did the Environmental Protection Agency. "If the administration goes through with this," said a former Yellowstone superintendent, "it will mark a new low in its pattern of ignoring science to benefit a special interest at the public's expense." Up to 140 snowmobiles will also be permitted in Grand Teton National Park.

This was but part of the Bushies' larger vision for America's public lands: they are to be commercialized, privatized, exploited by special interests. In 2005, **Gail Norton** (#18)'s Interior Department decided it was time to revise the management policy that guides park superintendents, which was last revised in 2001 and is usually reexamined only every ten or fifteen years. The new plan would eliminate the requirement that only motorized equipment with the least impact be used; strip away language about preserving the parks' "natural soundscape"; lower air-quality standards; allow increased jet skiing and snowmobiling; and remove the following from the park system's mission statement: "Congress . . . has provided that when there is a conflict between conserving [the national parks'] resources and values [for future generations] and providing for enjoyment of them [today], conservation is to be predominant."

While they were at it, the *New York Times* noted, these stewards of our natural resources handed down a directive that "would require park personnel who hope to advance above the middle-manager level to go through what is essentially a political screening"—presumably because park rangers, who understand the damage best, hate the motorized intrusions.

One if by land, two if by sea, three if by snow. The yahoos are coming!

#82: ARTHUR "ELEMENT OF HYPOCRISY" FINKELSTEIN

"GOP Consultant Weds His Male Partner"—*New York Times*, April 9, 2005. *There's* a headline you don't see every day. Not that there's anything wrong with it. It wouldn't be worth mentioning if the consultant hadn't, through most of the forty years of that domestic partnership, worked on behalf of some of America's most rabidly homophobic politicians; if he wasn't "the architect of Jesse Helms's political rise"; if he wasn't acclaimed as "the guy who slandered the term 'liberal' in American politics"; if he hadn't worked for presidents Nixon and Reagan; helped elect the likes of **George W. Bush**, New York Governor George Pataki, Senator Alphonse D'Amato, and Israeli Prime Minister Benjamin "To the Right of Attila Sharon" Netanyahu; advised Sharon; helped the Swift Boat Smearers for Bush smear John Kerry's military reputation; and announced that he would be spearheading the "Get Hillary" campaign to defeat Senator Clinton's reelection campaign in 2006.

All that, and more, is on Arthur Finkelstein's resume. If you haven't heard of him before, it's because he made sure you didn't.

As CNN reported in 1996: "He is the stuff of Hollywood: A man who can topple even the most powerful foes, yet so secretive that few have ever seen him." Finkelstein has been compared to criminal mastermind Kaiser Sose in *The Usual Suspects*, who laid so low that some doubted he really existed. CNN captioned its photo, "Only known photo of Arthur Finkelstein." This after twenty years in big-time politics.

Finkelstein, a Massachusetts resident, helped direct Republican strategy in thirty-three Senate races in 1996 alone. Typical Finkelstein ad lines: "Call liberal Paul Wellstone. Tell him it's wrong . . ." "That's liberal. That's Jack Reed. That's wrong. Call liberal Jack Reed . . ." "That's the Finkelstein formula," Democratic consultant Mark Mellman told CNN· "Just brand somebody a liberal, use the word over and over again." Clients called this "Finkel-think." Among Finkelstein's most outspokenly homophobic clients were Lauch Faircloth (R-NC), Jesse Helms (R-NC), Don Nickles (R-OK), and Bob Smith (R-NH)—four senators whose opposition helped defeat a bill banning antigay job discrimination. "I think it's clear that there is an element of hypocrisy where [Finkelstein] lives this kind of sedate, gay lifestyle while making millions of dollars off of candidates who bash gays," Stephen Rodrick, who outed the Fink in a 1996 article in *Boston Magazine*, told CNN.

Nor did being Jewish stop Finkelstein from repeatedly helping to remind voters in a 1978 South Carolina congressional race that the Democratic candidate, Max Heller, was Jewish. (A poll Finkelstein conducted for the Republican, Carroll Campbell, referred to Campbell as "a native South Carolinian" and Heller as "a Jewish immigrant." Five days before the election, an independent candidate jumped in—allegedly at the Repubs' behest—and attacked Heller for not "believ[ing] in Jesus Christ." Heller lost by less than six thousand votes.)

A classic Finkel-think tactic was the "independent expenditure" campaign, which, by remaining technically unaffiliated with any candidate, "can avoid spending limits while pummeling Democrats with ads GOP candidates can later disavow," *Time* explained. The beauty of this arrangement, a Fink colleague once explained, is that "a group like ours [Finkelstein's National Conservative Political Action Committee] could lie through its teeth, and the candidate stays clean."[17]

Finkelstein's wedding, which was disclosed by an associate, took place in December 2004. "None of Mr. Finkelstein's better-known political clients" attended, the *New York Times* noted.

#81: KIRK LYON AND THE AMERICA-HATING SONS OF CONFEDERATE VETERANS

Addressing the Sons of Confederate Veterans (SCV) in 1984, Senator (and future Senate Republican leader) Trent Lott said, "the spirit of Jefferson Davis lives in the 1984 Republican Platform." In a 1996 speech, **Gail Norton** [#18] lauded the Confederate Army. In a 1998 interview, John Ashcroft praised the pro-Confederate *Southern Partisan* magazine for "defending Southern patriots like [Robert E.] Lee, [Stonewall] Jackson and Davis."

With the blue pushed back into the corners of the land and the gray/red occupying all the rest—including Washington—you'd think pro-Confederate groups like the 31,000-member SCV would be lightening up and celebrating their long-delayed victory with barbecues, cross burnings, what have you. But no. They're more politicized than ever and as fired up as they were some seven score and five years ago to push the envelope of the Confederate

---

17 Eric Pooley, "The Mystery Man Who Inspired Dole's Latest Strategy," *Time*, October 7, 1996.

agenda (as Jeff Davis might have put it). They're not just reen-acting; they mean it.

Founded in 1896, the SCV long remained a group for genealogy fans, history buffs, and reenactors of Civil War battles, dedicated to honoring Confederate heroes and flying their flags. It pledged to be "strictly patriotic, historical, educational, benevolent, non-political, non-racial, and non-sectarian." In 1992, the SCV even passed a resolution condemning the Ku Klux Klan and "all others who promote hate."

All that began to change in the late nineties, when the NAACP and other groups launched campaigns to remove the Confederate flag from state capitols in Georgia, Mississippi, and South Carolina. In response, a so-called "reform wing" of the SCV aligned itself with extremist groups like the neosecessionist League of the South and the white-supremacist Council of Conservative Citizens (CCC). Soon, wrote Jason Zengerle in the *New Republic*, "the SCV's campaign to keep the Confederate flag flying morphed into a more general anti-government, anti-Northern crusade."[18] SCV camp meetings had always begun with a Pledge of Allegiance to the American flag, but now the Pledge and the Stars and Stripes were abolished from some meetings altogether. Now, they're "more likely to feature anti-government diatribes and odes to the unique 'Anglo-Celtic' nature of the South than plans to commemorate Robert E. Lee Day."

As Kirk Lyons, "Chief of Staff" of the SCV's largest division, the "Army of Northern Virginia," put it: "Polishing headstones and giving education seminars and going to reenactments doesn't cut it anymore. . . . We're at war."

With fewer stealth bombers than muskets, SCV must focus on legal battlefields. Lyons, a North Carolina lawyer who runs what

18 Jason Zengerle, "Lost Cause: The Confederacy's New Face," *The New Republic*, August 2, 2004.

he calls a "Civil Rights Law Firm for Confederate Southern Americans," is, wrote Zengerle, "the brains behind the dubious legal theory that 'Confederate Americans' are a distinct 'national origin' deserving of constitutional protection." Along with a string of unsuccessful lawsuits against companies and school districts that ban displays of Confederate symbols, Lyons—who says he wants to stop "the ethnic cleansing of Dixie"—has a long history of association with extremist groups: he has represented members of the Ku Klux Klan and in 1990 he married the daughter of a leader of the Aryan Nations. (*Mazel tov!*)

In 2002, Lyons narrowly lost an election for commander of his "Army," but a member who shared his views, Ron Wilson, was elected SCV's "commander-in-chief," vowing that under his leadership, the organization would help correct a "drifting, wobbly American society" and fight "the homosexual agenda, abortion, and other Godless causes." Wilson appointed to key staff positions a number of SCV members who also belonged to the League of the South and the CCC, and began a purge of SCV moderates. About 350 members from North Carolina alone were suspended for publicly supporting a small faction calling itself Save the SCV, whose members say the organization's current leadership is rife with racists and right-wing extremists. "They've gotten confused," said one of those purged. "Whereas the Confederate battle flag used to be the symbol of the cause, it's now *the* cause."

Actually, *he's* got it backwards. It's the current SCV leaders—and tens of millions of descendants of slaves—who understand what cause the flag symbolizes: "States rights" baloney aside, it is, and always has been, the "defense" of the white race. And with the war going the Confederates' way in recent years, why should they give it up?

#80: BILL DONOHUE: "HOLLYWOOD LIKES ANAL SEX AND ABORTIONS"

Didn't know that? Then you have much to learn from William Donohue, president of the New York-based Catholic League for Religious and Civil Rights, which purports to defend Catholics' right "to participate in American public life without defamation or discrimination." Donohue is also an adjunct scholar at the **Heritage Foundation** (#8), and the league has links with the violent, extremist **Operation Rescue** (#69). Indeed, right-wing Catholic groups like Donohue's have forged ever closer ties with the Protestant-Evangelical right, where *defamation* of Catholicism as "Satanic" and "a false religion" is commonplace (see, for example, #66): clearly a case of my enemy's enemy. As Donohue explained in December 2004, in one of four appearances that year alone on MSNBC's *Scarborough Country*:

> Hollywood is controlled by secular Jews who hate Christianity in general and Catholicism in particular. It's not a secret, OK? [It was *supposed* to be, but he's blown it.]. . . . That's why they hate this movie [#65, **Mel Gibson**'s *Passion*]. It's about Jesus Christ, and it's about truth. . . . Hollywood likes anal sex. They like to see the public square without nativity scenes. I like families. I like children. They like abortions."

Didn't Donohue's mission statement say "without defamation?" Oh, right—*of* Catholics. Same for the "discrimination" part, clearly: in 2003, Donohue defended Senator **Rick Santorum** (#23)'s remarks equating homosexuality with bestiality and incest, because treating "alternative lifestyles" (like "the gay death style") equally would spell doom. Doom. A few more Donohue-isms:

- "I'm pretty good about picking out who queers are." Hey, isn't that "gay-dar" gays have remarkable?
- "The new Puritans [those criticizing Gibson's *Passion*] . . . like gay sex. . . . [T]hey have no problems when it comes to sodomy. It's smoking they don't like and Catholicism." It's true—we Puritans want all cigarettes burned. But with so many priests having gay sex, how could we not like Catholics?
- "As for fidelity to the New Testament, Mel [Gibson] is not obligated to tailor his interpretation of the Bible according to someone else's politically correct straightjacket." Whether Mark's, Matthew's, Luke's, or John's.
- John Kerry "never found an abortion that he couldn't justify." In fact, that's what kept him too busy to answer the Swift Boat smear.
- On stem cell research: "[W]e might as well serve [human embryos] as appetizers at a human embryonic cocktail to people" [*sic* and sick].
- "The media elite have an aversion to religion." That must be why, in 2004 alone, Donohue appeared at least twenty-one times on cable news programs, including MSNBC's *Hardball* and CNN's *Paula Zahn Now*, and twice on network news shows. Where do you think he made all these bigoted, loony remarks?
- "They [the media elite] want Tom, Dick, and Harry to get married." No, no, that would be polygamy.
- "The left" won't tell "the truth about the gay deathstyle" because "they are censorial at heart." Unlike Bill "Anything Goes" Donahue: this civil-rights champion wrote a book attacking the American Civil Liberties Union, which has defended even Nazis' free-speech rights. It is the Catholic League that has meanwhile led efforts to ban artworks and films dealing frankly with matters such as homosexuality, AIDS, and the Catholic Church sex abuse scandal (see #76).

In August 2005, Donohue accused those who questioned the views of **John Roberts** (#36), **Bush**'s right-wing nominee for Chief Justice of the Supreme Court, of "Catholic baiting." It was all because "Roberts is Catholic. There is no other plausible reason." Never mind that many other Catholics have been confirmed; as Donohue admitted, "I'm going to try to do my job to intimidate the Senate Judiciary Committee."

It was the same with all of Bush's far-right judicial nominees, People for the American Way noted: "When Democrats opposed the confirmation of Miguel Estrada . . . the Right accused them of being 'anti-Hispanic'. . . . When they opposed the confirmation of nominees like **Janice Rogers Brown** [#61] and **Priscilla Owen** [#62], it was because Democrats were either anti-African American or anti-woman, or both." On Henry Saad, they were anti-Arab. The *Democrats*.

But allegations of "anti-Christian" or "anti-Catholic" bigotry have become the right's primary tactic. The Catholic-conservative group Fidelis warned Senate Democratic leaders to "keep religion out of future Supreme Court confirmation hearings." Of course, it was precisely Roberts's religious views that sold him to Christian conservatives. If the president were to nominate an avowed atheist, I suppose the religious right would still demand that religion be ignored. Or maybe they'd demand a *gay* atheist.

#79: BRADLEY SMITH 1

The function of the Federal Election Commission (FEC) is to enforce the election laws, particularly the campaign finance laws. Bradley Smith believes there should be no campaign finance laws and no FEC. Therefore Bradley Smith sits on the FEC. That's called a *syllogism*. At least in the Bush era. (You're learning a lot from this book.)

Actually, Smith was appointed to the FEC by Clinton. Although, as the libertarian magazine *Reason* said, "virtually all agreed that he was the wrong person for the job" ("akin to confirming a conscientious objector to be secretary of defense," said Republican Senator John McCain), Clinton made a deal with Republican senators Trent Lott and **Mitch McConnell** (#47): in exchange for Smith's nomination, the Repugs allowed *sixteen* of Clinton's judicial nominations to go forward. That's how badly they wanted Bradley.

Here's why: "The ideal system" of campaign finance regulation, Smith says flatly, "is no regulation." No limit to the influence of organized money over the political system—to the right of corporate special interests, wealthy candidates, and billionaires at large to buy the government they so richly deserve—and to do it anonymously.

Like other apologists for big-money domination of politics, Smith argues that campaign spending is *free speech*, guaranteed by the First Amendment. The Constitution, wrote Smith in his 2001 book *Unfree Speech: The Folly of Campaign Finance Reform*, "demands the abolition of all restraints on political contributions and spending"—everything from the 1907 Tillman Act, which banned direct political contributions by banks and corporations, to the 1971 Federal Election Campaign Act, which regulated campaign contributions and spending, required public disclosure of donors' identities, and created the FEC, to the McCain-Feingold campaign finance reform law of 2002, which banned unregulated "soft money."

A former law professor at (aptly enough) Capital University in Columbus, Ohio, Smith does not think the amount of money spent on campaigns ($945 million on federal races in 2004) is excessive. Without it, he argues, voters would receive less "information." Indeed, he says, the goal "should be to increase [campaign] spending." As long as it's not through a system of *publicly financed* elections: that, Smith opposes. (Whose special interests would *that* benefit?)

Smith says higher spending does not always result in electoral victory. True. In 2004, the candidate who spent the most won in only 95 percent of House races and 91 percent of Senate races. Smith says it cannot be assumed legislators are "corrupted" by large-scale fund-raising—and besides, "what reformers mean by 'corruption' is that legislators react to the wishes of constituents." Indeed. For example, when the Senate in 2002 voted 68 to 32 against higher vehicle fuel efficiency standards, the "yeas" had on average received more than three times as much as the "nays" in donations from the automakers' "constituency."

In 2004, eight out of ten political action committees (PACs) were corporate, of which 90 percent gave most or all of their money to Republicans. The oil and gas industry, for example, gave 80 percent of its contributions to R's—who in return gave the oil and gas industry the lion's share of the **Bush** energy bill: around $9 billion in subsidies and tax breaks. While D's enjoy more union support, business outcontributes labor by roughly nine to one. In December 2004, the FEC—which, thanks to two George W. Bush appointees, has a three-to-two Republican majority—changed the rules to make it easier for industry PACs to raise money. As of February 2005, the Repugs had a six-to-one cash advantage over the Dems.

Smith assured everyone he would enforce the laws he believes should not exist. But as he told *Reason*: "I don't think the Supreme Court has a monopoly on [interpreting] the Constitution." No wonder Chief Justice Commissioner Smith was worth sixteen mere circuit court judges.

#78: BRADLEY SMITH 2

Alas, as Bradley Smiths go, **Bradley A. Smith** (#79) is, relatively speaking, the *good* news. While researching him, I learned of

Bradley *R.* Smith, a leading Holocaust denier for more than two decades. Formerly media director of the "Institute for Historical Review," the world's leading clearinghouse of Holocaust denial propaganda, Smith now runs the California-based so-called Committee for Open Debate on the Holocaust (CODOH), which "argue[s] for an open debate on what we recognize as the First Great WMD fraud—the German gas-chamber fantasy." Smith's avowed aims are to "promote intellectual freedom," "help civilize Americans," and "address" "Jewish participation in anti-Christian, Marxist-Stalinist horrors, the unnaturally bloated Jewish influence in American cultural affairs and political life," "Jewish participation in the slave trade," "the primitive anti-Christian ugliness in the Talmud," and "how the story of Jewish 'genocide' is being promoted."

CODOH is especially active in "outreach" to college students through ads in college newspapers. As the Anti-Defamation League noted:

> If the student newspaper published the ad, it inevitably generated outrage, pain and, most important, publicity. If the paper refused the ad, Smith played the victim of the "Thought Police," wrapped himself in the First Amendment and loudly bewailed the death of the university with its ideals of open inquiry and academic freedom. Holocaust denial got extensive coverage on the campus, in the local, and occasionally, national media, and Smith assumed the guise of the champion of intellectual integrity.

CODOH's Web site also offers insights into Zionism and samples of Smith's "work in progress," *Adolf Hitler and Me: Reading Mein Kampf.* I hope he dies before he finishes it.

#77: GOD

(Speaking of the Holocaust. What about *that*?)

He thinks He's above the law. He's broken I don't know how many Commandments—dozens—as well as the First Amendment. He used to support church-state separation, which is partly why He kept so blessedly quiet for a couple of hundred years. But more recently—far from striking down people like **Pat Robertson** (#55), **Franklin Graham** (#84), and **Sun Myung Moon** (#54, for whom he wrote a letter of endorsement!)—God has been going around America telling right-wingers to keep up the good work and/or run for public office, and telling Republican politicians like **George W. Bush** and **Tom DeLay** ($6) that they have His full support. All this while retaining His religious tax exemption *and* raking in huge increases in church collections and in faith-based grants awarded by the very politicians He endorses. (Bipartisanship? He called it "date rape." Wait, no, that was **Grover Norquist** [#24]. Well, they're both far to the right and they look sort of alike. Which is another thing about God.)

Before the Enlightenment drove Him underground, as it were (He dislikes bright light), God served as the model and justification for monarchy. With Bush He seems to be doing so again. While He had no involvement in deceiving the country into war in Iraq (that was mainly **Cheney**), the evidence suggests He signed off on the use of torture at U.S. military prisons, on indefinite detention of suspects without charges, and on domestic spying (He's been doing *that* for ages, God knows) and that He took part in closed-door meetings of Cheney's energy task force.

And He's been claiming again to have created the world—guided its evolution, whatever. (Only now he's a "designer." *Pardonnez-moi.*) Even more worrisome, after a state visit to California (accompanied, reportedly, by #66, **Tim LaHaye**), He began calling Himself the Terminator.

Frankly, like they say about George Bush, I think He's drinking again.

He also inspired Christian rock. Now people are standing up at concerts and singing along with their eyes closed and their arms in the air. It's fucking unbearable. Then there's **Osama bin Laden** (#5). No, that's to do with Allah. Aahh, they're all the same.

#76: POPE BENEDICT XVI: THE DICK CHENEY OF CATHOLICISM

So global a figure would seem to fall outside this book's parochial, American scope. How much more unfitting it would be to bring up the Catholic Church's nearly two-millennia history of savage persecutions of nonbelievers, torture and burning of heretics, brutal suppression of science, and vast self-enrichment off the labor of masses controlled through fear of hell; its blessing of tyrannical regimes, wars, and jihads; its endorsement of the forced conversions, enslavement, or slaughter of whole continents of "heathens" and "savages"; its looking the other way during the Holocaust. . . .

(By the way, as a ferocious anti-"relativist," Benedict would deny that the acts of people of different cultures or eras must be judged by different moral standards.)

The Bavarian-born Joseph Ratzinger, who was promoted from cardinal to pope in May 2005, has long been one of the Church's most influential theologians. He strongly opposes birth control, abortion, stem cell research, and homosexuality. (Is the pope Catholic?) He has attacked those who find "feminist" meanings in the Bible and has told American bishops it's appropriate to deny Communion to supporters of abortion and euthanasia. His views on pedophilia among Catholic priests are more . . . complicated. But of this there is no doubt: *habemus conservativam*. We have a hard-core conservative on our hands, more so even than his predecessor.

Ratzinger was hence a logical choice to be named by Pope John Paul II in 1981 as prefect of the Congregation for the Doctrine of the Faith (CDF)—formerly known as the Holy Office of the Inquisition. In that capacity, Ratzinger played a key role in silencing liberation theologians and clergy in Latin America who championed human rights and sided with the poor against rich landowners and brutal military regimes. But this, again, falls far outside this book's scope.

Nor must we make an issue of Ratzinger's membership in the Hitler Youth, which was legally mandatory, if not quite unavoidable. (If it comes out that he still likes to get into the uniform for special occasions, well, then we do need to reexamine the issue. Along with that of his professed taste for red Prada shoes. Indeed, the whole question of pradaphiles in the Church.) Ratzinger has said resistance (to the Nazis, not the Prada) was "impossible." Please! Some credit at least for the many who did resist—lest an appearance of denial suggest that *habemus papam* who hasn't quite come to terms morally with his past.

In 2004, Ratzinger opposed Turkey's entry into the European Union because, he said, "Turkey is founded upon Islam." "The views the new pope has expressed," said the *Christian Science Monitor*, "suggest that he is not willing to deal with members of other faiths as equals." In 2000, his office warned of the danger of seeking "to justify religious pluralism" and said non-Catholics "are in a gravely deficient situation" vis-à-vis "salvation." Granted, you can't expect Coke to declare Pepsi just as good. But if Coke starts to suggest Pepsi drinkers will wind up in Hell, then, Houston, I mean, Rome, *habemus problemam*. (By the way, watch those empty spiritual calories.)

As head of the CDF, it was Ratzinger's responsibility to investigate sexual abuse of minors by priests. In the United States especially, allegations of abuse and of systematic cover-ups by senior Church officials have been rampant. Ratzinger took matters firmly in hand: in 2001, he sent a Latin-language letter to every bishop in the Church warning them, "under the penalty of excommunication," that abuse investigations were to remain "the strictest secret" of the Church for up to twenty-eight years. The archbishop who cosigned the letter said bishops were not obligated to report abuse allegations to police. Lawyers for alleged victims claimed Ratzinger conspired to obstruct justice.

In 2002, Ratzinger said "less than one percent of priests are guilty of acts of this type." (Other sources have said 1.5 to 2 percent.) According to a report by the Vatican itself, there were 4,450 such priests worldwide between 1950 and 2002. A study commissioned by the U.S. Conference of Catholic Bishops reported 10,667 victims in the U.S. alone over roughly the same period. At least 1,092 allegations were made against 756 Catholic priests in the U.S. just in 2004.[19] Needless to say, the true figures . . .

In 2005, Ratzinger was accused of ignoring for seven years charges that Father Marcial Maciel, the Mexican-born founder of the powerful, ultraconservative Legionaires of Christ order, sexually abused nine teenagers in his organization, and that he ignored these charges because Maciel was a close friend of John Paul II and raised a lot of money for the Church. The nine, now grown up, some of them priests in the U.S., presented their accusations to Ratzinger in 1997. According to one of those priests, Ratzinger's response was that Maciel had brought many "benefits" to the Church and that it was a "touchy problem." "One can't put on trial such a close friend of the Pope," Ratzinger said on another occasion. In 1999, his office declared the matter closed.[20]

One of the new pope's first acts (after shopping for shoes) was to appoint William Levada, archbishop of San Francisco—a

19 Jamie Doward, "The Pope, the Letter and the Child Sex Claim," *Observer*, April 24, 2005.

20 Ibid.

staunch conservative—as his successor to head the CDF. In 1997, Levada objected to a new city law that all companies must provide the same benefits for domestic partners as for spouses. In 2005, he led a protest march against gay marriage through the streets of San Francisco.

"Pray for me," Benedict said at his inaugural mass in St. Peter's Square. He must have a good idea how his heavenly credit report looks. (Popes receive them free.)

#75: KANSAS STATE BOARD OF EDUCATION

In 1998, Pope John Paul II announced that the Roman Catholic Church would no longer oppose the teaching of evolution. That seemed to leave American fundamentalist Protestants (among them our Bible-thumper-in-chief, #2) as *the* most backward segment of humanity (along with certain mullahs and their followers) in their views on science.

In 1999, the Kansas State Board of Education voted to erase any mention of evolution from the state science curriculum. That was reversed in 2001, after Kansas became such a laughingstock that three board members who supported the move were defeated in a Republican primary. But after conservatives won a six-to-four majority on the board in November 2004, they voted to require that students be taught—falsely—that evolution is a controversial theory among scientists and be presented with different "points of view," particularly **"intelligent design"** (ID, #34), a religious doctrine masquerading as science which posits that life is too complex to have evolved unaided by a Designer.

A statewide referendum on the theory of gravity is expected in 2007.

As cultural critic Tom Franks titled his 2004 book: *What's the*

Matter with Kansas? Well, nothing that isn't wrong with most of the country. In the early 1980s, Louisiana passed a law giving creationism equal teaching time with evolution. The Ohio Department of Education voted unanimously in 2002 for teaching "alternatives." In 2004, a suburban Atlanta school district put warning stickers on its biology textbooks calling evolution "a theory, not a fact." Battles over evolution are under way in at least forty-three states. In a November 2004 CBS News/*New York Times* poll, only 40 percent of the respondents (and 28 percent of **Bush** voters) said they believed humans had evolved; only 13 percent (6 percent of Bush voters) believed in evolution unguided by God; and 65 percent favored teaching creationism alongside evolution in public schools. And now, the Church of the Flying Spaghetti Monster (FSM) is demanding equal teaching time for *its* theory that the world was created by an FSM.[21]

In 1996, the Associated Press reported that fewer than half of American adults understood that the Earth orbits the sun yearly. Only 9 percent knew what a molecule was. (Talk about the descent of man . . .)

In fact, there is no serious *scientific* uncertainty about whether species arise through evolution—*or* whether Darwinian evolution, that is, "blind" natural selection, is capable of explaining all that we see in living things. Evolution is "just a theory" just as "relativity as described by Albert Einstein is 'just' a theory," wrote science writer David Quammen in *National Geographic.* "The notion that Earth orbits around the sun rather than vice versa . . . is a theory. . . . Each of these theories is an explanation that has been confirmed to such a degree, by observation and experiment, that knowledgeable experts accept it as fact."

It is religion, a *particular* religion, *disguised* as science, that is being introduced into public schools in Kansas and other states—as members of the religious right occasionally acknowledge—and

21 Venganza.org.

as U.S. District Judge John E. Jones ruled in December 2005 in a lawsuit by parents in Dover, Pennsylvania, against the local school board for requiring ID to be presented as an alternative to evolution. Jones said ID "is not science" and school board members showed "breathtaking inanity" in trying to inject religion into science classes.

However, it's a victory for the religious right that there even *is* a "scientific" debate on evolution—which is being brought into public school classrooms to *create* uncertainty about well-established science. The Kansas Board of Ed is helping make America a laughing-stock and advancing our retreat, as it were, toward the good, Christian, prescientific, geocentric, anthropocentric, ankle-deep-in-mud-and-manure, barefoot-and-pregnant Middle Ages.

"The best argument that the creationists have got is that it's only fair to teach both sides," a spokesman for the National Center for Science Education told *Salon*'s Michelle Goldberg. "The problem with that argument is that science is not a democracy and a lot of times there aren't two correct sides." Public desires don't determine the physical facts of the world. But, Goldberg noted, creationism "is the perfect culture-war issue because . . . in a country gripped by right-wing populism, it's not hard to stoke resentment against scientists who have the gall to think that they know more than everybody else."

Red-state conservatives do not reject evolution out of blind biblical fundamentalism (much less for scientific reasons) but because they understand that Darwin, along with Marx and Freud, threatens their moral, social, and political beliefs and ideals, their whole worldview. The sun is too hot for their crops so they demand it be moved farther away.

Instead of simply invoking the Bible to attack the theory of evolution, **Tom DeLay** (#6) blamed evolution for the Columbine school shootings (as does an exhibit in the recently opened, $25-million Museum of Creation in Kentucky, where other exhibits blame "mankind's sin" for disease and famine and homosexuals for AIDS). And there *is* something to DeLay's deranged claim. In the process of demolishing traditional religious beliefs about the world, science *has* created *the* moral dilemma of the modern age: Without religious belief, upon what foundation *does* morality rest? Aren't we left with the chaos of moral relativism and nihilism—with Kliebold and Harris, Abramoff and Scanlon . . . **Rove** and, well, DeLay?

But the sense of moral order that religious beliefs help some people maintain and the social order they supposedly help preserve (if you ignore the incessant religious violence throughout history) do not make those beliefs *true*. As George Bernard Shaw said: "The fact that a believer is happier than a skeptic is no more to the point than the fact that a drunken man is happier than a sober one." If scientific discoveries have made life morally, philosophically, and emotionally harder, *too bad*. (It is ironic how much the current religious revival is a child of 1960s youth culture: both disdain the painstaking labors it takes to really learn something—to add a single *fact* to the store of human knowledge—and instead seek a cheap high and instant truth in a pill or a prayer. I'd like to see a commercial: "This is your child's brain on the opium of the people.")

But what can we expect from Kansas if former Bush speechwriter David Frum of the **American Enterprise Institute** (#7) and *National Review*—no benighted evangelical but an educated, Canadian-born Jew—could say: "I don't believe that anything that offends nine-tenths of the American public should be taught in public schools . . . that public schools should embark on teaching anything that offends Christian principle." Well, that rules out teaching science. No problem—while we pray, the Chinese, Japanese, and Koreans will invent, make, and sell us everything we need. They don't seem to mind.

#74: NIHAD AWAD, IBRAHIM HOOPER, AND THE COUNCIL ON AMERICAN-ISLAMIC RELATIONS: CAIR-ING FOR TERRORISTS

"The Council on American-Islamic Relations (CAIR)," says the all-knowing Wikipedia, "is the largest Muslim civil rights organization in North America. Its stated goals are to promote a positive image of Islam in the United States, empower the American Muslim community, and promote understanding," and to advocate "on behalf of Muslims and others who have experienced religious discrimination, defamation, or hate crimes." Over the years, "CAIR has become an often-cited source for journalists who are seeking input or a quote" from the Muslim community. Washington, D.C.–based CAIR was founded in 1994 by Nihad Awad, Omar Ahmad, "and other former members of the Islamic Association of Palestine, which in turn was founded by senior Hamas figure Mousa Mohammed Abu Marzook, later deported from the U.S." It does get interesting quickly.

In 2003, the Ohio chapter of the American Civil Liberties Union gave its annual Liberty Flame Award to the Ohio chapter of CAIR "for contributions to the advancement and protection of civil liberties." **George W. Bush** included CAIR leaders in several public functions following 9/11. CAIR's online "Not in the Name of Islam" petition repudiates the use of terror.

Meanwhile, U.S. state attorneys have filed a number of lawsuits against CAIR and several CAIR participants, accusing them of supporting terrorism. Several CAIR members have been convicted on terror-related charges. And the administration has reportedly renounced its ties with CAIR over its alleged support for Hamas and Hezbollah, which are designated as terrorist organizations by the U.S., Canada, Britain, Australia, and the European Union:

- In 1994, Nihad Awad declared himself a supporter of Hamas, whose stated goal is to establish an Islamic theocracy in Palestine—meaning, of course, the area that is currently Israel, the West Bank, and Gaza; Hamas proudly advertises its suicide bombings and other acts of violence against Israelis, both military and civilian. The same year, CAIR coordinated a series of meetings for a Jordanian Islamic militant, Bassam Alamoush, who told a Chicago audience that killing Jews is "a good deed."

- In 1998, cofounder Omar Ahmad told a Muslim audience in California: "Islam isn't in America to be equal to any other faith, but to become dominant. The Koran . . . should be the highest authority in America, and Islam the only accepted religion on earth."

- CAIR termed the trial of Sheik Omar Abdel-Rahman—the blind Egyptian cleric deemed the ringleader of the 1993 World Trade Center (WTC) bombing and convicted of conspiring to blow up New York landmarks including the UN, the Lincoln and Holland tunnels, and the George Washington Bridge—a "travesty of justice"; indeed, CAIR listed the trial among "incidents of anti-Muslim bias and violence." (Not to try to prejudice you or anything, but among many other acts of violence, Sheik Omar's Egypt-based Islamic Group carried out the 1997 Luxor massacre, in which fifty-eight foreign tourists and four Egyptians were shot, beheaded, and/or disemboweled.)

- Awad reportedly wrote that "there is ample evidence indicating that both the Mossad [Israeli intelligence] and the Egyptian Intelligence played a role" in the 1993 WTC bombing.[22]

- In 1995, CAIR board member Imam Siraj Wahaj was named as an unindicted alleged co-conspirator in the attempt to blow up

22 Jake Tapper, "Islam's Flawed Spokesmen," *Salon*, September 26, 2001.

New York City monuments. In 1991, Wahaj warned that America would fall unless it "accepts the Islamic agenda." (But we want the Christian agenda!)

- Shortly after 9/11, CAIR's Web site solicited donations for what it called the "NY/DC Emergency Relief Fund." However, clicking on the donation link led to a Web site for donations to the Holy Land Foundation for Relief and Development, a charity whose assets were later frozen by the U.S. Treasury Department, which said "its primary purpose [was] to fund Hamas."
- Between 2003 and 2005, CAIR's director of community relations, its civil-rights coordinator, and a CAIR-Texas founding member were convicted, variously, on charges of credit card and bank fraud, providing material support to Al Qaeda and the Taliban, funding Hamas, and the illegal export of electronics equipment to state sponsors of terrorism.
- In 2004, CAIR was named as a defendant in a class-action lawsuit relating to the 9/11 terror attacks, alleging that CAIR funds terrorist groups and "silence[s] critics, analysts, commentators, media organizations, and government officials by leveling false charges of discrimination, libel, slander and defamation."

Indeed, while CAIR routinely attacks and occasionally sues critics of CAIR and of other Islamic groups—typically dismissing them as right-wing zealots and "anti-Muslim bigots" and accusing even Muslim critics of being, as CAIR spokesman Ibrahim Hooper said, "front men" for "the pro-Israel lobby"—CAIR has refused to condemn Hamas, Hezbollah, or even **Osama bin Laden** (#5). "It's not our job to go around denouncing," Hooper has said. "We're not in the business of condemning." I may be just a front man for the pro-Israel lobby, but condemning is certainly *one* of the businesses CAIR is in.

#73: BERNARD GOLDBERG'S *BIAS*

Goldberg has already received ample attention in my introduction. We don't want him to get a swollen head—which, given its rightward tilt, could make him dangerously unstable, endangering passersby. ("Goldberg Predicts Collapse of Liberal Media," went a headline on the right-wing Web site NewsMax.com. "Liberal Media Predict Collapse of Goldberg," we reply.) But we must add a few words about that bias—and about *Bias*, Bernie's book about the **so-called liberal media** (#13).

Goldberg claims that liberal bias is so entrenched among liberals in the media—who are surrounded almost exclusively by other liberals—that they are not even aware it *is* bias. Nothing like this happens in conservative circles. "Goldberg has also been criticized by many for not properly documenting his sources and often for taking information out of context," notes Wikipedia. Al Franken devoted an entire chapter in his book *Lies and the Lying Liars Who Tell Them* to factual inaccuracies in *Bias*. (*You* may cynically believe Franken's only aim was to become #37 in Goldberg's *100 People Who Are Screwing Up America*. I don't.)

"Many people see Bernard Goldberg's attacks on the unsubstantiated 'liberal bias' of CBS to be in retaliation after leaving the network," Wiki adds. Goldberg's first attack on CBS, where he was a reporter for thirty years, came in a *Wall Street Journal* (#49) op-ed piece he wrote in 1996—"after managing to hold his tongue for a quarter of a century," noted Michael Kinsley in *Slate*. "Fired? Not at all. Given a cushy job until a bigger pension kicked in at age 55, when he left of his own accord? Yup. Those liberal swine! No wonder Goldberg is regarded (by himself, among others) as a martyr."

The right's favorite Goldberg anecdote is his report of a conversation with CBS News president Andrew Heyward: "'Look, Bernie,' he said, 'of course there's a liberal bias in the news. All the networks tilt left.' But, 'If you repeat any of this, I'll deny it.'" There you have it—denial-proof proof of the vast left-wing conspiracy!

For the record, the liberal watchdog group Media Matters for America monitored *CBS Evening News* broadcasts between November 2004 and February 2005 and reported that appearances by Republicans and conservatives—not including forty clips of **George W. Bush**—were nearly 30 percent more frequent than those by Democrats and progressives. (And see #13.)

Radio? Get real. A study released in June 2004 by Democracy Radio revealed that national and local conservative broadcasts totaled over thirteen times as many hours per week as liberal programming. Radio is owned by giant, Republican-owned chains like **Clear Channel** (#50)—and, figuratively, by **Limbaugh** (#27), **O'Reilly** (#29), **Hannity** (#30), **Schlessinger** (#68), Bob Grant, Michael Reagan, Oliver North, Gordon Liddy . . .

Just what is "bias" anyway? Where is the center? Where was it in 1938 Germany? Was "bias" to be avoided then? This much seems certain: news reporting *should* try to avoid bias, and there's a lot more of it at **Fox News** (#28) than at CBS. Despite being, in Kinsley's view, "remarkably dense," Goldberg must understand all this. It follows that his problem isn't with the "bias" part but with the "liberal" part.

One of Goldberg's central claims is that TV broadcasters "pointedly identify conservative politicians as conservatives" but rarely use the word "liberal" to describe liberals. This—if true—would not be surprising, given what a slur conservatives have turned "liberal" into. But as reported in the *American Prospect* in 2002, a database search of more than twenty major U.S. daily newspapers—including the "liberal" *New York Times, Washington Post,* and *Los Angeles Times*—found that liberal legislators were more than 30 percent more likely to be labeled "liberal" than conservatives were to be labeled "conservative." The discrepancy—again, contrary to Goldberg's claims—was even wider in the labeling of actors: Barbra Streisand and Rob Reiner were labeled "liberal" four times as frequently as Tom Selleck and Bruce Willis were labeled "conservative." Warren Beatty was labeled more often than **Ahnuld** (#70), Norman Lear more often than Charlton Heston. Since 1992, reporter Geoffrey Nunberg found, newspaper references to "liberal bias" in the media outnumbered references to "conservative bias" by twenty-seven to one—not what you'd expect from a truly "liberal" press. All this, wrote Nunberg, only indicates how phobic the media have become about charges of bias from the right. The disparities in labeling are "a tribute to the success that critics like Goldberg have had in popularizing their picture of the media—and . . . to the extraordinary attention that the media have given to views like Goldberg's in the first place."

"Bernard Goldberg may not be wrong about the presence of bias in the media," Nunberg concluded—"he's just wrong that it's 'liberal.'" "Wrong" is one word for it.

#72: DAVID LESAR
AND THE GOOD CITIZEN HALLIBURTON

No, you *haven't* heard enough about Halliburton and its good corporate citizenship until you can recite it all from memory and have sworn to transmit it to your children and grandchildren.

Halliburton is the Houston-based energy, engineering, and construction giant that **Dick Cheney** headed from 1995 to 2000. With nearly one hundred thousand employees in around 270 divisions (including some twenty-three offshore tax havens) in scores of countries—regardless of race, creed, or state sponsorship of terrorism—Halliburton builds, repairs, supplies, and staffs oil and gas drilling rigs, pipelines, refineries, shipping terminals, roads, and military bases. It is said to have some sort of presence in almost every oil-drilling operation in the world. It maintains security forces recruited from among retired police and army officers in places like Colombia for deployment in places like Iraq. There is no question Halliburton does jobs of a scale few other companies can handle. It got this big in part by exploiting political connections no other company can equal. And it has abused its privileged position—cooked the books, overcharged clients (usually U.S. taxpayers), failed to deliver services, and violated U.S. trade sanctions—on an equally unequaled scale, costing taxpayers and shareholders billions, complicating U.S. foreign policy, and probably costing U.S. lives.

But the Cheney-Bush administration, with its cronyism and contempt for *free-market* capitalism, keeps defending Halliburton and awarding it no-bid contracts. Between 2002 and 2004, Halliburton went from the Pentagon's thirty-seventh largest contractor to number one, with some $18 billion in contracts for services in Iraq. It is quite simply the fattest, dirtiest, and most immovable hog feeding at the public trough.

From the 1940s through the sixties and especially during the Vietnam War, Halliburton's Brown and Root (B&R) division (once owned by **George W. Bush**'s grandfather Prescott Bush's firm, Brown Brothers Harriman) grew by building military bases. It has been joined at the hip to the Pentagon ever since. In the early 1990s, Halliburton pioneered the outsourcing of military "logistical support"—operating bases and providing mail, food, laundry, and trash services and who knows what else. (I am *not* alluding to the article "Brown and Root and the Bush-Cheney Drug Empire" by Michael Ruppert, formerly of Los Angeles Police Department's Organized Crime Intelligence Division, which I recommend *no one* read in the October 24, 2000, issue of FromTheWilderness. com.)

In 1992, the Pentagon, under Defense Secretary Cheney, commissioned B&R for a classified study on whether the military should use more private contractors! B&R thought about it long and hard, finally agreed, and got one of the first private army support contracts. Outsourcing took off. And in 1995 Cheney, with no business experience, became CEO of a multibillion-dollar firm. During his five years at Halliburton, the value of its federal contracts (and its political donations, mostly to Republicans) doubled. Upon leaving Halliburton in 2000, Cheney was its largest shareholder, owning a $45 million slice.

Halliburton has since been the subject of several federal investigations. On Cheney's watch, the firm was allegedly involved in a $180 million bribery scheme in Nigeria and overcharged the army for work in the Balkans. In 2002, it paid $2 million to settle charges it inflated costs on a maintenance contract at an army base in California. In August 2004, it paid a paltry $7.5 million to settle Securities and Exchange Commission (SEC) charges that it defrauded shareholders of billions by inflating revenue while under Cheney's management—maneuvers Cheney was aware of, Halliburton's new CEO, David Lesar, told *Newsweek*. All five of the SEC commissioners who approved the settlement—and said Cheney should not be held accountable—were appointed by Bush (or perhaps Cheney).

In 1998, Halliburton acquired Dresser Industries and its Kellogg division (which it merged with B&R to form KBR) and with it, Kellogg's asbestos-related litigation problems, thanks to which Halliburton booked $900 million a year in *losses* from 2002 through 2004—even as its Iraq business and its stock price were booming. (Taxes? What are those?) The stock, after falling nearly 80 percent in 2001 because of the accounting scandal (Cheney had sold $35 million, or 78 percent, of his common shares in August 2000), went from $10 to $70 beween early 2002 and 2005.

In speeches overseas in 1998 and 2000, Cheney attacked U.S. trade sanctions on Iran and Libya—which the State Department listed as state sponsors of terrorism—and complained that the policy prevented U.S. firms from "invest[ing] significantly in Iran." Apparently, it didn't: by 2004, the Treasury Department was investigating Halliburton for "serious and willful violations" of the sanctions laws while Cheney was CEO. Halliburton denied performing $30 to $40 million annually in oil-field service work in Iran: *that*, it said, was its Cayman Islands–registered subsidiary, Halliburton Products & Services Limited (HPSL)—which, it argued, was exempt from any U.S. embargo. In 2003, Halliburton generated about $80 million in revenue in Iran—part of Bush's "axis of evil," the most active state sponsor of terrorism, according to the State Department, and an emerging nuclear threat.

In January 2005, Lesar announced that the firm was pulling out of Iran—without mentioning that just a week before, subsidiary HPSL signed a new $30-to-$35-million deal to help develop Iran's natural gas fields. "They're still acting like the sanctions law are a big joke," a congressional investigator told *Newsweek*, which noted that the deal "appears to suggest a far closer connection with the country's hard-line government than the firm has ever acknowledged."[23]

During the 2000 campaign, Cheney claimed he had "imposed a 'firm policy' [at Halliburton] against trading with Iraq." As secretary of defense under Bush I, Cheney had been one of the architects of the post–Gulf War trade embargo on Iraq. But less than six years later, the *American Prospect* noted, he "apparently had more important interests than preventing Hussein from rebuilding his army." While Cheney was CEO, Halliburton acquired two foreign subsidiaries and used them to sell Iraq more than $73 million in oil-production equipment without violating U.S. sanctions. "Two former senior executives of the Halliburton subsidiaries say that, as far as they knew, there was no policy against doing business with Iraq. One of the executives also says . . . he is certain

---

23 Michael Isikoff and Mark Hosenball, "Business As Usual?" *Newsweek* Online, February 16, 2005.

Cheney knew about" the Iraqi contracts, the *Washington Post* reported.[24]

Halliburton was also accused during the 1990s of working with Nigeria's "kill'n'go" Mobile Police, who shot peaceful protestors at oil facilities and destroyed nearby villages. As our vice-champion of global freedom and democracy said back then, "The good Lord didn't see fit to put oil and gas only where there are democratic regimes" friendly to the United States. Well, if the *Lord* says it's okay, who cares about *laws* or human rights?

Even before the invasion of Iraq began in March 2003, Halliburton got an estimated $1 billion contract to put out oil-well fires there, without the competitive bidding normally required for government contracts. In addition, KBR was secretly awarded a no-bid contract worth up to $7 billion to upgrade Iraqi oil facilities —which, it turned out, also allowed the company to pump and distribute the oil for a time. By early 2004, Halliburton was getting more than one fifth of what the U.S. was spending in Iraq, or around $1 billion *a month*. KBR had billed the Army $9.6 billion (a sum expected to grow by $6 billion a year) for support services for which the army initially estimated and budgeted $3.6 billion.

Pentagon and congressional reviews in 2004 concluded Halliburton overcharged the army by $61 million for delivering gasoline for Iraq's civilian market—charging more than twice the going rate—and had failed to account for 43 percent of its total expenses. It was billing the army $100 for each 15-pound load of laundry—which came to $1 million a month in overcharges. KBR employees were housed in five-star, $110 hotel rooms in Kuwait while the troops lived in tents at a cost of $1.39 per day. Halliburton billed taxpayers for empty trucks driven up and down Iraq, and $85,000 vehicles were abandoned for lack of spare tires. Workers were told to "look busy" while doing virtually no work

24 Colum Lynch, "Halliburton's Iraq Deals Greater Than Cheney Has Said," *Washington Post*, June 23, 2001.

for salaries of $80,000 a year. In November 2004, the Coalition Provisional Authority (CPA) inspector general reported that a third or more of the government property Halliburton was paid to manage—including more than $18 million worth of vehicles, generators, and computers—was missing. (Seems to be a Halliburton habit. Just around the same time, the firm lost track of a 185-pound container of radioactive material—the kind used in dirty bombs—that it was importing into the U.S. and failed to report the loss for four months, in violation of federal regulations.)[25] Halliburton charged the Army for thousands of meals a day that it never served to troops. It even fell behind in delivering drinking water to the troops. Privatization = Efficiency!

In July 2004—the same month that the Government Accountability Office, Congress's investigative arm, reported that Halliburton had overcharged the government by more than $165 million—Senate Republicans voted down a proposal to impose stiffer penalties on contractors who overbill. In February 2005, the administration budgeted an additional $1.5 billion for Halliburton services and awarded the firm $9.4 million in bonus payments.

What does it take to stop getting contracts from the Bush administration? ("The wrong political connections" is correct.)

Even as Halliburton was being investigated for bribery, bid-rigging, felonious overcharging, and other criminal violations, upon what company did the Bush administration rush to bestow a $12 million contract for cleanup and reconstruction the day Hurricane Katrina made landfall in September 2005? "Dunkin' Donuts" is incorrect. Let no one accuse Bush & Co. of not responding to Katrina quickly. By late October, Halliburton's Katrina contracts were worth $125 million and climbing.

And the Lord visited upon them floods, pestilence, cronyism, overruns, price gouging. . . .

25 "Hey, Anybody Seen Our Nukes?" AmericanProgress.org, February 11, 2005.

#71: THE HOUSE OF REGNERY: WHITE PUBLISHING POWER

In 2004, the Southern Poverty Law Center (SPLC) reported that William Regnery II, an heir to the "conservative" Regnery Publishing fortune, was "moving into a new line of business: matchmaking for 'heterosexual whites of Christian cultural heritage.'"

So? That doesn't necessarily imply bigotry. Why do liberals persist in the slander that the conservative movement is fueled by racism, along with selfishness, greed, and nostalgia for the class and gender privileges and inequalities of yesteryear? Why? Why?

Are repugnant values regnant in the House of Regnery?

Founded by William's father, Henry, in 1947, Washington, D.C.–based Regnery Publishing specializes in books like *Unfit for Command: Swift Boat Veterans Speak Out against John Kerry*, the filthy and utterly discredited smear on Kerry's Vietnam War record that was published a few months before the 2004 election; *Unholy Alliance: Radical Islam and the American Left*, by **David Horowitz** (#31); *High Crimes and Misdemeanors: The Case against Bill Clinton*, by **Ann Coulter** (#32); *In Defense of Internment: The Case for "Racial Profiling" in World War II and the War on Terror*, by Michelle Malkin; *Persecution: How Liberals Are Waging War against Christianity*, by David Limbaugh; and such titles as *Reckless Disregard: How Liberal Democrats* [and not **Bush** and **Rumsfeld**] *Undercut Our Military, Endanger Our Soldiers, and Jeopardize Our Security*; *Leftism Revisited: From de Sade and Marx to Hitler and Pol Pot* (yes, Hitler was really a *leftist*); and *Fidel: Hollywood's Favorite Tyrant*. Other Regnery authors include **Phyllis Schlafly** (#20), **Marvin Olasky** (#40), **Wayne LaPierre** (#22), G. Gordon Liddy, Newt Gingrich, Oliver North, Pat Buchanan, William Bennett, Laura Ingraham, and, why, **Bernard Goldberg** (#73).

William II's grandfather, William I, helped organize the America

First Committee, which opposed the United States going to war against Nazi Germany. The group's leading spokesman was Charles Lindbergh, who accepted a medal from Herman Goering in 1938 and who asked at group rallies, where the Nazi salute was popular, "Are we going to let Jews run this country?" "The America First Committee is truly American and truly patriotic!" said Joseph Goebbels in a shortwave radio broadcast.

In 2001, William II founded the Charles Martel Society, which, according to SPLC, "plans research on how government programs negatively affect white families." The society, which Regnery heads and bankrolls, publishes a white-nationalist journal, *Occidental Quarterly*, whose editorial board is stacked with leaders of anti-immigrant organizations and hate groups like Jared Taylor's New Century Foundation. The magazine is filled with articles by white-supremacist luminaries such as Sam Francis of the Council of Conservative Citizens and Wayne Lutton, editor of the Social Contract Press. The Martel Society's activities are "all designed to push Regnery's view that the white race is veering toward extinction."[26]

Which is where his dating service comes in. In an appeal to potential investors, Regnery wrote that this would be a chance to ensure "the survival of our race," which "depends upon our people marrying, reproducing and parenting." The dating service, he added, will be only the first offering in a line of "services and products to whites."

WCW seeks WCM for movies, romantic walks, white power rallies, maybe more. No Steinbergs, Greenbergs, or Goldbergs. (Not to worry—**Bernard** is too busy attacking such forces of evil as Phil Donahue.)

---

26 "Reclusive Publishing Heir to Start All-White Dating Service," Southern Poverty Law Center, summer 2004.

#70: ARNOLD SCHWARZENEGGER: THE DUMBINATOR

Warning: This section contains bad puns based on every god-damned Schwarzenegger movie title, role, and trademark expression.

A specter haunts America: the specter of a Schwarzenegger presidential bid. And one haunts California: the certainty of a Schwarzenegger gubernatorial reelection bid in 2006. To be sure, the Governor's odds for either office lengthened in 2005 as his popularity dropped faster than a 300-pound barbell from the arms of a girlie-man. But that Ahnuld managed to become even a one-terminator governator is a *Raw Deal* (1986).

Arnold and Ronald (Reagan) are of course not just anagrams but analogs, if not *Twins* (1988): both are towering role models for all who aspire to high office with no qualifications except primitive showbiz skills, a macho persona, a conservative-populist posture, plenty of pesos, and above all, sheer celebrity. As much as the spectacle of a wrestler elected governor of Minnesota may have helped turn American politics into a circus or freak show, the Governatorship of California is a far more likely launching pad for a presidential *Running Man* (1987)—even one with foreignness issues, accent issues, Hitler issues, women issues, gay issues, Enron issues, other conflict-of-interest issues, steroid-use issues, makeup issues ("what's he using—wax?" wrote one blogger), heart-valve-surgery issues, abortion-issue issues (he's pro-choice), and good old-fashioned failure-as-governor issues. (As for the foreignness issue, in 2003, Senator Orrin Hatch [R-UT] proposed a constitutional amendment to allow naturalized Austrian-Americans to run for president. He might have included other naturalized Americans as well.)

Ahnuld has said he was inspired to become a Republican by watching the 1968 Nixon-Humphrey debates (there were no

Nixon-Humphrey debates) and hearing Nixon say, "open up the borders" (Ahnuld has opposed giving drivers' licenses and some social services to illegal immigrants) and "strengthen the military and get the government off our backs." (As it stayed off the backs of people drowning in New Orleans, for example?) Ahnuld's political aspirations were known from the early nineties. In 1991, he bought the rights, outtakes, and stills from *Pumping Iron*, the 1977 bodybuilding documentary he starred in. He apparently knew what he was doing; in 2003, two African-American bodybuilders came forward, claiming Schwarzenegger had said, among other such remarks, "If you gave these blacks a country to run, they would run it down the tubes."

It may be completely irrelevant that both of Ahnuld's parents were Nazi Party members—indeed, the diversity of our backgrounds is one of America's glories—but in 2004, a book proposal by the producer of *Pumping Iron* surfaced that quoted Schwarzenegger saying at the time, "I admire [Hitler] for being such a good public speaker and for his way of getting to the people and so on," "and what he did with it" or "not . . . what he did with it," according to the producer's conflicting reports.[27] According to a businessman and "longtime friend" of Ahnuld's quoted by *Spy* magazine, in the seventies Ahnuld "enjoyed playing and giving away records of Hitler's speeches." Ahnuld supported Kurt Waldheim's campaign for the presidency of Austria in 1986, even after it came to light that Waldheim had lied about his past as a Nazi Party storm trooper officer and a German Army officer in World War II.

In April 2003, with the prospect of a *Total Recall* of California governor Gray Davis, Ahnuld met with **Karl Rove** to discuss a possible run. That made sense: it was Davis's failure to protect

27 "Schwarzenegger Disputes Alleged Pro-Hitler Quote," CNN.com, February 24, 2004.

California from the massive electricity-price-gouging "crisis" engineered in 2000 and 2001 by Enron and a few other big-time **George W. Bush**–supporting corporate pirates that led to the recall effort.

In fact, who had Ahnuld met with in 2001 to plan the recall campaign, according to journalist Greg Palast? Then–Enron CEO Ken Lay and some of Lay's other "political buck-buddies." The meeting was about how to stop Davis's and Lieutenant Governor Cruz Bustamante's lawsuits to make Enron and the other power pirates pay back their $9 billion in illicit profits. The solution? A recall campaign and election that would replace Davis with a new, Enron-friendly governor. "If Arnold is selected," wrote Palast, "it's 'hasta la vista' to the $9 billion [threat]."

And so it came to pass. With characteristic seriousness and dignity, Ahnuld announced his candidacy on Jay Leno's *Tonight Show*, saying, "There is a total disconnect between the people and the politicians" (as opposed to the close connection "between the people and multi-millionaire Austrian weight-lifters," a blogger wrote), and issuing his first of many "hasta la vista, Gray Davis"s ("showing that he does have one clear connection with the people of California, who can't tell the difference between politics and show biz either"). He was instantly anointed by the **so-called liberal media** (#13) as the leading candidate.

And the rest is *Jingle All the Way*. After running on the *True Lies* promise that he would not "take any money from anybody" because "I have plenty of money myself" and because "the people should make the decisions rather than special interests," Ahnuld proceeded over the next two years "to collect campaign contributions from private interests at a greater rate than any politician in California history, including Gray Davis, whom he criticized on that very issue,"[28] amassing around $57 million from real estate,

---

28 Wikipedia.org.

financial, entertainment, technology, retail, and agribusiness interests.

As of August 2005, the Schwarzenegger administration had negotiated around $3 billion in settlements with the various energy companies involved in the $9 billion ripoff. The Governator also proposed further deregulating the energy markets and "rewriting" the California law that makes companies liable to repay illegal profits.

On top of his Hitler problems, Ahnuld's 2003 campaign was plagued by "Gropegate" (the two scandals merging in a new Doonesbury character, "Herr Gröpenführer"). Sixteen women came forward with allegations that he was a sexual *Predator* (1987), the accounts ranging from breast-groping at a gym to spanking to wild orgies.

Only months before the election, Ahnuld told *Entertainment Weekly* about his inspiration for a scene during the filming of *Terminator 3*: "I saw this toilet bowl. . . . How many times do you get away with this—to take a woman, grab her upside down, and bury her face in a toilet bowl?" That apparently endeared him to the California Republican Women's Caucus, which endorsed him, saying he "supports family."

But more important than his behavior on movie sets, wrote columnist Robert Scheer, is whether Schwarzenegger, who "appears [to] delight in the extreme violence he peddles" in his films, makes any connection between that and the violence of our society.

None of this has prevented the *Kindergarten Cop* (perhaps with an eye on dose red states) from policing "family values" as governor. In 2004, while claiming to be pro–gay rights, he opposed a move by San Francisco's mayor to allow gay marriages, and in September 2005, he vetoed the California gay marriage bill that had passed both houses of the legislature. Meanwhile, he attacked worker's compensation and state pensions for nurses, teachers, police, and firefighters. Perhaps "values" will see them and their families through.

But the *Collateral Damage* (2002) from Ahnuld's wilder days keeps on coming. In August 2005, the *Washington Post* reported that the publisher of two bodybuilding magazines for which Ahnuld has been executive editor for years had paid a former TV actress $20,000 to keep silent about a seven-year extramarital affair Ahnuld had with her beginning in 1975, when she was sixteen years old. As the age of consent in California is eighteen, Ahnuld may have committed statutory rape.[29]

Two more charges must be brought: He encouraged the production of civilian Humvees (see #67) by custom-ordering the first one in 1992; and in the closing days of the 2004 election campaign, he stumped for George W. Bush in Ohio, the state that determined the outcome.

Let's hope Ahnuld is the *Last Action Hero* (1993) to rise to such political heights—and that he rises no higher. But we can't rule out a *Triumph of the Will* (1936). Because having been named Mr. Olympia, Mr. World, and Mr. Universe multiple times *could* have some effect on a person's ego and feed ambitions for, you know, vuhld domination and all dose tings.

#69: RANDALL "HATE IS GOOD" TERRY AND OPERATION CHRISTIAN TERROR

The antiabortion group Operation Rescue (OR) is best known for conducting protests, often violent ones, at clinics that perform abortions, including illegally blocking access, invading the offices, and subjecting patients and staff to intimidation and harassment. But from humble beginnings in 1988, when it was started by Randall Terry, an evangelical-Christian ex–used car salesman, the Dallas-based group (another gift from Texas) has grown into an

29 Ibid.

all-purpose antifreedom organization that opposes gay and lesbian rights, all methods of and information about birth control and family planning except abstinence, the right to die with dignity (in 2005 Terry served as spokesman for Terri Schiavo's parents), even art that its members find offensive. Groups of OR members have raided bookstores and torn up dangerous books (such as acclaimed photographer Jock Sturges's book *Radiant Identities*, which included photographs of nude children and adolescents). "Because what matters is what *we* believe," goes OR's slogan. Or it should.

Actually, Terry expressed the group's outlook best when he told members in 1993: "I want you to just let a wave of intolerance . . . a wave of hatred wash over you. Yes, hate is good."

"Our goal is a Christian nation," Terry continued. "We have a Biblical duty, we are called by God, to conquer this country. We don't want equal time. We don't want pluralism." During the 1992 election, Terry warned his followers that "to vote for Bill Clinton is to sin against God." Terry got five months in prison for arranging to have a dead fetus delivered to Clinton at that year's Democratic convention. On other occasions, he called Planned Parenthood founder Margaret Sanger a "whore" and an "adultress" and said of doctors who perform abortions: "When I, or people like me, are running the country, you'd better flee, because we will find you, we will try you, and we'll execute you. I mean every word of it." And: "It's us against them. It's the good guys versus the bad guys." And: "There is going to be war," and Christians may be called to "take up the sword to overthrow the tyrannical regime that oppresses them."

Abu al-Terry's followers seem to have taken his exhortations seriously indeed. From 1982 to 2005, there were 169 bombings or arsons of U.S. abortion clinics. In 2003, one of Terry's earliest and most avid followers, James Kopp, was convicted for the 1998 murder of a doctor who performed abortions in Buffalo, New York.

In a 2001 book, Jerry Reiter, a former OR media coordinator turned FBI informant, wrote that at an OR "command post" (housed, he noted, in offices of Jerry Falwell and #56, **Ralph Reed**'s Christian Coalition), he was given books advocating "dozens of not-so-peaceful activities," including the bombing of abortion clinics. Calling OR "the most radical, most dangerous people in the country," Reiter told the *St. Petersburg Times* he became an FBI informant "because I knew that lives were on the line." After the trial and conviction of a terrorist called Michael Griffin, who in 1993 shot and killed Dr. David Gunn as he arrived for work at a Pensacola, Florida, abortion clinic (Griffin may have recognized Gunn because OR had displayed his face and phone number on a "Wanted" poster), Reiter recalled being told by another antiabortion extremist and former minister, Paul Hill, to expect "an IRA-type reign of terror" in which individuals or small groups would "do what the leaders want to see done, but since there won't be any direct orders given, no one can prove conspiracy." The next year, Hill shot and killed a doctor and a volunteer at another Pensacola clinic.

In 2000, Terry was censured by the church in Binghamton, New York, where he had been a member for fifteen years, for a "pattern of repeated and sinful relationships and conversations with both single and married women." Terry denied the allegations but was chastized by Reverend Flip Benham, who took over as OR's national director in 1994. Like, make war, not love!

In 2003, according to the evangelical-conservative *World Magazine*, Terry solicited contributions on his Web site without disclosing they were to help pay for his new $432,000 home in Florida. He told *World* he and his family needed a place to be safe and to "entertain people of stature, people of importance." The same month that he put a down payment on the house, a New York State court found that he was not paying a fair share of child support to his ex-wife. Terry seems interested in exploring *every* way of attacking women's rights.

After his adopted son came out as gay in 2004, Terry disowned him and said his son was gay because of abuse he suffered before Terry "rescued" him at the age of eight. (Terry also teaches that 90 percent of lesbians were sexually assaulted in their youth and that, on average, gay men die at the age of forty-two.) Both of Terry's adopted daughters became pregnant outside of marriage, effectively ending their relationship with him. One later became a Muslim. Terry does make converts.

Indeed, in 1999, Benham converted OR's name formally to the more modest Operation Save America, perhaps to distance it from Terry. A less incendiary OR? Well, Reverend Flip boasts as many arrests as Terry. And the OR Web site sells a T-shirt with "Intolerant" across the front, and on the back, "Homosexuality is a sin. Islam is a lie. Abortion is murder. Some issues are just black and white." Made of pure poppycock. Sizes XS–XXL. Black-and-white only.

#68: DR. LAURA "DO WHAT I SAY, NOT WHAT I DO" SCHLESSINGER

Judge Laura—I mean, *Dr.* Laura—is (like "**Dr. Phil,**" #91) decidedly of the non-nonjudgmental school of broadcast psychotherapy. So if any of the following apply to you: ☑ gay; ☑ having sex outside of marriage; ☑ living together before marriage; ☑ single parent; ☑ mother working outside the home; ☑ kids in day care; ☑ married quickly or at a young age; ☑ divorced too "easily"; ☑ had or are contemplating abortion; or ☑ had or are contemplating euthanasia, Dr. Laura is there, three hours a day on nearly three hundred radio stations, to make you feel stupid, sinful, and utterly ashamed of yourself in front of 8 million listeners. Well, Schlessinger does insist her show—which at its peak was second only to **Rush Limbaugh** (#27)'s in the ratings—is *not* an advice show but a "moral education" show. Goodbye to the poison of moral relativism, for there is always a clear-cut right and wrong, and Judge Laura—despite knowing next to nothing about you and your situation—will tell you which is which. (*You*, in your sniveling, liberal-induced confusion, probably thought you needed sympathetic, impartial, open-minded counsel.)

Thus sayeth Dr. Laura (a Ph.D. in *physiology*):[30]

- "Stay-at-home" moms make the best parents.
- Most two-paycheck couples work for luxury goods, not to make ends meet.
- "This degree [her Ph.D.] entitles me to state the obvious: Homosexuality is a deviation from the biological norm of heterosexuality"—"aberrant," "dysfunctional," a "biological error." "Of course a society should discriminate." "A huge portion of the male homosexual populace is predatory on young boys." Homosexuals can and should be "turned" heterosexual ("reparative therapy").
- Only heterosexual couples with a stay-at-home mother should be permitted to adopt.
- The only excuse for divorce is one of the "three A's"—abuse, addiction, or adultery. Most bad marriages are the wife's fault.
- Women who engage in sex outside marriage are "presenting themselves virtually as unpaid whores." (Whereas, I guess, if you're married and supported, you're, like, *paid*.)
- All contraception is unreliable. The morning-after pill causes "disease."
- Abortion is murder. The pro-choice movement, especially Planned Parenthood, is "evil" and "deceptive."
- Any woman, "no matter how loving and how nurturing," who "intentionally bring[s] a child in the world with no father" is "downright criminal and immoral. . . . It's like having a pet."

30 Main source: Wikipedia.org.

- Hollywood's "impulse to spread vulgarity, violence, and mayhem can often be even greater than their interest in making money." (Their real aim must be to destroy America's moral fiber and make the liberal-communist takeover easier.)
- "I am so sick and tired of all the Arab-American groups whining and complaining about some kind of treatment. . . . What culture and what religion were all the murderers of 9/11? They murdered us." Just one big "they."
- September 2004: "This is not a political show, and I don't want it to be a political show." Six minutes later: "We have insurgents, terrorists, Muslim terrorists in Baghdad murdering children to make sure [Senator John] Kerry's elected." (Evidence and reason suggested the terrorists preferred Bush—the better to accelerate the global religious conflict; see note on Al Qaeda letter, p. 231.)
- "I am a prophet . . . I am a prophet."[31] "I have never, ever said that I was a prophet! That's a total, complete lie."[32]

Schlessinger has written a dozen books which together have sold millions of copies. Her most popular, *The Proper Care and Feeding of Husbands*, despite the title's pseudo-feminist mockery of men, encourages wives to keep their husbands happy by showing respect and cheerfully providing sex and meals and all the other household services, and warns women against "self-centeredness" (which is "a result of the women's movement"). That a man can "have it all"—work and family—"goes unquestioned," reviewer Sacha Zimmerman noted in the *New Republic*. "But a woman who complains about housework on top of a long day at the office is the most selfish, self-centered person on earth." All this is evidently lapped up by Mullah Laura's core audience, which

31 Janet Wiscombe, "I Don't Do Therapy," *Los Angeles Times Magazine*, January 18, 1998.

32 "Corpus Argumenti Lauretti," TVTalkShows.com.

The Nation's Katha Pollitt described as "half lost sheep, half grad-
uates of the Taliban School of Female Deportment."

After her show was sold to **Clear Channel** (#50) in 1998, Schlessinger's opinions shifted further rightward. That year, she and
her entire family converted to Orthodox Judaism. Talk about
divorcing too easily: in 2003, after five years of dispensing advice
couched in Jewish teachings, she announced she was no longer a
practicing Jew. She complained that, while the letters she receives
from Christians "have been very loving, very supportive," from
Jews, "I don't get much back." (According to her friend and fellow
conservative talk show host Michael Medved, "Laura [was] naive
to think, 'gosh, I'll be the queen of the Jews.' ") Schlessinger
hinted at a possible turn to Christianity, "a move that, radio
insiders say, would elevate her career far beyond the three hundred stations that currently syndicate her show," the *Forward*
reported.

"Honor thy father and mother," quoth Dr. Laura. "Even bad parents deserve to be honored if only at a minimal level." Yet, in 2002,
she remained unaware of her own mother's death for two months,
while her mother's corpse lay undiscovered in her home, not far
from Dr. Laura's studios. And at a community prayer breakfast in
2003, Schlessinger announced that she had just spoken to her
sister for the first time in twenty years. Some family values.

"Do what I say, not what I *did*," Schlessinger says. But it is
what she says day after day that is the problem—and not only for
its intolerance and hypocrisies: "Whether it's Dr. Laura or Dr. Phil
(when did we start calling doctors by their first names?)," wrote
Zimmerman, "a ten-minute [radio or TV] conversation will likely
never get to the root of any serious problem. In fact, such micro-
scopic advice could be hugely damaging." Unfortunately, Zimmerman concluded, "an easy answer is always more appealing
than hard work." Actually, Schlessinger's answers are not
appealing at all.

#67: SUAV (SCREWING UP AMERICA VEHICLE) BUYERS

The Hummer screams to the world the words that stand as one of Schwarzenegger's signature achievements as an actor: "Fuck you, asshole!" Maybe this class of vehicles should be called FUVs.

—Gregg Easterbrook in *The New Republic*,
referring to the fact that it was **Ahnuld** (#70)
who persuaded GM to sell a civilian Hummer
and who purchased the first one

SUV buyers, wrote Easterbrook in a 2003 book review titled "Axle of Evil: America's Twisted Love Affair with Sociopathic Cars," buy them "perhaps because they think that SUVs make them safer, or perhaps because [they] privately long to bellow at the world to get out of their way." The first of those reasons is fallacious. As for the latter, it is exactly this mentality the auto industry has identified and targeted in designing SUVs.

Easterbrook's article (from which, unless otherwise indicated, the quotes below are taken) is a review of Keith Bradsher's *High and Mighty: SUVs—The World's Most Dangerous Vehicles and How They Got That Way*. The "High and Mighty" refers as much to the mentality of SUV purchasers as to the size of the monsters now damaging America's economy, air, and climate, menacing its highways, and clogging its city and suburban traffic. (For while SUV buyers may *fantasize* about perching triumphant in their SUV atop a Wyoming mesa, overlooking a spectacular, carless landscape, or just want to be *perceived* as adventurous, only 1 percent of SUVs are ever driven off-road.) The U.S. government deserves plenty of blame for giving SUVs—at the bidding of the **auto industry** (#16)—special exemptions from pollution and safety rules. But ultimately, it is those who buy SUVs who make

them "the very emblem of contemporary selfishness." SUV ownership is indeed "sociopathic" in at least four distinct ways:

1. SUVs pollute the air and emit global-warming greenhouse
   gases far more than regular cars. Cars get cleaner every year—
   and so did the air in U.S. cities, until the SUV boom. SUVs' typical score on the EPA's 1-to-10 scale of clean-air performance:
   0 or 1.
2. These shameless gas-guzzlers increase America's dependence
   on oil imports, with all that that implies economically, geopo-
   litically, Iraqily. Typical SUV mileage is officially 12 to 14 miles
   per gallon in the city. Actual mileage may be a *complete* joke.
3. "These Godzillas are instruments of death for non-SUV-driving
   motorists." In fact, an SUV marketing specialist told Bradsher
   this is part of the "sell line": "If there is a crash, I want the other
   guy to die."
   • The driver of a car struck in the side is 6.6 times as likely to
     die as the driver of the striking car; when the striking car is
     an SUV, its weight drives the death ratio to 30 to 1.
   • SUVs are exempt from all kinds of safety requirements that
     apply to regular cars. They are permitted, for example, to
     have less durable tires and much poorer brakes, meaning
     longer stopping distances. SUVs' height—which is intended
     both to make them intimidating looking and to give them the
     ground clearance to qualify as trucks and escape cars'
     mileage rules—not only produces their notorious rollover
     rates but blocks other drivers' view of the road and causes
     the SUV's headlights to dazzle oncoming drivers. When the
     government tried to get SUV headlights lowered,
     automakers complained that this would make the vehicles
     look less evil, and regulators caved.
   • The many SUVs built on truck frames do not handle well.
     And in accidents, the frame is apt to separate from the
     body, becoming "an iron guillotine aimed at the other car's

passenger compartment." To further increase their asshole appeal (AA), SUVs have been given sports-car-like accelerating power, which SUV drivers "certainly do not need . . . except to act anti-socially" and which makes the vehicles harder to control and more prone to spin out.

- Highway deaths declined through the 1980s and early 1990s. Then the decline flattened out, even as safety devices came into use and drunk driving declined. Why? "The 'kill rate' caused by the presence of ever more SUVs on the road was swamping all safety gains." Adding phynancial to physical injury, these Ubu-like SUV owners generally do not pay higher insurance premiums than owners of regular cars, despite having much higher "loss rates." Sedan drivers subsidize wealthier, SUV-owning SOBs.

4. Finally, the FUV factor itself: From the start, SUV customers were mostly people "who wanted to be different or obstreperous or macho behind the wheel." Bradsher summarized the industry's own marketing research about SUV buyers: "They tend to be people who are insecure and vain. They are frequently nervous about their marriages and uncomfortable about parenthood. They often lack confidence in their driving skills. Above all, they are apt to be self-centered and self-absorbed, with little interest in their neighbors." An "auto-marketing guru" said people buy SUVs "because they want to look as menacing as possible"; "selfish modern buyers think they can cut off other drivers more easily in wheels that seem threatening." Manufacturers used focus groups "to determine which features and styling cues suggest an anti-social message and then zeroing in on them." They boosted SUVs' AA by adding sheer bulk (the typical SUV occupies as much space as 1.4 regular cars) as well as ominous-looking, identity-concealing blackout windows (forbidden on regular cars) and mammoth grill guards (which increase the chance that an SUV will kill someone in an accident)—and by engineering aggressive-looking body shapes.

Designed "to bring out the worst in their owners while simultaneously making them feel that they are invincible," SUVs, wrote Easterbrook:

> have converted driving . . . into a nerve-wracking Darwinian battle . . . Can it be a coincidence that road rage started to become a national concern in the mid-1990s, just as these pharaonic contraptions began flooding the roads . . . [and] that road rage gets worse annually . . . in sync with the annual rise in the [SUV ownership]? . . . What does it say about the United States that there are now millions of people who . . . will pay thousands of dollars extra for vehicles that visually declare, "I have serious psychological problems . . . ?"[33]

#66: TIM LAHAYE AND JERRY JENKINS: LEFT AND RIGHT BEHIND

As you've probably heard, any day or second now, you will find yourself living through a time of "Tribulation," a veritable hell on earth (no, *worse* than your present life), culminating in your slaughter, followed by *actual* Hell for eternity. If, however, you have personally accepted Jesus Christ as your savior, you will not be "left behind" but, "in the twinkling of an eye" (I Corinthians 15:52)—in what is called the "Rapture"—will be beamed up to a better place.

This is the biblically based prophesy proffered in the twelve-volume *Left Behind* (LB) series of apocalyptic Christian novels by

---

33 Gregg Easterbrook, "Axle of Evil: America's Twisted Love Affair with Sociopathic Cars," *New Republic*, January 20, 2003.

Reverend Tim LaHaye and his novelist partner, Jerry Jenkins. By December 2004, the LB novels, at least six of which debuted at number one on the *New York Times* best-seller list, had sold more than 60 million copies worldwide and earned their propheteering authors $50 million each. The related *Kids* series, audio books, and comic books generated another $100 million in annual revenue. LaHaye has also written around fifty nonfiction books, including several self-help books and a sex manual (shortcut to the Rapture?) that has 2.5 million copies in print. In 2002, he signed a $42 million deal for a new series about an evangelical Indiana Jones—without telling Jenkins about it. LaHaye's new novelist-partner would not, like Jenkins, get a 50 percent cut. "Left behind" can mean many things.

Are R&T (Rapture and Tribulation) moguls' earnings tax-exempt, one wonders? After all, the novels are, in LaHaye's words, "blessed" by God, and are part of LaHaye's ministry on Earth. But are they part of the Tim LaHaye Ministries? God (and the IRS) knows.

In 2001, LaHaye was picked by *Evangelical Studies Bulletin* over even Billy Graham as "the most influential Christian leader for the past quarter century." He is also a major *macher* of the *political* right. A graduate of Bob Jones University (along with his wife Beverly LaHaye, founder of the right-wing Concerned Women for America), LaHaye was a founding board member of Jerry Falwell's Moral Majority, which warns that America faces doom, doom, thanks to secular humanists, militant homosexuals, and "baby killers." LaHaye helped form the Institute for Creation Research to promote biblical creationism; founded the American Coalition for Traditional Values (ACTV), which received funding from **Sun Myung Moon** (#54); chaired Moon's Coalition for Religious Freedom (and worked with Moon to try to nominate Falwell instead of George H. W. Bush as the GOP's 1988 presidential candidate); and, with **Paul Weyrich** (#9), organized the Council for National Policy (CNP), a highly secretive group of far-right leaders that ABC News called "the most powerful conservative organization in America you've never heard of." CNP *is*, mysteriously enough, tax-exempt.

But we've left behind *Left Behind*. At the start of the LB cycle, one third of the passengers on a transatlantic flight suddenly disappear, "raptured," leaving only their clothes behind—some of them expensive, barely worn designer items. These are quickly stowed away securely by an alert flight attendant. Actually, one of LaHaye's "researchers" explained on CBS's *60 Minutes*, "There is a lot of debate over [whether] artificial body parts, and contact lenses, and clothes would be 'Left Behind' or not." There is debate, too, over whether body parts such as brains have already been removed and sent on ahead.

There is no question, however, according to LB, that before their fiery end, those left behind will endure seven years of chaos, violence, and the accent of a Rumanian-born Antichrist who finds fitting employment as secretary-general of the UN. There he establishes world government; promotes abortion, family planning, assisted suicide, and global disarmament (his global force of storm troopers are called "peacekeepers") as well as higher taxes and expansion of social services, and calls for (Lord save us) "an equal playing field for everyone." "Yes," noted Steven Waldman in *Slate*, "the Antichrist is a tax-and-spend liberal." Eventually, he launches—from his Baghdad headquarters—the catastrophic assault on Israel that according to the theology must precede Christ's return. As Michelle Goldberg remarked in *Salon:* "No wonder the born-again lobby is . . . opposed to any peace plan."

The novels' sheer looniness is exceeded only by their pulpiness, as betokened by hunky heroes with names like Ray Steele and "Buck" Williams (a thirty-year-old virgin clearly waiting for the right Ms. Fire-and-Brimstone to come along). "You're tense," one character tells her man, offering a soothing, Christian massage and *mes*sage: "Relax, love. Messiah is coming." (I'd say, "What next, a Harlequin Romance Christian division?" except it already exists. You really *can't* make this shit up.) For the guys, there are enough red-blooded combat scenes and explosions to satisfy the most diehard Tom Clancy fan or *Christian Soldier of Fortune* subscriber. There is also, wrote John Cloud in *Time*, "a yuppie aspirational quality to the books, which are full of pretty people with cell phones and seats in first class. In other words, *Left Behind* serves those readers who are just as worried about being left behind in this life as in the next."

But note what buys one a Rapture ticket. Church leaders, Ray Steele explains, led people astray because they merely "expected them to lead a good life . . . to be kind, to live in peace. . . . How far from the mark!" *All* that matters is faith in Jesus. Naturally, all Jews but for 144,000 who repent Israel's "specific national sin" of rejecting Jesus' messiahship are left behind to perish in LaHaye's final solution. Meanwhile, LaHaye's world crawls with dark Jewish conspiracies. The Antichrist's rise is engineered by a cabal of bankers and supported by Israeli liberals. "It's bizarre that more attention hasn't been paid to the series' open hostility to the Jewish religion, if not the Jewish people," wrote Michelle (but not Bernard) Goldberg. "Christian paranoia has become so mainstream that few see fit to remark on it anymore."

Catholicism? "A false religion," LaHaye has declared. (The feeling is mutual. See #65.)

LaHaye's Christianity is, as one blogger put it, "a reimagining of Jesus . . . as a vengeful, merciless slaughterer of infidels with blood dripping from his lips." "You'd never know that Jesus preached the Sermon on the Mount—or that he specifically and repeatedly warned his followers against idle speculation about the 'End Times,' " wrote Gene Lyons of the *Arkansas Democrat-Gazette*.

LaHaye has also written that witchcraft is a real menace (see his views on and odd little parallels with **J. K. Rowling**, #96) and that homosexuals' traits include "deceit," "selfishness," "incredible promiscuity," and "sadism-masochism." In his book *The*

Unhappy Gays, which LaHaye calls "a model of compassion," he wondered who was more "cruel and inhuman"—"those who practiced Old Testament capital punishment" on gays or those who accept them instead of putting them out of their misery.

Jenkins acknowledged that "our message is inherently offensive and divisive . . . especially since 9/11." Uh, *yeah.* . . . "If Saudi Arabians wrote an Islamic version of this series," wrote the *New York Times*'s Nicholas Kristof, "we would furiously demand that sensible Muslims repudiate such hatemongering." *60 Minutes*'s Morley Safer moronically called LB "a triumphant tale—unmistakably Christian, undeniably American." LaHaye: "I think if you cut us, Jerry and I would bleed red, white and blue. [Can we try?] We believe that God has raised up America to be a tool in these last days." Well, *we* believe his vision is about as American as Al Qaeda.

Beyond the embarrassment one might feel over sharing a nationality and a species with adults who believe this dreck, one might worry that, say, a mechanic who thinks it will all be over any day now might not inspect the wiring in that Boeing quite so thoroughly. . . . As for the believers who occupy the Bush administration and Congress—well, is there any point doing anything about global warming when a much hotter fate awaits most of us, while the faithful few will enjoy a cool, comfortable eternity? Does it matter if the Iraq War sends the whole region up in flames? And we sure as hell don't need to bother rebuilding New Orleans.

But we must respect others' religious beliefs (even if *they* don't), mustn't we? After all, around 70 million Americans call themselves evangelicals. According to a *Time*/CNN poll in 2002, 59 percent of Americans believe the end-time prophecies in the Book of Revelation, on which the LB novels are based, will come true, and 17 percent said they believe it will happen in their lifetime. This is no small cult. As I believe Freud said, if one person believes it, it's a psychosis; if two, it's a *folie à deux*; if a hundred, a cult; a million, a religion.

#65: MEL GIBSON

The most common complaints about *The Passion of the Christ*, Mel Gibson's (literally) excruciatingly bloody 2004 movie about Jesus' last hours, are about just that—the gore. Gibson, who bankrolled and cowrote the film but denied directing it—"The Holy Ghost was working through me," he explained—detests modern, watered-down, easygoing, feel-good Christianity, preferring a Christianity in which blood and pain, not Jesus' teachings of gentleness and goodness, are the crucial elements. Gibson's gore fest sought to shock Christians out of their comfort and complacency, to inflame their awareness of evil, and to instill in certain other people an appropriate sense of guilt. Thus, as *The Nation*'s Katha Pollitt writes, "The Bible's brief [one sentence] mention of Jesus's flogging . . . becomes a ten-minute homoerotic sadistic extravaganza that no human being could have survived, as if the point of the Passion was to show how tough Christ was." The *New Republic*'s Leon Wieseltier called *The Passion* "pious pornography . . . a profoundly brutalizing experience . . . a repulsive masochistic fantasy, a sacred snuff film [that] leaves you with the feeling that the man who made it hates life."

Yes, yes, to be sure. . . . But this film grows ugly long before the gore begins to flow. Less than a half hour into it, I thought: there haven't been this many nasty, ugly, plotting, scheming, big-nosed Jews on screen since the Nazi studios shut down.

Gibson's physiognomic exceptions are the *good* Jews: Jesus, who probably looked as Semitic as Gibson's Judas Iscariot but is played by the handsome, blue-eyed, Aryan-nosed Jim Caviezel, and his followers, including Mary Magdalene, played by the beautiful Monica Bellucci. These visual characterizations, Pollitt noted, follow a long tradition of Christian iconography including "the Oberammergau Passion Play that Hitler found so touching." Granted, the Roman soldiers we see doing the scourging and crucifying aren't a pretty bunch, either. But Pontius Pilate—whom the first-century historian Josephus described as savage and corrupt —is portrayed as a noble, rational Roman, a decent chap caught between a mob of violent, bloodthirsty Jews and the emperor's orders to prevent civil unrest. Gibson washes Pilate's hands *for* him. Pilate's wife is not only beautiful but full of goodness and sympathy for the members of the Christ household: an incipient Christian herself.

According to Boston University professor of scripture Paula Fredriksen,[34] the film—which Gibson claimed is a scrupulously accurate retelling of the Gospels—is rife with glaring historical and scriptural inaccuracies (including its very badge of authenticity, the Latin and Aramaic languages used; Romans and Jews spoke Greek to each other). Pollitt noted that the Gospels contain no scenes such as Gibson's in which the Jewish guards whip Jesus with chains and dangle him, choking, from a bridge; or in which the high priest Caiaphas "and his most Fagin-resembling sidekick" show up to watch Christ's scourging; "or in which Satan (played by a woman, for a nice touch of misogyny) flits among and merges with the crowd as it shouts, 'Crucify him! Crucify him!'" "And why," Pollitt asked, "does [Gibson] show an earthquake splitting the temple interior as Christ expires (in the Bible, a curtain is torn), if not to justify as God's vengeance the historical destruction of the temple by the Romans a few decades later and all the sufferings of the Jewish people since?"

This, I believe, is *The Passion*'s main achievement *and aim:* to shift blame for the killing of God back onto the Jews; to make this ancient charge—the cause of seventeen centuries of violent persecution—respectable again. After all:

• Gibson is a bankroller of ultra-right-wing "traditionalist" Catholicism, a sect that rejects the pope and the Vatican II

34 Paula Fredriksen, "Mad Mel: The Gospel According to Gibson," *The New Republic*, July 28, 2003.

Council of 1965, which absolved the Jewish people of responsibility for Jesus' death. (In the "traditionalist" view, the evangelicals who championed *The Passion* are also condemned to hell since they are not Catholic. Indeed, so is the entire mainstream Catholic Church.)

- Gibson's father, Hutton Gibson, is a prominent traditionalist Catholic author and Holocaust denier (the European Jews, he claims, simply moved to Australia) who called Vatican II "a Masonic plot backed by the Jews." "The man never lied to me in his life," said Mel in an interview. Asked if *he* believed the Holocaust happened, Mel said many people died in World War II, and some were Jews: standard denial-speak.

- When **Bill O'Reilly** (#29) asked Gibson if the movie might upset "any Jewish people," he answered: "Anybody who transgresses has to look at their own part or look at their own culpability." (Okay—drop murder one and I'll confess to man two and conspiracy to crucify.)

- Gibson cited as historical sources for the movie the writings of two nuns who authored anti-Semitic works—Mary of Agreda, a seventeenth-century Spaniard, and Anne Catherine Emmerich, a nineteenth-century German who explained quite clearly that Jews murdered Christian children to obtain their blood.

- Gibson restricted his pre-release screenings to prominent conservatives, including one Jew (the noted ~~biblical scholar~~ "idiot with a modem,"[35] Matt Drudge). Abraham Foxman of the Anti-Defamation League, who asked to see the film, was refused. Why—unless Gibson knew his "statement of love," as he called the film, would offend Jews? "His game from the start," wrote the *New York Times*'s Frank Rich (whose "intestines" Gibson subsequently said he would have "on a stick"), "has been to foment the old-as-Hollywood canard that the 'entertainment

35 MSNBC anchor Keith Olbermann.

elite' (which just happens to be Jewish) is gunning for his Christian movie." But Gibson "counter"-attacked Jewish critics before a single one had criticized the film. "The star's pre-emptive strategy is to portray contemporary Jews as crucifying Mel Gibson."

- He and his flacks, on the other hand, studiously avoided comment on Christian, and particularly Catholic, criticism of the film. A panel of three Jewish and six Roman Catholic scholars who read the (leaked) script found that Jews were presented as "bloodthirsty, vengeful and money-hungry." They were shocked by the screenplay's resemblance to the notorious medieval Passion plays.

The U.S. Conference of Catholic Bishops, on the other hand, gave the movie a thumbs up, despite its violating just about every one of the conference's own criteria for the portrayal of Jews in dramatizations of the Passion. According to Vatican officials, Pope John Paul II himself blessed Gibson's work, saying: "It is as it was." (Other witnesses thought what he mumbled was, "What a waste of seven euros.") And evangelicals proved eager to support any "Christian" effort against sinful, secular Hollywood. This, Pollitt noted, despite the film's " 'popish heresies'. . . . Do evangelicals not have theology anymore—anything goes as long as it's 'conservative,' and puts Jesus on top?"

Only a similar political imperative could have moved right-wing Jews like film critic Michael Medved (an orthodox Jew) and **David Horowitz** (#31) to champion the film and deny its anti-Semitism. Horowitz (whose organization has collected several million pieces of silver from major Christian-right figures and foundations): "An awesome artefact . . . an overpowering work." (**Bernie Goldberg**: silence.)

As troubling as the film's widespread acceptance in the United States is (box-office gross: $370 million; you wouldn't think Gibson needed to license a line of crucifixion-nail jewelry), more worrisome still is its influence abroad. In Italy, where Gibson shot it, a cartoon in the newspaper *La Stampa* showed Israeli tanks about to roll over the baby Jesus' manger. "Do you want to kill me once more?" read the caption. While all expressions of Christianity are banned in some Muslim countries, and the Koran even denies that Jesus was crucified, *The Passion* was approved for screening in Jordan, Syria, Lebanon, Palestine, Indonesia, even the fundamentalist-ruled United Arab Emirates, where it broke opening-day records. Across the Middle East, demand was so huge that in some multiplexes, every theater showed it. In Kuwait, the Associated Press reported, a top Shiite cleric urged that it be shown because it "reveals crimes committed by Jews." In Jordan, "Hanan Nsour, a veiled, 21-year-old Muslim," emerged "in tears and pronounced her verdict: Mel Gibson's crucifixion epic 'unmasked the Jews' lies and I hope that everybody, everywhere, turns against the Jews.' " Yasir Arafat likened Jesus' suffering to the Palestinians'.

Well done, Mel. You might even have gained a few converts. To Hamas.

#61–#64: BROWN, OWEN, MYERS, AND PRYOR: OYEZ OYEZ OYEZ . . . (OY-OY-OY . . .)

Janice Rogers Brown, Priscilla Owen, and William Pryor may be all too typical of **George W. Bush**'s judicial nominees, but these three powerful appellate court judges are nonetheless extraordinary— extraordinarily right-wing, pro-business, antiworker, anticonsumer, anti-environmental, antisecularist, and anti–abortion choice. In short, extraordinary in the precise sense that was meant in spring 2005, during Nuclear War I, when Bill Frist and his fellow Senate Republican leaders agreed to forego the "nuclear option" and not do away with the Senate's judicial filibuster rule as long as the Dems used it against Bush nominees only in "extraordinary circumstances." Which to the Repuglicans clearly meant *never*. As part of the deal, the Dems agreed to let Brown, Owen, and Pryor go to the floor for a vote, where they were confirmed to lifetime appointments. Together, they could be screwing up America for one hundred person-years. The Dems portrayed the deal as a victory. You decide.

Brown (D.C. Circuit court, which is second in influence only to the Supreme Court) was described by the *Washington Post* as "one of the most unapologetically ideological nominees of either party in many years." "Far out of the mainstream of accepted legal principles" (*Atlanta Journal-Constitution*). Her views, if adopted, "would signal the death-knell for a vast range of health labor, and environmental standards" enacted during the last century (Center for American Progress).

Brown supports sharp limits on corporate liability, absolutely opposes affirmative action, and believes, despite being black, "that racially discriminatory speech in the workplace, even when it rises to the level of illegal harassment, is protected by the First Amendment." (Several Supreme Court precedents found just the opposite.) While all for government control of the womb (and bedroom), here's what a woman mentioned as a possible Supreme Court nominee believes: "Where government moves in . . . [t]he result is: families under siege; war in the streets . . . the loss of civility and the triumph of deceit . . . [and] a debased, debauched culture which finds moral depravity entertaining and virtue contemptible." The New Deal—which brought us Social Security, the minimum wage, and fair labor laws—"marks the triumph of our own socialist revolution." (*¡Viva la revolucíon!*) And: "Today's senior citizens blithely cannibalize their grandchildren because they have a right to get as much 'free' stuff as the political system will permit them to extract." Now if we could just get the seven-year-olds back into the factories and get those old cannibals to give up that filthy habit. . . .

Owen (Fifth Circuit, covering Texas, Louisiana, and Mississippi) was previously a regular dissenter—from the far-right—on the right-wing Texas Supreme Court. The *Houston Chronicle* cited Owen's "distinct bias against consumers and in favor of large corporations." She enabled Enron, for example, to avoid paying millions in school taxes by allowing it an accounting advantage that an appellate court had deemed unfair and unconstitutional. Even **Alberto Gonzales** (#19), then Owen's colleague on the court, repeatedly criticized her for ignoring the law and for "unconscionable judicial activism"—such as in a case where Owen would have effectively rewritten the law to protect manufacturers of products that cause injury. In another case, the majority opinion called her dissent, which would have exempted certain private landowners from environmental laws, "nothing more than inflammatory rhetoric" and "pure excrement." (I made that last bit up.)

As Alabama attorney general, Pryor (Eleventh Circuit, covering Alabama, Florida, and Georgia) called *Roe v. Wade* "the worst abomination of constitutional law in our history" and defended unconstitutional restrictions on abortion with no exception to protect the health of the pregnant woman. Pryor believes it is constitutional to imprison gays and lesbians for consensual, adult shagging in the privacy of their own homes. On the Circuit Court bench, he cast a vote that blocked a challenge to the Florida law prohibiting gays and lesbians from adopting children—the only such statute in the country and the only categorical adoption ban on the state's books (even people with a history of drug abuse or domestic violence may apply to adopt). The state senator who sponsored the measure said "its purpose was to send a message to the gay community that 'we're really tired of you' and 'we wish you'd go back into the closet.' " As *we* wish Pryor would do. A very airless closet, crowded with closeted gays and lesbians and **obnoxious cell phone users** (#101).

Let's also out William Myers, whom Bush nominated and renominated for the Ninth Circuit but, as of late 2005, had failed to be confirmed. The Ninth Circuit, covering nine Western states and three fourths of all federal lands, is the nation's most significant appeals court when it comes to environmental precedents. So Bush nominated an extreme anti-environmentalist and a longtime lawyer-lobbyist for the ranching, mining, timber, and other industries, which seek to exploit public lands. Myers fought Clinton's "Roadless Policy," designed to protect public lands from development; argued that the Clean Water Act, the Endangered Species Act (ESA), and federal protection of wetlands are unconstitutional; and attacked the setting aside of wilderness areas for national parks. As the Interior Department's chief lawyer from 2001 to 2003, he met at least thirty-two times with ranching, mining, and other industry lobbyists—oh, and once with an environmentalist. He helped weaken the ESA; attempted to change Interior regulations to allow a foreign-owned, 1,600-acre, open-pit gold mine to be established in the California Desert Conservation Area and on Indian lands; and, after a mining company was caught mining public land in California, quietly tried to have the land given to the company for free. He left Interior amid a departmental investigation that he gave a politically connected Wyoming rancher "virtually carte blanche authority to violate federal grazing laws," AmericanProgress.org reported. Myers was the first judicial nominee ever opposed by the conservative National Wildlife Federation in its sixty-eight-year history. In short, the Bush nominee (and **Goldberg** omittee) *par excellence.*

#60: JAMES BAKER
AND THE CARLYLE GROUP:
INTERNATIONAL MEN OF MYSTERY

The Carlyle Group. The name sends shivers up millions of spines. Keeps young conspiracy scholars stoked through long nights of Web searches. Terrifies small children: "Be good or the Carlyle Group will get a $45-billion, no-bid government contract to spank you."

No company is more politically connected, especially with the Reagan-Bush crew, than Carlyle, a Washington-based merchant bank and defense contractor. Carlyle chairman Frank Carlucci was defense secretary under Reagan and college roommate under **Donald Rumsfeld**. (Not an altogether *bad* connection for a defense contractor.) George Bush, Sr., was a Carlyle "senior advisor" from the mid-1990s until 2003 and was instrumental in attracting major Saudi investors, including members of the bin Laden family. Carlyle executives also include former British prime minister John Major and former Philippine president Fidel Ramos. Carlyle-owned arms manufacturer United Defense "is making a gold-plated mint off the war in Iraq," noted William Pitt of TruthOut.org. "It's the best 18 months we ever had," Carlyle's chief investment officer told the *Financial Times* in November 2004. "We made money and we made it fast."

And watching over this secretive global empire, his tentacles extending into the darkest corners of Bushdom, is the Bush family consiglieri, James A. Baker III: chief of staff and Treasury secretary under Reagan, secretary of state under Bush I, and today, senior counsel and $180 million equity stake owner in Carlyle as well as senior partner at Baker Botts, the law firm founded by his grandfather. Like **Dick Cheney**, Baker belongs to an elite who can boast of harming U.S. interests in their government roles *and* (often conflicting) business activities alike.

As Treasury secretary in the 1980s, Baker took no action on the emerging savings and loan crisis, "leaving the situation to explode under his successor's watch," noted NNDB.com.

In 1989, thirteen months after Saddam Hussein gassed Kurdish villagers in northern Iraq, then–secretary of state Baker "sent a nice note to Iraqi Foreign Minister Tariq Aziz, seeking 'to strengthen the relationship between the United States and Iraq whenever possible.' "[36]

36 NNDB.com.

In July 1990, Saddam met with the U.S. Ambassador to Iraq, April Glaspie, and asked her whether the U.S. would have any objection to his "defend[ing] our claims on" Kuwait. Glaspie: "We have no opinion on your Arab-Arab conflicts, such as your dispute with Kuwait. Secretary Baker has directed me to emphasize the instruction . . . that the Kuwait issue is not associated with America." The rest is 1990–1991 Gulf War and 2003–2073 Iraq War history.

Baker managed the 1980 Reagan-Bush campaign against Jimmy Carter—helping prep Reagan for the debates using notes his staff stole from the Carter campaign.[37] He helped reelect Reagan in a landslide in 1984; managed Bush Senior's 1988 campaign; and helped "elect" Bush Junior in 2000. As the Bush-Cheney campaign's senior counsel and media front man during the Florida recount battle, it was Baker's strategy to keep repeating "the vote has been recounted" (it had *not* been, in many counties, contrary to Florida law)—and to have the election decided in the U.S. Supreme Court "instead of through more traditional means such as counting the ballots."[38]

On the morning of 9/11, Baker was in the Ritz-Carlton Hotel in Washington, D.C., where he and George H. W. Bush, along with Shafiq bin Laden, **Osama** (#5)'s half-brother, and other major Carlyle investors, were attending the company's annual conference. After 9/11, Baker's law firm represented Saudi defense minister Prince Sultan bin Abdul Aziz and Saudi Arabia in a $1 trillion lawsuit filed by families of those killed and injured in the 9/11 attacks, alleging that the Saudis funneled millions of dollars to Islamic charities suspected of financing Al Qaeda and other terrorist groups. Baker Botts's offices are in Houston, Washington, D.C., and Riyadh, Saudi Arabia. I mean, with friends and clients like these, you just have to wonder how serious the Bushies are going

---

37 Christopher Hitchens, "The Stupidity of Ronald Reagan," *Slate*, June 7, 2004.
38 NNDB.com.

to be about rooting out Saudi terrorist connections—as Michael Moore, **Bernard Goldberg**'s villain #1, will tell you *ad nauseam* if not *ad absurdum* (and as Goldberg will not tell you at all).

Further fueling the belief that every U.S. war is about oil, Baker's law firm represented a consortium of oil and gas companies seeking to build a pipeline through post-Taliban Afghanistan. Intriguing. Even more so is the fact that Baker was meanwhile employed by the Bush Justice Department (DOJ) as Counsel for Intelligence Policy, responsible, according to the DOJ, "for advising the Attorney General on all matters relating to the national security activities of the United States," including obtaining warrants for electronic surveillance and physical search from the secretive, scary Foreign Intelligence Surveillance Court (also see #35, **John Yoo**).

In 2003–2004, Baker served as Bush's special envoy to convince foreign countries to relieve the debts owed to them by Iraq, the most debt-laden country in the world—even as Carlyle sought a deal, using Baker's name and position, to help Kuwait *collect* up to $57 billion owed by Iraq in return for a $1 billion investment in Carlyle. The deal directly contradicted the U.S. aim of drastically reducing Iraq's debt burden, endangered Iraq's prospects for stability, and possibly violated multiple conflict-of-interest regulations, including criminal statutes.

After the deal made front-page news around the world in November 2004 (though barely a blip in the U.S. **so-called liberal media** [#13]—not a word in the *New York Times*), Carlyle denied its involvement in this "unsuitable" activity, even though the Kuwaitis confirmed it. In its business proposal to Kuwait, the consortium handling the deal mentions the Carlyle Group first and forty-seven times in all and James Baker by name at least eleven times to advertise the consortium's "personal rapport with" and ability to "reach key decision-makers in . . . key capitals." "It's influence peddling of the crassest kind," an international lawyer told Naomi Klein, who broke the story in *The Nation*.

As secretary of state, Baker played a role in running up Iraq's foreign debts in the first place, personally intervening in 1989 to secure a $1 billion U.S. loan to Saddam Hussein, Klein noted. Baker was also a key architect of the first Gulf War as well as of the cease-fire that required Saddam to pay huge reparations, including $30 billion to Kuwait.

Meanwhile, "Baker has not managed to get a single country to commit to eradicating Iraq's debts. Iraq's creditors know that while Baker was asking them to show forgiveness, his company was offering Kuwait a special side deal to push Iraq to pay up. It's not the kind of news that tends to generate generosity and good will."[39] And as other Iraq creditors began cutting separate deals, Baker was nowhere to be found; he was busy negotiating the rules of the presidential debates for Bush.

#59: JOHN BOLTON: AMERICA'S BARKING FACE AT THE UN

Under its unofficial motto, "Fuck you" (see **Cheney**), the **Bush** administration's way is to appoint top officials to agencies and organizations whose very functions—such as regulation of business or protection of the environment—they view with contempt. It is fitting and proper, therefore, that America's UN ambassador be a man renowned for his hostility to the UN and to diplomacy itself.

In 1994, John Bolton, whom foreign service officers call the "anti-diplomat," said, "There's no such thing as the United Nations"; the international community "can only be led by the only remaining superpower"; and "if the UN secretariat building in New York lost ten stories, it wouldn't make a bit of difference." (What did he have in mind, flying a jetliner into it?)

39 "James Baker's Double Life," *The Nation*, November 1, 2004.

In other displays of finesse, in 1999 Bolton called for full diplomatic recognition of Taiwan, dismissing the "fantasy" that China would respond with force. (And if he's wrong? That's right, we liberal girlie-men *would* prefer to avoid nuclear war with China. If that's alright.) In 2003, the State Department removed Bolton—then under secretary of state for arms control and international security—from its delegation to North Korea after he called the country's tyrannical dictator a tyrannical dictator at the start of delicate disarmament talks.

Bolton pressed for war with Iraq but opposed sticking around afterwards to do any peacekeeping or nation-building; the United States should oust Saddam and, according to one member of Bolton's team, "get the hell out immediately" (which would have left Islamist radicals and pro-Saddam Baathists in charge of much of the country). Bolton tried to fire intelligence analysts who wouldn't stretch the truth on Iraqi weapons programs, and led an administration effort to oust Mohamed El Baradei as head of the International Atomic Energy Agency for being *right* on Iraq's alleged nuclear program. Bolton told the media that after Iraq, the U.S. would "deal with" Iran, Syria, and North Korea, and in the case of Iran, "all options are on the table."

Noting Bolton's "utter failure" in nuclear talks with North Korea and Iran—where, partly in response to U.S. "diplomacy," an Islamist, anti-U.S. hard-liner, determined to pursue a nuclear program, has since been elected president—the *New York Times*'s Thomas Friedman asked, "why would you appoint him to be ambassador at an institution he has nothing but contempt for to do a job he has no apparent skills for?" Why? Because he was a favorite of Cheney, and precisely because, as the *Times*'s Maureen Dowd noted, "In Bush 43's Washington, bristling and bullying are the cardinal virtues."

Along, of course, with political service to Bush. The Bush-Cheney 2000 campaign dispatched Bolton to Florida during the vote-recount battle. As Lawrence Kaplan, a qualified admirer of Bolton, wrote in the *New Republic*:

> Upon his arrival . . . Bolton reportedly barked, "I'm with the Bush-Cheney team, and I'm here to stop the count." When he did exactly that, a grateful Dick Cheney [said] Bolton's job in the new administration should be "anything he wants." . . . Rewarded with a high-ranking State position . . . before long, he had engineered America's withdrawal from the Anti-Ballistic Missile (ABM) Treaty, established a harder line against North Korea and Iran, scuttled a draft protocol on enforcing the Biological Weapons Convention, waged a successful campaign to oust the chief of the Organization for the Prohibition of Chemical Weapons, and set the stage for America's abandonment of the International Criminal Court (ICC) [which Bolton called "the happiest moment of my life"]. And that was only year one.

The Bush administration's rejection of these treaties helped to earn it the loathing of most of the world and the adoration of the right, for whom international pariahhood means the U.S. is on the right track.

Unlike most of his fellow Project for the New American Century (see #4) alumni, Bolton is no neoconservative. Neocons are aggressively hawkish but, as heirs of certain liberal ideas, believe America has a mission to spread democratic ideals. For Bolton, raw U.S. interests are all that matter. "Rather than the construction of a new world order," Kaplan wrote, "a vision like Bolton's merely requires tearing down the old. This happens to be his specialty. . . . Hence, [he is] holding up one leg of America's grand strategy, while the rest collapses around him."

And what kind of "U.S." interests, exactly, does Bolton stand for?

- In 2001 Bolton effectively torpedoed a UN treaty to regulate the international traffic in small arms—which is vital to the terrorism and drug-trafficking industries—by invoking America's "cultural tradition of hunting and sport shooting."

- He reputedly architected the U.S. deal with Libya that reopened the country's huge oil reserves to **ExxonMobil** (#12) and ChevronTexaco in exchange for dictator Muammar Qaddafi's renunciation of his nonconventional weapons programs but without addressing his regime's jailings, torture, and killings of political opponents—despite the Bush administration's avowed aim of a "global democratic revolution."

- Upon his UN appointment, Bolton promptly proposed the abandonment of the UN's Millennium Development Goals, adopted in 2000, which called on developed nations to work toward giving 0.7 percent of their national incomes for development aid to poor countries by 2015. Bolton's proposal, said the *Los Angeles Times*, would be "a death sentence for millions."

Unable to win Senate confirmation, Bolton was installed at the UN in August 2005 in one of Bush's many recess appointments— just when Bush was proclaiming the need "to begin repairing our damaged relations with the rest of the world," noted Senate minority leader Harry Reid. "What message are we sending to the world community?" asked Republican Senator George Voinovich. (Answer: see first sentence of this entry.)

Former Senator Jesse Helms (R-Neanderthal) once said, "John Bolton is the kind of man with whom I would stand at Armageddon." With Bolton's help, we may get there soon enough.

#58: SENATOR TOM COBURN AND THE RAMPANT LESBIANS OF OKLAHOMA

Oklahoma Republican Tom Coburn is refreshingly different from most Congress members. During his six years in the House and after winning his Senate seat in 2004, he refused to give up his practice as a family physician/obstetrician in Muskogee, even when the Senate Ethics Committee demanded that he do so. (Senators are barred from "affiliating with a firm, partnership [etc.] for the purpose of providing professional services.") Washington "careerism," Coburn has written, is "a constant corrupting force" in the government system, and citizen legislators are more likely than career politicians to impose fiscal restraint.

And Coburn practices what he preaches to a degree that in Washington is downright eccentric. In the House, he opposed spending even for his own state. He voluntarily term-limited his House tenure to three terms and has pledged to serve only two terms in the Senate. "You can't justify criticism of the system if you participate in the system," he said.

Then again, Coburn is, as a political scientist told *Salon*, "one of the real far-right guys" among Newt Gingrich's "revolutionaries," one who "really drank the Kool-Aid with the class of '94," when Coburn was first elected to Congress, and who now "packages this political agenda in his image as a kindly family doctor," wrote *Salon*'s Robert Schlesinger. To *The Nation*'s Max Blumenthal, Coburn is "the clueless physician-cum-political hobbyist described by his underling as someone who 'doesn't know anything.'" To me—to you—he's a damned disgrace to Okies from Muskogee everywhere.

Coburn won his Senate race—which he termed a "battle of good versus evil"—with the help of a TV ad showing images of Hispanics and dark hands receiving welfare payments. The ad, which attacked the Democratic candidate's record on immigration, reminded some people of Senator Jesse Helms's notorious 1990 ad showing white hands crumpling a piece of paper, under the message, "they had to give [the job] to a minority because of a racial quota." No coincidence: both ads were (forgive me) the handiwork of the sleazebags at **Maverick Media** (#42). Coburn's campaign had the support of high-powered Christian-right groups like **James Dobson** (#15)'s Focus on the Family and the National

Right to Life Committee—and perhaps even higher-powered backing: Coburn said he had a "spiritual impression" that he should seek the seat.

As a congressman, Coburn's fiscal zeal was such that he tried to stop federal disaster relief for his own state after a 1999 tornado. (After Hurricane Katrina in 2005, he asked, apparently suffering a little mental hurricane: "Is it the responsibility of the federal government—does the State of Louisiana going—is it going to require some responsibility?" *Nah.*) In his first year as a senator, Coburn championed legislation to eliminate funding for the UN program for sustaining biological diversity and voted "no" on a Republican-sponsored amendment to increase health and education funding by $2 billion (around one third of America's *monthly* expenditure on the war in Iraq, which Coburn avidly supports). After just eight months, *National Review* exulted, Coburn's "presence in the Senate has moved the fiscal debate rightward." Recalling Helms's ability to bring proceedings to a halt when the Senate appeared to be moving leftward, Rep. Mike Pence (R-IN) rejoiced: "Jesse Helms has finally found his heir."

America faces an even greater threat than debt, according to Coburn: "The gay community has infiltrated the very centers of power in every area across this country, and they wield extreme power. That agenda is the greatest threat to our freedom that we face today. Why do you think we see the rationalization for abortion and multiple sexual partners? That's a gay agenda." In 1997, Coburn proposed a bill that would have required reporting the names of those who tested positive for HIV/AIDS to public health authorities. "Lesbianism is so rampant" in some Oklahoma schools, Coburn warned in 2004, that "that they'll only let one girl go to the bathroom." As a blogger wrote: "You might think that to become both a doctor and a senator, you'd have to be something other than a complete idiot. You'd be wrong." Coburn's tirades about the gay menace contributed to the pressure that led to **Bush**'s endorsement of a constitutional amendment to ban gay marriage.

Coburn echoed Bush's bogus and racially insulting rationale for privatizing Social Security, but made it even dumber. By a "genetic predisposition," said the doctor, the average life expectancy of black men is less than the retirement age of Social Security. (a) It isn't. (b) That "genetic predisposition" is called *poverty*, and all that it implies: the *average* life expectancy of black men is lower than whites' mainly because so many die *early* in life—due to social problems conservatives don't care to address. The Bush scheme would, however, address Wall Street's need for more profits.

"I favor the death penalty for abortionists," says Coburn, who opposes abortion even in cases of rape—on *fiscal* grounds, apparently: "Do you realize," he has said, "that if all those children had not been aborted, we wouldn't have any trouble with Medicare and Social Security today?" Meaning those fetuses would have wound up paying into the system. Just two questions: Would they ever get old and *require* social services? And could women who fail to breed taxpayers be charged with tax evasion?

Apparently, Coburn's own constituents disagree with him on embryonic issues. When his Senate Web site asked them whether they supported federal funding for "destructive embryonic stem-cell research" or for "ethical alternatives" instead, 54 percent voted to "destroy embryos for research" and just 27 percent for the "ethical alternative."

More awkwardly still for Coburn, it came to light in 2004 that in 1990, he sterilized a twenty-year-old female patient without her permission, according to a civil malpractice suit she filed against him. Coburn claimed he had her oral consent but admitted he had charged the procedure to Medicaid despite knowing that Medicaid does not cover the cost of sterilization for anyone under the age of twenty-one—which is called health care fraud—and that he told the patient "that she shouldn't talk about it." Coburn, noted *Salon*'s Schlesinger, has built his congressional career on extreme opposition to abortion and to government programs—and

Medicare and Medicaid fraud has been one of his signature issues. He introduced the Health Care Anti-Fraud Act of 1995.

If only Coburn could keep as quiet about other matters:

- In 1997, he denounced NBC's showing of *Schindler's List* as "an all-time low, with full-frontal nudity"; the movie, he said, encouraged "irresponsible sexual behavior." I didn't know anyone found Holocaust movies sexually arousing. Obviously some do.

- After the 1999 Columbine High School massacre, Coburn opposed Clinton's proposal for making adults liable if they allow their children to buy guns and harm others: "If I wanted to buy a bazooka to use in a very restricted way, to do something, I ought to be able to do that." Senator, *think*: when you incinerate a group of people, one could be carrying an embryo.

- In his opening statement at Chief Justice **John Roberts** (#36)'s Senate confirmation hearings, Coburn, *The Nation*'s Blumenthal noted, "exclaimed in a trembling voice, 'My heart aches for less divisiveness, less polarization, less finger-pointing, less bitterness, less partisanship.' " Physician, **** thyself. Coburn then told Roberts he had used his "medical skills of observation of body language" and determined "that your answers have been honest and forthright." And he had a question about something of obvious interest to him—the concept of brain death: "Would you agree that the opposite of being alive is being dead?" Roberts took a moment, and then agreed.

Almost as estimable is Coburn's chief of staff, Michael Schwartz. In the 1980s, Schwartz worked for **Paul Weyrich** (#9) and was one of the organizers of the violently antiabortion group **Operation Rescue** (#69). Following the Terry Schiavo affair in 2005, Schwarz told a Christian-right gathering that he favored "the mass impeachment of judges," but after a little thought, amended that to, "I want to impale them!" He has also denounced the Supreme Court for giving Americans "the right to commit buggery."

When you remember that Oklahoma's other senator is **James Inhofe** (#33), you begin to think that Ohhhhh-klahoma! Where the wind comes sweepin' down the plain / And the wavin' wheat and blazin' heat / must do somethin' to the brain.

#57: THE UNTEACHABLY IGNORANT, BUSH-VOTING AVERAGE AMERICAN

Our countrymen have all the folly of the ass and all the passiveness of the sheep. . . . They are determined not to be free.

—Alexander Hamilton

He'll support any war he's told to, against countries he couldn't find on a map. (At least until the going gets tough or he gets bored and wants to, like, change the channel.) Wave a U.S. flag at him and he'll charge at anyone labeled "enemy"—or rather, let some poor kid do it. She knows if we don't fight "them" over there, we'll have to over here, but isn't *too* particular about who "them" is. He knows that his God (the one his team prays to before the game) can wipe the ground with *their* God. And that the world hates us because we're the greatest. He'll vote for whichever wrestler—I mean, candidate—acts meanest and toughest. Because those French have been pushing America around for too long. She likes **Bush** because he's a straight shooter (though *now* she's not so sure). When **Fox News** (#28) tells her liberals are waging a "war on Christians and Christmas," she believes it. (Ha-ha. We're really waging war against *Easter*.) He owns guns in case They come streaming out of their neighborhood and close in on his suburban homestead, slavering after his womenfolk. She *knows* the government takes her money and gives it to the undeserving poor. (They give it to the undeserving rich.) He thinks the tax he pays is (as his president says) *his* money, not money he *owes* for services and infrastructure that make the entire economy, including his job, possible—services he wants more of but doesn't want to pay for.

When a story disappears from the evening news, to her, it no longer exists. (She *does* always know how things stand with Jennifer, Brad, and Angelina.) He's fat, and likes it that way: Thin might look gay. She believes in angels, a government cover-up of UFOs, you name it, but isn't sure about evolution—but *is* sure she wants *her* religious beliefs taught in the public schools. He wants to know what the fuck *you're* looking at. The rights she enjoys become "special rights" when a group she doesn't like demands them.

Speaking of special rights: he consumes six times as much energy as the world per capita average, as much grain as thirty-five Indians or five hundred Ethiopians (mostly fed to animals for his meat), and twenty tons of basic raw materials annually. She consumes 1,300 gallons of water per day. (You're *not* just imagining those long showers.) They'll spend enough on their daughter's wedding to feed, shelter, and clothe 155 rural Africans for a year. He aggressively drives an SUV bearing a Proud to be American sticker because that doesn't mean giving a shit about your *fellow* Americans, their safety, or the air they breathe. She spends six hours a week shopping and forty minutes playing with her children. He'll spend one year of his life watching TV *commercials*.

They're only stereotypes, but they can be extremely dangerous. Avoid leaving food or beer out in the open. If you see one, back away *slowly*.

#56: RALPH REED

*I used to tell people he was going to be either president of
the United States or Al Capone.*

—Marcy Reed, Ralph Reed's mother

By time you read this, Reed—lobbyist, former Christian Coalition
director, **George W. Bush** campaign adviser, Abramoff crime
family member, and aspiring president of the United States—
could be a resident not of the White House but of another well-
guarded federal facility. But shame on any *Screwing Up America*
list maker who does not include this poster child for GOP/reli-
gious-right sleaze.

Pity we can't show you a picture. The combination of Christian
earnestness, supercilious smirk, and stiletto-up-the-sleeve
menace is very, very special. On this, and this alone, we can agree
with Reed's fellow Georgian, Steve Scoggins of the far-right
Georgia Heritage Council, who wrote: "There was always something just a little phoney about him. Was it his sissie GQ baby-
face? Or maybe the oiliness of his diction? To me he just came
across as a caricature, too much of the exaggerated Boy Scout
with a phoney 'aw-shucks' that alternated with righteous confidence." Said the Religious Freedom Coalition, which in 1998
awarded Reed its Lifetime Achievement Award for Bigotry and
Villainy: "Reed, who has the aura of a choirboy who slips behind
the rectory to strangle cats, is one of the most sinister figures ever
to gain power on the Christian Right."

In June 2005 a former Georgia Republican state representative,
Bob Irvin, published "an open request" to Reed to "Please withdraw your candidacy for Georgia lieutenant governor" in 2006
(which Reed, then aged forty-four, reportedly saw as a stepping-
stone to much higher things) to avoid "destroying our [GOP]
majority coalition." Reed, said Irvin, is "someone who is available
for hire to influence political outcomes," who "took millions of

dollars from gambling interests in Louisiana and Mississippi" and from Enron to lobby for electricity deregulation. "His M.O. is to tell evangelical Christians that his cause of the moment, for which he has been hired, is their religious duty. . . . I resent Christianity being used simply to help Reed's business." Reed is "an ideologue" who has "no connection with the real world" and "has never made a dime" outside of politics.[40] Jack Abramoff—*Jack Abramoff*—told his accomplice Michael Scanlon that Reed "is a bad version of us!"

Abramoff and Scanlon are the lobbyists who were indicted in 2005 for their role in an Indian gambling–related scam. Abramoff, a Bush Pioneer (see #52) and crony of Reed, **Tom DeLay** (#6), and **Grover Norquist** (#24), was also named a "person of interest" in the related murder investigation of the owner of a casino boat company. Abramoff and Scanlon, a former DeLay spokesman, allegedly bilked at least $80 million out of six newly wealthy Indian tribes for lobbying and PR work the tribes never received. Meanwhile, the two directed the Indians to donate $10 million to GOP politicians and right-wing organizations, and exchanged messages calling tribal leaders "morons," "troglodytes" and "monkeys."[41] From 2000 to 2002, Abramoff teamed up with Reed to charge a Louisiana tribe millions to organize a "Christian" crusade against gambling in order to shut down a rival tribe's casino—then charged the rival tribe $4.2 million to lobby lawmakers to reopen it. Reed and Abramoff also allegedly gave illegal donations to DeLay and other senior high-ranking Republicans in return for political favors.

Reed began working with Abramoff and Norquist in the early 1980s when the three took control of the College Republican National Committee (CRNC), purging "dissidents" and rewriting

40 Bob Irvin, "Reed an Albatross for GOP," *Atlanta Journal-Constitution*, June 15, 2005.

41 Editorial, "Sleaze in the Capitol," *New York Times*, January 1, 2005.

the bylaws to consolidate their control. According to Nina Easton's book *Gang of Five*, Reed was known as the "hatchet man." Around the same time, Reed, a student at the University of Georgia, wrote a column for the student newspaper titled "Gandhi: Ninny of the 20th Century." If that weren't enough, the article allegedly plagiarized another, and Reed was fired from the paper. Then the CRNC determined that Reed had rigged the election of an ally to succeed him as president of the local College Republicans.

Reed was clearly destined for great things in the conservative movement.

But one vital element was missing. Lo and behold, just a few months later, Reed recalls, "the Holy Spirit simply demanded me to come to Jesus." Instead of telling the Holy Spirit to fuck off, he went to an evangelical church the next morning and became a born-again Christian.

In 1984, Reed started a students' group in North Carolina supporting the reelection of Senator Jesse Helms. In 1985, he was arrested during a demonstration he organized against an abortion clinic in Raleigh. After that, Reed cultivated a temperate, polished, smooth, oily, shiny, scaly persona. Which is why he was hired in 1989 as executive director of **Pat Robertson** (#55)'s Christian Coalition (CC)—Robertson was prone to say what he and his movement really think. As Reed said, "The most important strategy for evangelicals is secrecy." And: "I want to be invisible. I do guerrilla warfare. I paint my face and travel at night. You don't know it's over until you're in a body bag." Very much as Jesus would have put it.

Reed of course wants the government to allow prayer in schools, religious symbols in government buildings, taxpayer funding of religious organizations like CC, full evangelical control of all U.S. military forces, strategic weapons, and so on (that one's just a guess)—the whole theocrapic program.

The CC was widely credited with helping the GOP win control

of the House in the 1994 congressional elections. However, in 1996, the Federal Election Commission alleged that on Reed's watch, the CC violated federal campaign finance laws in 1990, 1992, and 1994. The Internal Revenue Service then revoked the CC's tax-exempt status (which it had enjoyed by virtue of being, you know, nonpartisan and nonpolitical). And federal prosecutors began investigating allegations of further financial mischief by Reed involving CC overpayments to a close friend and direct-mail vendor.

As the investigations continued, Reed resigned in 1997 and set up shop as a political consultant and lobbyist. He was accused of running some of 1998's most vicious and racist campaigns. Drawn no doubt by the promising-sounding name, he joined the campaign of Mitch Skandalakis for lieutenant governor of Georgia, helping him win the primary with charges against his opponent such as "desecrated Indian graves." Skandalakis lost the general election after running ads calling the black mayor of Atlanta a "buffoon," promising to "kick Atlanta's ass," and accusing the Democratic candidate of drug abuse, for which he was sued for libel and paid $50,000 in damages. Skandalakis subsequently pled guilty to lying to federal investigators in a public corruption investigation and was sentenced to a six-month prison term.

"Hey, now that I'm done with the electoral politics," Reed e-mailed Abramoff, "I need to start humping in corporate accounts! I'm counting on you to help me with some contacts."[42] Reed went on to lobby for such distinguished clients as Enron (arranged for Reed by **Karl Rove**, allegedly to secure Reed's backing for Bush in 2000); the cable TV industry, which hired the Christian activist to help fight newly proposed federal decency standards; Chris Whittle's "educational" Channel One News, which even a conservative group said pumps classrooms full of "commercials for junk

42 Susan Schmidt and James Grimaldi, "Panel Says Abramoff Laundered Tribal Funds," *Washington Post*, June 23, 2005.

food and sleazy movies"; and Microsoft, which was being prosecuted for antitrust violations and which Reed helped to lobby Bush *while* he worked on the Bush 2000 campaign. (Not kosher.) But as Reed wrote in an October 2000 memo to Enron soliciting more business, "it matters less who has the best arguments and more who gets heard—and by whom."

As a consultant to the 2000 Bush-**Cheney** campaign, Reed was credited with orchestrating the successful attacks on Senator John McCain in the crucial South Carolina primary, which included a "push poll" suggesting McCain begat an illegitimate black child. In 2001, Reed was elected state chairman of the Georgia Republican Party with the help of secret financing from an Indian tribe represented by Abramoff and a large block of pro-Confederate "heritage activists," including the **Sons of Confederate Veterans** (#81), whom Reed promised to help restore the Confederate battle emblem to the state flag. They now say he "double-crossed" them on the issue. In 2002, Reed helped Republican Saxby Chambliss unseat Georgia's Democratic Senator Max Cleland. Chambliss, who never served in the military, ran ads (created by #42) that questioned the patriotism of Cleland—a triple amputee and decorated Vietnam veteran—and juxtaposed images of Cleland and **Osama bin Laden** (#5). In that year's Ralph Reed financial scandal, Reed was accused by Republicans of diverting state party funds to his own firm.

I'd say Marcy Reed's prediction (see quote introducing this entry) has come true.

#55: PAT ROBERTSON
AND "RELIGION" INC.

"Did you know that Pat Robertson can leg-press 2000 pounds! How does he do it? Where does Pat find the time and energy to host a daily, national TV show and head a world-wide ministry" while pursuing business ventures with African dictators, calling for the assassination of other foreign leaders, denouncing Islam, blaming disasters on gays and abortion, and adding to his Christ-like, $200 million to $1 billion net worth? "One of Pat's secrets is his age-defying protein shake, a delicious, refreshing shake, filled with energy-producing nutrients." (Safflower oil, protein powder, and vinegar.)

Most of that comes from an ad on Robertson's own Christian Fraudcasting Network (CBN) Web site. In 2005, Robertson, the televangelist, right-wing political activist, and entrepreneur, came under fire (nothing he's not used to—and nothing compared to the *eternal* fire awaiting him) for promoting Pat Robertson's Age-Defying Shake in his *tax-exempt* TV ministry. But compared to Robertson's other business ventures, his spiritual snake-oil racket, and his poisoning of the body politic, this is rather like going after Al Capone for tax evasion.

Not that Capone's business empire compared. Robertson's, based in Virginia, has included ownership of radio stations, an oil refinery, a gold mine in Liberia, and a diamond mine in Congo. CBN is seen in 180 countries and broadcast in seventy-one languages. Robertson's CBN Cable Network is now owned by Disney, which renamed it ABC Family but continues airing Robertson's *700 Club* program twice a day.

In one of his best-selling books, *The New World Order* (1992), Robertson showed that, with the right energy-producing nutrients, even the busiest televangelist-tycoon can find time to dispense nutcase conspiracy theories about Freemasons and "international bankers," drawn from notorious anti-Semitic works such as Nesta Webster's *Secret Societies and Subversive Movements* and Eustace Mullins's *Secrets of the Federal Reserve*.

Robertson first "spoke in tongues" (part of his "charismatic" faith) after finding Christ in the late 1950s. When he first spoke with *forked* tongue is unknown. In one of his books he described himself as a "Yale-educated tax lawyer" even though he failed to pass the bar exam.[43] He has variously claimed his IQ to be 159, 139, and 137 (which at least trends in the right direction). During his 1988 presidential campaign, Robertson's literature said he was a combat Marine who had served in the Korean War. Others in his battalion have said he never spent a day in a combat environment. According to former Republican Congressman Pete McCloskey, who served with him, Robertson's father, a U.S. senator, intervened to keep his son out of combat, and Robertson spent most of his time in Japan, tasked with keeping the officers' clubs supplied with liquor. Another veteran alleged that Robertson had sexual relations with prostitutes and sexually harassed a Korean cleaning girl.

Today he merely screws up America. Robertson used his 1988 campaign organization to start the Christian Coalition (CC), which aimed at controlling the Republican agenda and electing conservative Christians and quickly became one of the most powerful *political* organizations in America. The tax-exempt, nonpartisan CC illegally endorsed candidates in 1990 and 1992 and illegally coordinated its activities with the Bush I reelection campaign, according to a 1996 lawsuit by the Federal Election Commission. Robertson and CC are credited with helping **George W. Bush** win the crucial South Carolina and Michigan presidential primaries in 2000 with the help of smear attacks against John McCain (see #56, **Ralph Reed**). As their reward, they demanded and got John Ashcroft as attorney general.

In 2001, ten black employees sued the CC, claiming it treated them with Jim Crow–style segregationist rules, even keeping them from attending company-sponsored prayer sessions. A white employee then sued, claiming he was fired for refusing to spy on the black employees.

---

43 "The Two Faces of Pat Robertson," Religious Freedom Coalition of the Southeast.

That year, Robertson stepped down as the CC's president. As evangelical leader Gary Bauer said, "I think [it's] because the position has already been filled. [Bush] is that leader right now."

And now, the world according to Pat (also see the Introduction to this volume):

- "The Christian Coalition will be the most powerful political force in America. . . . We have enough votes to run this country . . . we're going to take over!"
- "[T]he great builders of our nation almost to a man have been Christians, because Christians have the desire to build something.   The people who have come into (our) institutions (today) are primarily termites. They are into destroying institutions that have been built by Christians. . . . The termites are in charge now . . . and the time has arrived for a godly fumigation." (Zyklon B? It was originally a pesticide. . . .)
- On apartheid South Africa: "I think 'one man, one vote,' just unrestricted democracy, would not be wise."
- "Christ is the head of the household and the husband is the head of the wife, and that's the way it is, period."
- Congress "can ignore a Supreme Court ruling if they so choose."
- "The feminist agenda is . . . about a socialist, anti-family political movement that encourages women to leave their husbands, kill their children, practice witchcraft, destroy capitalism, and become lesbians."
- "NOW [National Organization for Women] is saying that in order to be a woman, you've got to be a lesbian."
- "You say you're supposed to be nice to the Episcopalians and the Presbyterians and the Methodists. . . . Nonsense. I don't have to be nice to the spirit of the Antichrist."
- "I am just totally against these [African-American] leaders who stir up the divisions and the hatred . . . talking about all these offenses and things that happened." (I know. Kicking up a fuss about slavery, Jim Crow . . .)

- "The minute you turn the document [the Constitution] into the hands of non-Christian people and atheistic people they can use it to destroy the very foundation of our society." (So, no non-Christians to be permitted in government, obviously.)
- On 9/11: Americans "have allowed rampant secularism and occult, etc. [miracles are central to Robertson's faith] to be broadcast on television. We have permitted [abortion]. . . . We have a court that has essentially stuck its finger in God's eye and said we're going to legislate you out of the schools. . . . [So] God Almighty is lifting his protection from us." But the effects of "judicial activism" are "probably more serious than a few bearded terrorists who fly into buildings." Roberton's fanatical opposition to abortion evidently does not apply to certain racial or national groups. With regard to China's one-child policy, which often involved *forced* abortions: "[The Chinese are] doing what they have to do."

The acceptance of homosexuality, Robertson says, could result in hurricanes, earthquakes, tornadoes, terrorist bombs, and "possibly a meteor" striking the earth. Conversely, Robertson used the power of prayer to steer hurricanes Gloria in 1985 and Felix in 1995 away from his companies' Virginia Beach headquarters. (Whose side were Robertson's prayers on in Katrina versus sinful New Orleans and 9/11 versus damned New York? Subpoena the prayer logs, I say.) In 2005, he launched Operation Supreme Court Freedom, a televised nationwide twenty-one-day prayer campaign asking people to *pray for vacancies* on the Supreme Court, where, he said, "black-robed tyrants have pushed a radical agenda." After the announced resignation of Justice Sandra Day O'Connor, he declared that "God heard those prayers." (Any involvement in the Rehnquist vacancy, one wonders?)

During the U.S. involvement in the Liberian Civil War in 2003, Robertson repeatedly voiced support on *The 700 Club* for Liberian president Charles Taylor without mentioning his own $8 million investment in a Liberian gold mine—or that Taylor had been indicted by the UN for war crimes, or that prosecutors said he had harbored members of Al Qaeda responsible for the 1998 U.S. embassy bombings. Robertson's response to the State Department's oppostion to Taylor: "What we need is for somebody to place a small nuke at Foggy Bottom" (State's headquarters). Imagine if a Muslim preacher in America said that.

After Roberts pleaded on his show for cash donations to his tax-exempt, nonprofit organization Operation Blessing to help airlift refugees from Rwanda to Zaire in 1994, the organization's planes were discovered to be transporting diamond-mining equipment for Robertson's for-profit diamond mining venture in Zaire, established in cooperation with Zairian dictator Mobutu Sese Seko. An investigation by the State of Virginia determined that Robertson "willfully induced contributions from the public through the use of misleading statements and other implications," and called for a criminal prosecution. However, the Virginia attorney general—a Republican whose largest campaign contributor was, let's see . . . oh yes, Pat Robertson—intervened and overruled that recommendation.

Operation Blessing—a "humanitarian" group headed by a "man" who has "faith" that Muhammed was "a killer" and Hindus are "devil worshippers"—was one of the first recipients of a federal grant under Bush's "Faith Based Initiative."

By the way, *I've* been drinking Pat's Age-Defying Shake, and— unlike everything else about Robertson—it hasn't made me really sick once!

#54: SUN MYUNG MOON AND THE LUNAFICATION CHURCH

Reverend Moon: Messiah, or tax-evading, money-laundering, anti-Semitic, homophobic, right-wing, billionaire cult leader and media mogul—or both?

On Easter morning in 1935, when he was fifteen, while praying atop a hill in his native Korea, Moon, whose parents were converts from Confucianism to Christianity, had a vision of Jesus Christ, who instructed him to complete his—Mr. Christ's— mission of saving humankind. Moon began preaching around 1945. In 1954, he registered the Holy Spirit Association for the Unification of World Christianity, better known as the Unification Church (UC).

Moon first sent missionaries to the United States in 1959, and moved there in 1971. By the mid-1970s, our airport terminals were infested with flower-wielding "Moonies." Moon was accused of using mind control to brainwash college students into severing ties with their families and the outside world and devoting themselves to raising money for his church. Thanks largely to Moon, a new industry was created, and with it, thousands of jobs and a new Yellow Pages section: "Deprogramming." However, those job gains were balanced by losses in the ministerial sector as the UC conducted mass weddings—with all the matches arranged by Moon. An estimated seventy thousand Americans are or have been Moonies. That rather modest number, however, doesn't begin to describe the dark side of the Moon.

In the late seventies, congressional investigators reported "breathtaking financial misdoings" by UC, including a scheme to raise money for a church PR fund that disguised itself as a fundraiser for sick children. In 1982, Moon was indicted for criminal tax fraud for failing to declare some $160,000 of income. He was found guilty, served thirteen months in prison, and paid a $15,000 fine. His supporters blamed the tax case and media criticisms of Moon on political—that is, liberal—bias. In 1997, Moon was convicted in Japan after thousands of elderly Japanese said Moonies had defrauded them of their life's savings. But as the Moonies point out, Jesus, too, was persecuted by liberals.

But Jesus is not widely alleged to have had involvements with the CIA and with the Korean CIA, whose U.S. activities, according to a 1977–1978 congressional investigation, systematically violated numerous federal and state laws.

Moon's right-wing political activites in America date back at least to the Watergate scandal, when he took out a full-page newspaper ad defending Richard Nixon. During the 1980s, UC missionaries campaigned for Ronald Reagan, and Moon helped fund the contras through Oliver North's Nicaraguan Freedom Fund.

In 1982, Moon began to publish the right-wing *Washington Times*—"to fulfill God's desperate desire to save this world," he wrote. The *Times* became the preferred local paper of Beltway conservatives. The paper, whose editors and columnists include Pat Buchanan, Lawrence Kudlow, and Tony Blankley, is, exactly as Senate Democratic Whip Richard Durbin said, "an absolute party organ of the Republican Party." Recovering conservative journalist David Brock, who worked for the *Washington Times's* sister publication *Insight*, has written that *Times* news writers were encouraged to give news stories a conservative slant and that the paper's "journalistic ethics were close to nil." Assistant Editor Robert Stacy McCain drew fire for his apparent Confederate sympathies. One *Times* columnist spoke at a conference hosted by Jared Taylor's white-supremacist-nationalist New Century Foundation.

The Washington Times Foundation is allied with Christian-right figures like **Tim LaHaye** (#66) and Jerry Falwell, to whom Moon lent $3.5 million to bail out his struggling Liberty University. The foundation donated $1 million to the George H. W. Bush presidential library and has paid the former president untold amounts in fees for speaking to Moonie-run groups, which he praised for "strengthening the family"! (Interesting spin on "sever all ties with your family.")

In Korea, Moon owns a controlling interest in an auto manufacturer closely tied to the South Korean government. His U.S. properties include the University of Bridgeport in Connecticut, the New Yorker Hotel in Manhattan, fishing fleets in several states, a video postproduction company, the Goodlife TV Network, and, since 2001, the UPI newswire service. Despite all these business and political activities, the UC manages to maintain its tax-exempt status.

Moon's political respectability and influence have never been greater. **Bush** officials like former Attorney General John Ashcroft and director of Faith-Based and Community Initiatives James Towey have spoken at Moon events. A UC organization, Free Teens USA, has received Bush Faith-Based grants to promote abstinence-only sex education. One Moon lieutenant was appointed an AmeriCorps director, another, a deputy U.S. trade representative. In March 2004, Moon and his wife were literally crowned by members of Congress at a Capitol Hill ceremony, during which Moon declared himself "none other than humanity's Savior, Messiah, Returning Lord and True Parent" and said he had saved the souls even of Hitler and Stalin, who had "received the Blessing" through him and would vouch for him from the spirit world.

This was in accordance with the 2002 UC document "Clouds of Witnesses," which proclaimed that at a recent conference in Heaven, the founders of the world's five major religions—Jesus, Confucius, Buddha, Mohammed, and twelve Hindu divinities—plus Marx, Lenin, Stalin, and Deng Xiao Ping—had declared Moon the Messiah and pledged to follow him. The document includes a description of the seating arrangements, and concludes with a letter of endorsement from **God** (#77). (He writes in the first-person omniscient. His style? Well, it ain't no King James Bible.)

Moon teaches that "the church and the state must become one. "Jesus failed because he never attained worldly power; but the American government and people "will bow down" before *him*, Moon. In 1996, the ferociously anticommunist Moon praised Communism for producing obedient followers trained "to follow once an order came from above," for "individualism is what God hates most." Gays are "dung-eating dogs" who would have no place in a "peace kingdom." Rape victims are impure—and "if someone is trying to invade you [sexually], you would rather kill yourself than go through the fall. At least you won't go to hell that way." The Jews killed Jesus Christ, and as a result, "through the principle of indemnity [a central Moon teaching], Hitler killed 6 million Jews." But the debt is not yet repaid: All remaining Jews must "repent and follow and become one with Christianity through Rev. Moon."

Calling **Bernard Goldberg**: Have *you* been saved? It's never to late to repent and amend your *100 People* list. No, no, you're right—loyalty to the right *über alles*.

#53: THE COORS FAMILY: "THE [FAR-]RIGHT BEER"

What monstrous financial force lurks beneath many of the most powerful and radical right-wing organizations in America? Who personifies the evil axis of beer and backwardness, brew, Bushism, and bigotry, ale and apartheid, lager and labor-busting, suds and scabs, hops and homophobia? A certain family brewing fortune, of coors.

In 1969, the Colorado-based Coors Brewing Company was found guilty of racial discrimination for refusing to hire Hispanics. Reforms (as well as damages) ensued. But thou shalt distinguish the company from the Coors family (whose members have headed the company since Adolph Coors founded it in 1873, but today own only about 27 percent) and from the family foundations. In response to years of bad publicity and boycotts, the company has long since instituted an employment nondiscrimination policy and has offered domestic partnership benefits to gay and lesbian employees since 1995. (Family scion Scott Coors is in fact a person of gayness.) Only a hopeless cynic would suggest these policies merely (a) reflect the fact that Hispanics, gays, and lesbians have been known to drink beer; and (b) serve to insulate the company (and its sales) from the family's reputation, and the company's ongoing antiunion policies.

A strike against Coors in the 1970s by the Brewery, Bottling, Can and Allied Industrial Union ended with the company breaking the union by hiring hundreds of nonunion workers. Coors has broken nineteen unions since then, blocked federal inspectors from investigating workplace hazards that caused the death of employees, and supported the antiunion National Right to Work Committee.

In 1973, then-company president Joseph Coors, aka Adolph Herman Joseph Coors II, provided the initial funding for the **Heritage Foundation** (#8), which became America's most influential right-wing think tank. The Heritage publication *Mandate for Leadership*—which advocated increased military spending, cutbacks for education, welfare, health services, food stamps, child nutrition, and legal services for the poor, and the expansion of "low-intensity" warfare—served as the blueprint for the Reagan administration.

Coors named as coeditor of the Heritage publication *Policy Review* Roger Pearson, who authored books asserting the biological inferiority of blacks and the genetic danger faced by the white race and calling for scientific breeding of "only the fittest" in society. Pearson formerly edited a magazine devoted to "a responsible but penetrating inquiry into every aspect of the Jewish Question" (ah, yes, *die Judenfrage*), which included articles such as "Early Jews and the Rise of Jewish Money Power" and "Swindlers of the Crematoria." (In a letter, President Reagan thanked Pearson for his "substantial contribution to promotion and upholding those ideals and principles that we value at home and abroad.")

In 1974, Joe Coors financed the founding of **Paul Weyrich** (#9)'s Free Congress Foundation. Other Coors-funded right-wing causes have included the election campaigns of Barry Goldwater,

Orrin Hatch, and arch-segregationist Strom Thurmond; the Hoover Institution; the American Defense Institute; the Rutherford Institute; Accuracy in Media—which alleged, for example, that PBS (#48) airs "blatantly pro-Communist propaganda"; the equally immoral Morality in Media; **Pat Robertson** (#55)'s Regent University; the pro-Contra, **Sun Myung Moon** (#54)–funded Nicaraguan Freedom Fund (other backers included Oliver North and that son of a Hur, Charlton Heston); the far-right John Birch Society; the anti-environmentalist Mountain States Legal Foundation (see #18); **Phyllis Schlafly** (#20)'s STOP ERA campaign; the Center for Individual Rights, which fought the University of Michigan's affirmative-action programs; California's anti–affirmative action Proposition 209, approved in 1996; and Robert Simonds's National Association of Christian Educators. Simonds:

> There are 15,700 local school boards in this country. It is our intent to take them over one by one . . . and then we will determine what is taught . . . who is hired and who is fired . . . we will be the stealth candidates, and you must carry out our mission in such a way that the public won't know what we're about until we've won control. I'm a fundamentalist Christian, and as far as I'm concerned, that's the only kind of Christian there is.

In the 1980s, Joseph Coors, wife Holly, and sons Jeff and Peter were members of the board of governors of the secretive Council for National Policy (see #9)—along with a former Ku Klux Klan leader, supporters of South Africa's apartheid government, and Christian Reconstructionists, who call for the execution of homosexuals, adulterers, and goddamn motherfucking blasphemers.

Joseph's brother and company chairman William Coors described Joseph as "a little bit right of Attila the Hun." Consider who that came from: in a speech to a group of mainly African-American businessmen in 1984, William said: "Probably the

greatest favor that anybody ever did you was to drag your ances-
tors over here in chains, and I mean it." He then said of African
political leaders: "They lack the intellectual capacity to succeed.
. . . [Take] Rhodesia, where the economy was absolutely booming
under white management. Now, black management is in Zim-
babwe, and the economy is a disaster. . . . Lack of intellectual
capacity—that has got to be there." *There?*

In the 1980s, Coors—which advertises beer made with "pure
mountain spring water"—was identified as one of the largest water
polluters and dumpers of hazardous waste in Colorado, for which
it was cited by the Colorado Department of Health in 1985, 1986,
and twice in 1990. That year, there was a criminal investigation
into whether officials at the company's can plant knowingly concealed pipes leaking toxic chemical solvents into groundwater,
allegedly causing higher-than-usual incidences of low birthweights
and early childhood cancer. According to the Environmental Protection Agency, Coors dumped 20 million gallons of toxic liquid
waste into a landfill near Denver, which was still contaminated in
2005 when Coors and six other companies agreed to pay $14 mil-
lion in cleanup costs to settle a U.S. government lawsuit.

Worst offense of all? In 2005, Coors Brewing swallowed the
brewer Molson, a Canadian icon based in my hometown, Mon-
treal. Another step toward the U.S. conquest and enslavement of
Canada. Oh, so *now* you're ready to boycott.

#52: JACK "OLLIE" OLIVER AND BUSH'S
OILY MONEY MACHINE

Oliver, perhaps more than anyone, may be credited with raising
the money that put and kept **Dick Cheney** and **George W.
Bush** in the White House. By virtue of that achievement,
Oliver—even though he has moved (for now) from politics to

corporate lobbying—continues to Screw Up America daily. In addition, the Republican money machine he helped build endures, and—unless *all* its key players wind up in jail—will continue to SUA for years and elections to come. It is that machine, as much as Oliver, that is on trial here today.

As national finance director for the Bush-Cheney 2000 campaign, Oliver broke all presidential fund-raising records, raising more than $100 million—including $37 million in the campaign's first four months, which gave Bush critical early momentum. According to his Republican National Committee (RNC) bio, Oliver "quickly became a fund-raising phenomenon, a reputation he cemented in the 2004 race" when, as Bush's finance vice chair, he helped raise $240 million. "A little-known 34-year-old from Missouri is managing the most formidable cash machine in American political history," *Time* reported. Including funds for the RNC, Oliver helped raise $1 billion. Between the two campaigns, Oliver served as deputy RNC chair and (**Karl**) "**Rove**'s guy" at the RNC.

In 1999, Oliver headed former Missouri governor and future attorney general John Ashcroft's political action committee during Ashcroft's exploratory campaign for president. The PAC was later accused of criminal election law violations, about which Oliver was deposed in 2003 by the Federal Election Commission.

By the time Rove recruited Oliver to the Bush campaign, its basic fund-raising scheme had been worked out. Four Bush associates met in 1998 "to figure out how to capitalize on the extensive network of rich and powerful people that the governor [Bush], his father, brothers, uncles, grandfather and great-grandparents had built up over the past century," the *Washington Post* reported. Unlike donations to Texas state candidates, individual contributions to presidential candidates were limited to $1,000. The "gang of four" came up with the idea of bestowing upon those who raised or "bundled" at least $100,000 in contributions of $1,000 or less the title of Pioneer and encouraging them to vie to raise the most money and recruit other Pioneers. A key innovation was the

tracking number each donor would write on her check so the
fund-raiser and his industry would be properly credited and
rewarded. Pioneer Thomas Kuhn, the electric utility industry's
chief Washington lobbyist, wrote a letter to industry associates
citing Oliver as emphasizing "the importance of having our
industry incorporate the #1178 tracking number in your fund-
raising efforts." Here was a quantum improvement in the purchase of political influence. *Anonymous* influence: campaigns
have to disclose the names of donors but not of fund-raisers.

In 2004 (by which time the individual contribution limit had
been doubled to $2,000), "Ollie," as Bush called Oliver, helped
create two new categories of fund-raiser: The $200,000-plus club
would be known as Rangers; those who raised an additional
$300,000 for the RNC, as Super Rangers. "The name of the game is
maxing out the dollars," Oliver told a gathering of some three hundred Pioneers and Rangers. Rove helped recruit bundlers by
holding "pre-sale events" in which he schmoozed with the mil-
lionaire and billionaire guests.

"Sale" of what? And who were these Pioneers of corruption?
What virtually all had in common, the *Washington Post* reported,
"is that they, their clients, [and] their corporations . . . are major
beneficiaries of the Bush administration's tax-cutting and deregulatory policies." They were dominated by corporate CEOs, lobbyists, investment bankers, and at least forty-four energy company
executives. They included the heads of the **American Petroleum
Institute** (#12); Southern Co., which owns five electric utilities
and was a prime beneficiary of Bush's rollback of Clean Air Act
pollution rules (see #37); credit card giant **MBNA** (#86), Bush's
biggest corporate donor in 2004, which was lobbying for tougher
personal bankruptcy laws; thirty-seven real estate developers,
who benefited from Bush's rollbacks of environmental rules;
twenty-one drug and HMO industry executives and lobbyists—the
chief beneficiaries of Bush's health care privatization schemes;
and doctors, corporate defense lawyers, and others who stood to

benefit from Bush's proposals to limit lawsuits and medical malpractice damages.

"Sale" of what? "I can call Karl [Rove], and . . . about half of the Cabinet, and they will either take the call or call back," one lobbyist-Ranger told the *Post*. Another, Jack Abramoff—who pleaded guilty to fraud and conspiracy charges in 2005 (see #56)—had roughly two hundred contacts with the Bush administration in its first year and at least two meetings with Jack Oliver. More than a hundred lobbyists have received high-level Bush administration appointments—typically to agencies that oversee the very industries they were paid millions to lobby for—a geometric increase over the number of lobbyists hired by previous administrations.

Almost all of the top Bush fund-raisers were in the top 1 percent of the nation's incomes, many in the top one tenth of 1 percent—by far the biggest beneficiaries of Bush's tax cuts. Citizens for Tax Justice estimated that four Bush Rangers—the chairmen and CEOs of Merrill Lynch, Bear Stearns, Goldman Sachs, and Pfizer—each got annual Bush tax cuts ranging from $300,000 to $610,000, and those savings would grow over time. The financial firms would also be the principal beneficiaries of Bush's Social Security privatization scheme.

At least 173 Rangers and Pioneers or their spouses received Bush administration appointments. Four got cabinet positions, including Commerce Secretary Don Evans, Homeland Security Secretary Tom Ridge, and Labor Secretary **Elaine Chao** (#46). Twenty-nine received ambassadorships—compared to five of Clinton's $100,000-plus donors. At least thirty-seven were named to transition teams that helped select key regulatory appointees. Ken Lay, CEO of Enron, Bush's biggest contributor in 2000, was one of three Pioneers named to the Energy Department's transition team, which in turn picked key regulators of their own industry, such as **Jeffrey Holmstead** (#37). Two of Lay's picks were appointed to the five-member Federal Energy Regulatory Commission.

Speaking of "Kennie Boy," at least 148, or 23 percent, of Bush's Pioneers and Rangers have been involved in corporate scandals or helped run companies involved in them—including **Pilgrim's Pride** (#92), American Home Products/Wyeth, Credit Suisse First Boston, Goldman Sachs, JP Morgan, Merrill Lynch, UBS, and Marsh & McLennan—and at least forty-two represented polluting companies or industries.[44] Well, who needs to buy influence more?

"Patronage decisions for Pioneers and other friends of the president are made largely by Rove" and White House chief of staff **Andrew Card** (#17), the *Washington Post* reported. But "in making decisions immediately after the election, Rove consulted Jack Oliver . . . [whose] main function was to tell Rove 'what people had really done' to raise money."

Sometimes the quid didn't follow the quo. Or it took more quid. Quo. Whatever. In May 2001, Nebraska trucking company owner and Pioneer Duane Acklie wrote to Nebraska governor Mike Johanns that Jack Oliver told him weeks ago he would be receiving an ambassadorship. Why was he still waiting while other Pioneers had already received theirs? His complaints were forwarded to Bush, Rove, and Card. No action. But in 2003, a week after Acklie organized a $400,000 fund-raiser for Bush, W. appointed him chair of the Student Loan Marketing Association ("Sallie Mae"), where the trucker would oversee billions of dollars of student loans.

While lobbying for Verizon, Union Pacific, Northwest Airlines, Ernst & Young, Lehman Bros., and Anheuser Busch, Oliver has indicated he would like to run for political office. If so, he will already know all about the most important element in American politics, and already have a close relationship with his most important constituents.

---

44 "Payola Pioneering," Texans for Public Justice, October 1, 2004.

#51: MARK HYMAN AND SINCLAIR BROADCASTING

The Sinclair Broadcast Group (SBG) is second only to **Rupert Murdoch** (#14)'s **Fox News** among lying-scum propagandizers for right-wing, Republican, and **Bush** administration policies, according to industry surveys. Okay, according to one liberal critic.

Maryland-based Sinclair is America's largest operator of local television stations, with some sixty-two stations in thirty-eight markets. It owns or operates two stations, or "duopolies," in twenty markets—more than any other media company. SBG's broadcasts are received by 24 percent of American households. Many of its viewers have never heard of Sinclair; but the ABC, CBS, NBC, Fox, UPN, and WB stations they watch are either owned outright by or affiliated to and operated by SBG. It is a similar structure to that of radio-station owner **Clear Channel** (#50), another division of VRWC (Vast Right-Wing Conspiracy) Inc.

Three top SBG executives, including CEO David Smith, are sons of Sinclair founder Julian Smith. All three are donors to conservative Republican candidates. The company's most public face has been that of Mark Hyman, vice president for corporate relations. Thanks largely to Hyman, SBG has been in the vanguard of the increasing concentration of media ownership by a handful of Republican-run corporations—and of the media-wide trend toward cutting costs and controlling the news by reducing local news staffs and substituting prepackaged, centrally produced, right-slanted news segments which are inserted into and disguised as local news. Local communities, meanwhile, lose their own media voice. One trick SBG boasts of is using local news sets that match those at its "News Central" operation in Maryland, where the "local" coverage of national news originates.

Since 2001, all SBG stations have broadcast editorial segments by Hyman called *The Point*, on which he has attacked media organizations like National Public Radio and the *New York Times* for "aiding and abetting the enemy" (the Constitution's definition of treason) by reporting on Afghan civilians accidentally killed in U.S. attacks; called the French "cheese-eating surrender monkeys" (has Bush found his next ambassador to Paris?) for refusing to back Bush's war to eliminate the imminent Iraqi threat to America; called antiwar protestors "whack-jobs" and "communists"; and accused John Kerry of supporting communists, falsifying military records, and dodging the army draft by enlisting in the navy.

In April 2004, Sinclair decided that eight ABC stations it owned would not be allowed to broadcast an airing of a *Nightline* tribute to the 721 U.S. soldiers killed up to that point in Iraq. (*Sshh . . . don't metion casualties!*) An SBG statement claimed the tribute was "motivated by a political agenda designed to undermine the efforts of the United States in Iraq." It also demanded to know why Ted Koppel had not read the names of those killed on 9/11. Well, uh, he did. But as an SBG VP told a reporter, "The average viewer who watches the show is not going to remember that."

During the 2004 election campaign, a Sinclair station in Madison, Wisconsin, refused to air ads produced by the Democratic National Committee. Sinclair meanwhile directed local anchors to tape and broadcast spots "declaring support for efforts of President Bush and other government leaders," the *Baltimore Sun* reported.

Two weeks before the election, Sinclair—reportedly at Hyman's behest—forced all of its stations (many of which are in critical swing states) to air an anti-Kerry documentary called *Stolen Honor*—in prime time and as a *news* program. Produced by Carlton Sherwood—a reporter for **Sun Myung Moon** (#54)'s *Washington Times*, the author of a book defending Moon and a friend of and media consultant for Bush's Homeland Security secretary Tom Ridge—and cross-promoted by the Swift Boat Liars for Truth (see #3), the film blamed Kerry's 1971 congressional testimony about atrocities committed by U.S. troops in Vietnam for prolonging the war and for the suffering of American POWs. As Don Hazen wrote on *AlterNet*, "Imagine the uproar if ABC told its affiliate stations to pre-empt its primetime programming for a special showing of *Fahrenheit 9/11* or perhaps more appropriately *Going Upriver*, the powerfully positive biography of John Kerry that focuses on the same time period as *Stolen Honor.*" Former Federal Communications Commission chairman Reed Hundt called it one of the lowest moments in the history of American television. "Ordering stations to carry propaganda? It's absolutely off the charts," Hundt told *Salon*. "It's about a company that's forgotten the standard of behavior for broadcast television."

Hyman fired Sinclair's Washington bureau chief and lead reporter, Jon Leiberman, after he publicly criticised the plan to air *Stolen Honor*. Other Sinclair employees have been threatened or fired for protesting the propagandizing of Sinclair's news coverage. Leiberman told David Brock of Media Matters for America, "it was becoming impossible—and I'm not exaggerating—impossible for us to interview any moderate or any Democrat in Washington."

Liberal media bias. **Bernie** (#73) will tell you all about it. (But see #13, **the so-called liberal media**, just in case.)

#50: LOWRY MAYS & SONS AND ~~CLONE~~ CLEAR CHANNEL COMMUNICATIONS

"Clear Channel is destroying radio." "Dirty tricks and crappy programming: Welcome to the world of Clear Channel, the biggest station owner in America." "Radio's big bully." "Looking for classy radio programming? Don't look here." "Ruining radio in so many different ways." "Known for allowing animals to be killed live on the air, severing long-standing ties with community and charity events, laying off thousands of workers [and] homogenizing playlists." "The same fifty mindless cookie-cutter songs played in an endless, soul-numbing loop, the same conservative talk shows, even the same deejays doing the same shows for simultaneous broadcast in a half-dozen markets nationwide." "All about quantity, not quality." "The [#44] **Wal-Mart**ification of radio." "Too greedy and too powerful." "The evil empire." Worst of all: "Strong ties to President **Bush**."

The preceding comments by various critics do necessarily reflect the opinions of this book and its author and have been echoed by media critics and radio listeners across America. As it swallowed hundreds of independent stations and smaller networks over the past decade, San Antonio–based Clear Channel (CC) (yet another gift to America from Texas) became synonymous with the death of diversity, of local programming and coverage, of political fairness and independence, and of *quality* in American radio. Owning at least 1,240 U.S. stations—ten times as many as its nearest competitor—in three hundred cities; dominating 248 of the 250 largest markets; owning major stakes in Hispanic Broadcasting Services, the largest U.S. radio network for Latinos, a radio research company, regional radio news networks, syndicated programming, trade magazines, the nation's largest concert promotion and venue company, thirty-seven U.S. TV stations, 776,1000 outdoor advertising displays (CC is the world's largest billboard company), and interests in 240 radio stations in sixty-five other countries—CC is, as a former DJ put it, "the largest ownership monstrosity in the history of broadcasting." Airing and syndicating **Rush Limbaugh** (#27), **Sean Hannity** (#30), **"Dr. Laura"** (#68), and the right-wing maniac Michael Savage, buying all its national and international news from **Fox** (#28), and featuring shock jocks like Mikey Esparza, "who offered, on the air, kidnapping tips and satirical songs glorifying sex with children"[45]—this while banishing Bush critics and recording artists who do business with rival companies—

---

45 Dan Fost, "Clear Channel Radio Owners Force Shock Jocks to Eat Their Words," *San Francisco Chronicle*, October 3, 2002.

CC epitomizes the right-wing yahooism, corporate domination, and moral muck of the Bush era.

CC founder and chairman L. Lowry Mays—the most powerful person in radio, according to Radio Ink, and one of the Forbes 400 wealthiest Americans—is a friend of Bush *père* and a $100,000-plus "Pioneer" fund-raiser for Bush *fils*. His sons, CC president and CEO Mark Mays and chief financial officer Randall Mays, are also major Bush and GOP donors. As are other CC executives and CC's political action fund—to which Lowry Mays asked CC workers to return part of their paychecks in 2002. In 1999, Bush Pioneers Tom and Steven Hicks merged their 460-station AMFM, Inc., with CC; Tom—Bush's fourth-largest career donor—became CC's vice chair. *His* claims to fame include making Bush a multi-millionaire in 1999 by buying his Texas Rangers baseball team (whose value had been doubled by taxpayer funding of a new stadium) and doling out lucrative contracts to private investment firms with close ties to himself and then-Texas governor Bush while managing the $13 billion University of Texas endowment as Bush-appointed head of the UT Investment Management Co. (of which Lowry Mays was a fellow board member).

CC's metastasis from a few dozen stations in 1994 was enabled by that year's Republican takeover of Congress and the resulting passage of the 1996 Telecommunications Act, which did away with the decades-old limits on radio ownership (two stations in any one market and twenty-eight nationwide). Previously, wrote Eric Boehlert in *Salon*, "Government policy enforced the notion that radio was broadcast on the public airwaves and had an accompanying public trust. Local stations were supposed to be assets to local communities." But now, as former Federal Communications Commission chairman Reed Hundt said, "The question was, 'Who's your constituency, the listener or the owner?' There was no question of who the Republican constituency was."

In 1998, CC acquired the 428-station Jacor radio chain—*and* Jacor's management and mentality, most notoriously in the person of Randy Michaels, who took over CC's radio operations. Long before Howard Stern, Michaels "had achieved legendary status inside the business as a shock jock . . . and an effective but often tasteless programmer," wrote Boehlert, "farting on the air, cracking jokes about gays and tantalizing listeners with descriptions of 'incredibly horny, wet and ready' naked in-studio guests." What CC inherited in Michaels and his crew, a trade magazine publisher said, were "basically good ol' boys from the frat house. They want to see who can be the rudest and crudest." In the nineties, when he was Jacor's vice president of programming and an on-air personality at a Tampa, Florida, station, Michaels—who was said to roam the station halls with a rubber penis tied around his neck, accosting female employees—was sued for sexual harassment by a female jock who alleged, among other things, that false rumors were spread about her giving male employees blow jobs. In February 2001, a jock known as "Bubba the Love Sponge" at another Jacor/CC station in Tampa broadcast the castration and killing of a boar from the station's parking lot. The station posted pictures of the act on its Web site. It was the third time in a year that an animal was killed or tortured on-air at a CC station.

Under the Mayses' intense cost-cutting pressure (company employees call it "Cheap Channel"—"Everything needs to show a profit yesterday," one observer said), CC stations substantially increased the number of commercials, often cramming fifteen or twenty minutes' worth into each hour, while Michaels introduced a process known as "cyber-jocking"—eliminating hundreds if not thousands of DJ positions by simply sending out one show to dozens of stations, which could now be run by a single, low-paid board operator. "Today, traveling across the country," wrote Boehlert, "radio listeners hear not only the same songs over and over but the same jocks from coast to coast." One consequence was dramatized in 2002 when a train derailed in Minot, North Dakota, spilling 200,000 gallons of ammonia and creating a toxic cloud. When authorities tried to get in touch with the six local commercial radio stations—all of which were CC-owned—to get word out to residents to stay indoors, nobody answered the phones and there was no one there to make a live on-air announcement.

CC's size and "vertical integration" has meant tyranny over both the radio and the music business. In 2001, CC informed non-CC stations that its popular syndicated talk shows, including Limbaugh's and Dr. Laura's, were being yanked and moved to CC stations. CC leverages its ownership of 60 percent of rock radio to make sure its concert-promotion division lands certain tours. Bands that choose rival radio stations to sponsor their tours may find their songs pulled off CC playlists. For record labels, getting a song *onto* a playlist has long involved paying independent promoters or "indies" who in turn pay the radio stations to play their songs: payola in all but name. Increasingly, the "indies" are large corporations—the largest of which, Tri State Promotion and Marketing, entered into an exclusive agreement with CC in 2001. The CC/Tri State alliance could now make record labels pay through the nose, because, one source told Boehlert, "today you cannot have a hit record without Clear Channel or Tri State."

In the days leading up to the Iraq invasion, CC abandoned any serious claim to be a news organization rather than a White House cheerleader by organizing pro-war rallies around the country, as well as protests and boycotts of the Dixie Chicks after the group's Texas-born lead singer, Natalie Maines, told a London audience, "Just so you know, we're ashamed the president of the United States is from Texas."

So, when CC dropped the "vulgar, offensive and insulting" Howard Stern show in February 2004—three days after Stern declared on his show, "I'm one of those 'Anybody but Bush' guys now"—CC's statement that it had no political agenda met with some skepticism. Granted, the next day, CC execs were to testify at congressional hearings and promise a new zero-tolerance policy on "indecency" (referring, of course, not to wars started on false pretenses but to the Janet Jackson–Super Bowl atrocity a few weeks earlier). Still, the only thing about Stern's show that had changed was his stance on Bush.

One almost wishes CC would stick to castrating and killing animals instead of doing it to radio and free speech.

#49: THE *WALL STREET JOURNAL* EDITORS

The Wall Street Journal is like Pravda. . . . You don't want to underestimate the importance of the Leninist model. . . . They don't tolerate dissent.
—Conservative political scientist John Mearsheimer

When people think of the daily deluge of disinformation and propaganda put out by the right-wing media, they usually think first of **Fox News** (#28). Fair and balanced enough . . . but the *Wall Street Journal* (WSJ) editorial and op-ed pages deserve equal recognition —if not more, given the contrast between the paper's aura of respectability and authority and its actual, well, Foxicity.

Just on the day I happen to be writing this, the paper and its online editorial page, OpinionJournal.com, offered the following:

- An editorial blaming the rioting by Muslim youth in France on the country's "high taxes . . . powerful public-sector unions . . . GM-like benefits in pensions, early retirement, working hours and vacations, sick- and maternity leave," and my favorites, "job security" and "the debilitating effects of unemployment insurance." The editorial warned "above all, those who want America to emulate the French social model by mandating health and other benefits." Health benefits = mayhem in the streets!
- A piece by deputy editor Daniel Henninger blaming the rioting

on the resistance of "French elites—like their counterparts in
. . . the rest of Western Europe . . . to such modernizing forces
as the Doha [free] trade round, agro-bioengineering and fast
food"—that is, their insufficient love of globalized, capitalist
"creative destruction." "[F]or nearly 400 years," wrote Henninger, America has been "high on change. Lucky us. In
Europe, every village and town has roots that run 1,000 or
more years deep." Horrors! And all those French nuclear war-
heads just going to waste. . . .

- The text of **Karl Rove**'s speech to the **Federalist Society**
  (#25) the night before, on the theme of "judicial imperialism."
  (Lead example: the Supreme Court banning the death penalty
  for persons under eighteen.)

- An editorial lambasting successful ballot initiatives in that
  week's elections—measures that, for example, discouraged
  military recruiting in public schools and colleges and enacted
  strict gun-control laws in San Francisco, and that banned fast-
  food chain restaurants from Ogunquit, Maine, to preserve the
  town's beauty and "character." (WSJ's quote marks. Why not
  on "beauty" as well?)

- An item by OpinionJournal.com editor James Taranto about
  the terrorist bombings in Jordan two days earlier, with the
  smart-ass heading: "Al Qaeda continues to squander the
  world's goodwill."

- Two days earlier, Taranto wrote that the Democrats' decisive
  election wins that week—including the gubernatorial race in
  Virginia, a red (**Bush**) state, the defeat in California of all four
  of **Ahnuld** (#70)'s ballot measures, and the defeat of every
  Dover, Pennsylvania, school board member who favored
  teaching "intelligent design" (see #34)—had no larger, national
  significance re 2006 or 2008. (WSJ columnist Fred Barnes
  wrote the same the next day. This at a moment when Bush's
  approval rating stood at a new low of 36 percent and fewer
  than 30 percent said the Iraq War had made the United States

safer.) *But*: "Republicans can take heart from their victory in
the Manchester, N.H., mayor's race"—where "the haughty,
French-looking" John Kerry, "who by the way has not been
indicted for war crimes in Vietnam" (neither, by the way, has
Taranto), had appeared on the losing Democrat's behalf.

* According to Taranto, Princeton law professor who, comparing
  Bush Supreme Court nominee Samuel Alito to Justice
  Clarence Thomas (#11), wrote that "their IQs are so radically
  different. . . . We're not talking about someone in Sam's intellectual league," was guilty of "uninhibited expression of racial
  prejudice" and "insult[ing] the intelligence of specific black
  people by stereotyping them as having low IQs"! (Talk about
  insulting people's intelligence.)

The next day brought an OpinionJournal editorial headed "A
'Tortured' Debate: A ban on aggressive interrogation would
amount to unilateral disarmament in the war on terror," which
began by suggesting that critics of the use of "torture" (Opinion-
Journal's quote marks) in U.S. military prisons are encouraging
Osama bin Laden (#5) with "signs of flagging U.S. will to fight
the war on terror." It went on to attack Republican senator and
former POW John McCain's amendment (which the Senate passed
90 to 9) banning "cruel, inhuman or degrading" treatment of prisoners (which the editorial called "stressful interrogation techniques") and to defend the Bush administration's denial of
prisoner-of-war status and Geneva protections to terror suspects.
("I have not seen a well-stated rationale for *not* declaring them
prisoners of war," said Lt. Col. [Ret.] H. Wayne Elliott, former
chief, International Law Division, Judge Advocate's General
School, U.S. Army. But what would *he* know.)

A search of "Wall Street Journal" on MediaMatters.org will
yield hundreds of appalling *Journal*isms. But let's do just one
more. In January 2004, when the 9/11 Commission, echoed by 9/11
victims' families, had been asking the White House for weeks for

more time to complete its work—to no avail—a WSJ editorial titled "The 9/11 Ambush" attacked the "membership and behavior of the current 9/11 commission": "Richard Ben-Veniste, one of the commission's highly partisan Democrats, is . . . claiming that the Bush administration hasn't been cooperative enough. . . . Commission Democrats . . . were asserting that literally millions of pages hadn't been delivered to their desks with sufficient alacrity." In fact, it was Republican, Bush-appointed commission chairman Tom Kean who had repeatedly warned the administration to stop withholding key documents and witnesses, Republican commissioner Slade Gorton who criticized the administration's "lack of cooperation," and Republican commissioner John Lehman who said he "can't for the life of me understand why this administration is so negative on this commission." (He couldn't?) Half the commission's ten members, including its chairman and its staff director, Philip Zelikow—a close associate of **Condoleezza Rice** (#10) and former member of the administration's transition team—were Republicans. The WSJ mentioned none of this.

Behind the WSJ editors' "preposterous arguments was simply this," said the *New Republic* (TNR): "They didn't want a report on September 11 to come out in the middle of an election." (In fact, they suggested the commission "close up shop" until "after the election.") In other words, TNR continued:

> [The editors] saw nothing wrong with the GOP holding its convention in New York in early September, in a blatant attempt to capitalize on the anniversary of September 11 . . . [or] with President Bush making his interpretation of that awful day the centerpiece of his reelection bid. But they deemed it unacceptably political for a bipartisan commission to issue its report during the election campaign, so voters would have an independent analysis against which to judge the GOP's September 11 spin?

But I forgot—we're supposed to find bias only over at the **so-called liberal** (#13) *New York Times*. (Whose publisher, Arthur Sulzberger, is Bernie Goldberg's villain #2. Yes, for *liberal* bias!)

#48: KENNETH TOMLINSON AND THE RIGHT'S WAR ON INDEPENDENT PUBLIC BROADCASTING

Note: Since this was written, Tomlinson has resigned as Corporation for Public Broadcasting chairman over his hiring of Fred Mann (see below). However, his policies, his chosen CPB president, many like-minded board members, and the Bushies that appointed them remain in effect.

[Fiddle plays Scots-Irish-Appalachian dirge. Voiceover (Hal Holbrook?):]
Saturday, July 16; near the Rappahannock

My dearest wife Mary,
   Much has changed since I wrote last. Tonight we turned to the local PBS channel and found the lineup so dominated by right-wingers that I declare, Mary, we thought we had tuned to Fox. The gentlemen in Washington must have decided that not a single liberal voice is to remain on the air.
   We hear that we may fight tomorrow. Pray for me, my dearest wife, and for public broadcasting, as I pray daily for you and the children.

—William Jedediah Clarke,
Third Massachusetts Infantry

Under **Bush**, the right has come closer than ever to winning its civil war against public broadcasting—that bastion of diversity, tolerance, subversive Anglophilia, dangerously boring performances of opera, Broadway shows, and geriatric Motown revues, pioneering children's programming, in-depth public affairs programming, science, history, hard-hitting, independent journalism, and—gravest threat of all to the social order and to Judeo-Christian values— Buster the cartoon bunny (whom Bush education secretary Margaret Spelling attacked for visiting eleven-year-old Emma and her two mommies in one segment). No—worst of all: almost no commercials; yes, the filthy communistic concept that there should be one broadcasting organization *not* subject to the political and commercial pressures of private, for-profit, Republican-connected owners and sponsors.

The Corporation for Public Broadcasting (CPB) was intended to serve as a "firewall" to protect public broadcasting from political pressure. The CPB is funded by Congress and in turn helps fund the Public Broadcasting Service (PBS) and National Public Radio (NPR). Earlier Republican efforts, such as Newt Gingrich's in the 1990s, focused on killing off public broadcasting by eliminating its federal funding. The Bush gang has taken a more hands-on approach: hijacking the CPB by packing its board with Republican cronies and ideologues who would lead the crusade to impose a right-wing agenda on PBS and NPR. (One Bush-appointed board member had, along with her family, donated more than $324,000 to Republican causes since 1989; another was a top fund-raiser for Gingrich.) In 2003, the board elected Kenneth Tomlinson, a former *Reader's Digest* editor and a friend of **Karl Rove**, as chairman.

At a meeting in November 2004, Tomlinson told members of the Association of Public Television Stations and PBS officials that "they should make sure their programming better reflected the Republican mandate." Tomlinson later claimed his comment was in jest. Couldn't imagine how it was taken the wrong way!

In March 2005, Tomlinson hired a White House communications official to set up a new "office of the ombudsman" to oversee public broadcasting content. She helped draft its guiding

principles while she was still employed in the White House by
Rove. Two new ombudsmen were hired: a Republican fellow
Reader's Digest veteran and a fellow at the conservative Hudson
Institute. A few months later, Tomlinson picked a former cochair
of the Republican National Committee, Patricia Harrison, as
CPB's new president. "While Harrison has no known qualifica-
tions for the post," noted Joe Conason in the *American Prospect*,
GOP chair Ken Mehlman "has said that her training programs for
GOP volunteers ensured the Bush victory in 2000." The right-wing
Washington Times described her as "a cruise missile" who caused
"general havoc" for the Democrats.

As Conason put it, "Tomlinson's excuse for all this Soviet-
style partisan patronage, cronyism, and abuse is 'liberal bias.' "
And indeed, the evidence that public broadcasting is filling
Americans' minds with liberal propaganda, along with sexual
perversion, atheism, and hatred of America, is staggering . . . ly
absent. Consider:

- PBS brims with such liberal-leftist propaganda as *Antiques
  Roadshow* and *Masterpiece Theater*. Other left-wing PBS
  series over the years have included William F. Buckley's *Firing
  Line*, *The McLaughlin Group*, *Peggy Noonan on Values*, Ben
  Wattenberg's *Think Tank*, Adam Smith's *Money World*, *Wall
  $treet Week*, and *National Desk*, hosted by conservatives
  Laura Ingraham, Fred Barnes, and Larry Elder.
- In 2003, a GOP pollster commissioned by the CPB found that
  80 percent of Americans considered PBS programming "fair
  and balanced"; 90 percent agreed PBS "provides high quality
  programming"; and more than 50 percent said PBS is more
  trustworthy than CNN, Fox News, and other mainstream news
  outlets. The CPB chose not to release the results to the press,
  PBS, or NPR.
- In 2005, NPR listeners self-identified as one third liberal, one
  third conservative, one third independent. NPR, which doubled

its audience from 1999 through 2005, is one of the most trusted media outlets in the country, according to a CPB.

- How much is all this communist subversion costing? The federal subsidy for public broadcasting in America is $1.80 per citizen, compared with almost $27 in Britain.

No show on TV has exercised the right (in a double sense) more than PBS's *Now*, formerly hosted by Bill Moyers. *Now*— arguably PBS's best public affairs program ever—*is* liberal, as American broadcasting goes. To Tomlinson, a solitary liberal show evidently outweighed all the conservative and corporate programs PBS has carried over the years—not to mention what's available almost exclusively on every other network. Something had to be done.

The Public Broadcasting Act instructs the CPB to "assure the maximum freedom" of public broadcasters by not interfering with editorial content. Tomlinson chose to ignore that stipulation and to focus instead on a long-contested clause that calls for "strict adherence to objectivity and balance in all programs." Citing that clause, the CPB in early 2005 withheld $26.5 million in PBS funding.

In 2003–2004, Tomlinson secretly paid $14,700 in taxpayer money to a conservative activist, Fred Mann, to monitor *Now* and report on the political leanings of the guests. (Tomlinson lied that the contract was approved by former CPB president Kathleen Cox, who was not even president yet.) In a report riddled with spelling errors and even weirder political labeling, Mann characterized a *Now* segment on financial waste at the Pentagon as "anti-Defense," and labeled/libeled/liberaled Republican senator Chuck Hagel—who had earned a 100 percent approval rating from the Christian Coalition—as an "L" because he questioned Bush policy on Iraq. Tomlinson evidently planned for House Republicans and right-wing talk jocks to brandish Mann's report as definitive proof of a liberal tilt at PBS.

After House Speaker **Dennis Hastert** (#43) demanded that Moyers add Newt Gingrich or right-wing pundit **Tucker Carlson** (#93) as cohost of *Now*, and Moyers said he would rather resign, *Now* was cut from an hour to a half-hour; Carlson was given his own half-hour on PBS; and another show was added—*The **Wall Street Journal*** (#49) *Report*. While *Now* featured many conservative guests, the *Report* was a round-table discussion featuring the paper's ROA (right-of-Attila) editorial board, *period*. This show, for some strange reason, was exempt from the "objectivity and balance" clause.

Matt Labash, a former senior writer for the conservative *Weekly Standard*, told *The Nation's* Max Blumenthal: "We've created this cottage industry. . . . Criticize other people for not being objective. Be as subjective as you want. It's a great little racket." "But until Ken Tomlinson," wrote Blumenthal, "no conservative imagined that the [CPB] would provide taxpayer funding for the 'great little racket.' "

#46 & #47: ELAINE CHAO AND MITCH McCONNELL: IN BED WITH BIG BUSINESS

I'm teaming Labor Secretary Chao and Senator McConnell because (a) they're husband and wife, or vice versa; and (b) they're both heroes in the cause of big-business, big-money control of government. It's really kind of a ménage à trois.

McConnell—Republican of Kentucky and majority whip (the second-ranking Senate Republican)—has devoted much of his political career to fighting against campaign finance reform and raising money for himself and the GOP. While he served as national GOP chairman from 1997 to 1999, McConnell raised a record $37 million in unregulated "soft money." From 1997 to 2002, his own campaigns took in nearly $6 million—88 percent of which came from business, 0.4 percent from labor. These could perhaps be among the reasons that McConnell "thinks that big-money politics is good and works to the benefit of the Republican Party," as a spokesman for Common Cause said. McConnell's seven-year-long struggle to block the McCain-Feingold campaign finance bill, which would ban soft money, earned him the Republicans' admiring nickname, "the Darth Vader of Campaign Reform"—and did not end when the bill was finally passed in 2003: McConnell simply sued the Federal Election Commission to challenge the new law. But please understand—McConnell's fight was about the loftiest of principles: As he declared on the Senate floor, "spending is [free] speech." To diminish the right of corporations and the rich to buy elections is to threaten liberty and democracy itself.

Chao, before joining the **Bush** administration in 2001, was a policy analyst with the right-wing **Heritage Foundation** (#8), where she attacked affirmative-action programs and minimum-wage laws as undermining "free enterprise." Not to suggest she had closer ties to owners and management than to labor, she also served on the boards of Northwest Airlines, Clorox, C.R. Bard, Dole Foods, Bank of America, and hospital chain HCA.

Her tenure at Labor has been fabulously productive—for *employers*. In just its first six months, the Bush administration issued a barrage of rule changes that directly attacked unions and wiped out a decade's worth of progress on workplace regulations. Chao prefers *voluntary* compliance by employers over actual enforcement of workplace laws, which is so, I don't know, coercive. Accordingly, the first major bill Bush signed as president was a repeal of workplace safety standards enacted under Clinton. The improvements they mandated would have cost businesses around $4 billion a year. *Not* making them would cost an estimated $50 billion in lost wages, sick days, and lowered productivity—but workers themselves would shoulder much of those costs. No-brainer. In subsequent heinous acts, Chao & Co.:

- Repeatedly sabotaged efforts to raise the federal minimum wage.
- Ruled that payments for work required in order to be eligible for welfare were no longer covered by minimum-wage laws or entitled to any other legal benefits.
- Passed new rules allowing companies to cut off 8 million workers from overtime pay. Why? Because, Chao explained, employers were spending $2 billion a year on "needless litigation" by workers trying to receive the pay they were promised. Her department also *offered employers suggestions on how they could avoid paying legally mandated overtime*—such as cutting hourly wages to compensate.
- Repealed Clinton rules that denied government contracts to chronic corporate violators of environmental, labor, and safety laws.
- Repealed Clinton regulations that helped miners dying from black lung disease claim benefits from the mining industry.
- Barred the 56,000 federal baggage and passenger screeners from joining a union, saying collective bargaining was "not compatible with the flexibility required to wage the war against terrorism." Said a union leader: "The fight against terrorism is about preserving our freedoms—including our right to organize—not destroying them."
- Fired all seven members of the Federal Services Impasses Panel, which handled disputes between federal agencies and employees' unions over work conditions, and named a Heritage Foundation vice president to chair the panel.
- Appointed Eugene Scalia (in a dark-of-night recess appointment) as Labor Department solicitor, the department's top lawyer. In ten years as a "labor lawyer," Scalia, the son of Supreme Court Justice **Antonin Scalia** (#11), almost always represented corporations in fights *against* workers' rights.
- Again using recess appointments, added a business lobbyist and an antiunion labor lawyer to the five-member National

Labor Relations Board (NLRB), whose job is—or was—to enforce labor relations laws and investigate and remedy unfair labor practices. Among fifteen or twenty antilabor rulings in just the last few months of 2004, the NLRB made it more difficult for temporary workers to unionize; ruled that graduate students working as teaching assistants do not have the right to unionize at private universities; and made it more difficult for unions to obtain financial information from companies during contract talks.

Following the release of another in a long series of dismal jobs reports in February 2004, Chao revealed how she views the economy by saying on CNN: "Well, the stock market is, after all, the final arbiter. And the stock market was very strong this morning in reaction to the news." Shareholders of the world, rejoice. Workers of the world: Who told you to be *workers* instead of owning stocks and bonds?

#45: DEMOCRAT PUSSIES

Meaning, of course, the Democratic "leaders" who caved in to **Bush** and the GOP on issue after debate after issue throughout Bush's first term—until his approval ratings dropped far enough that they deemed it safe to come out and venture a criticism or two. As though their own timidity hadn't helped sustain Bush's support. Who wants to vote for pussies, particularly in "wartime"? "For if the trumpet give an uncertain sound, who shall prepare himself to the battle?"—Corinthians 14:8.

It goes at least as far back as the Gore campaign's excessively gentlemanly conduct in the face of the Bushies' barefisted thuggishness during the 2000 Florida recount battle; Gore's failure to demand a full statewide recount; his unduly gracious, let's-all-come-together final concession—as though there was even a shred of bipartisan spirit on the other side; and the D's joining with the R's to instruct Americans to put behind them the small matter of whether the individual moving into the White House was the one who really won the election.

Under the Repugs' accusations of cowardice and weakness on national security, the Dems, well, cowered. Instead of counterattacking and exposing the Bushists' exploitation of September 11 and terrorism for the sham, the weapon of mass distraction that it was, Dems' acceded to Bush's deceptions on and rush to disastrous war in Iraq. During the 2004 campaign, John Kerry issued the amazing statement that he would still have voted to authorize war had he known then what he knew now about Iraq's alleged WMDs—so desperate was the decorated Vietnam War hero to match the manliness of the draft-dodger-in-chief on the "war on terrorism." This failure alone could have cost Kerry the election. But there was worse. As Joseph Finder wrote in the *New Republic*: "If Kerry loses . . . his failure to speak honestly and strongly about Bush's pre-9/11 failures will likely go down as his most significant mistake."

Between those two first-term termini, there were countless other examples of Democrats' pusillanimity or pussihood—their fear of taking clear, strong, liberal stands, even on "Democratic," economic and social-justice issues. Even if such positions were opposed by most Americans, Dems would have a duty to clarify and fight for what they believe. What makes their failure all the more appalling is the fact that large majorities of Americans—including Bush voters (who, according to surveys, tend not to know Bush's actual positions)—*favor* clearly "liberal" policies on Social Security, Medicare, energy, the environment, military spending, education, health care, and abortion rights—not to mention Iraq. But consider the 2004 Democratic Platform. Iraq: "People of good will disagree about whether America should have gone to war." A woman's right to choose: one paragraph. Gay marriage: no stand at all.

Since the 2004 election, the Dems have caved on **John Roberts** (#36) and cut a deal with the GOP in the Senate on judicial nominations that the Dems stupidly or deceitfully proclaimed as a victory (see #61–#64).

An embarrassment of political riches for the Democrats—and they've been too embarrassed to talk about them: environmental and workplace safety rollbacks; offshoring of jobs; elimination of overtime pay for millions of workers; lack of health insurance; new personal bankruptcy laws virtually dictated by the credit card industry; energy and "climate change" nonpolicies dictated by the oil, gas, and coal industries. I could go on, but I can't see through my tears. I'm allergic to pussycats.

Alas, it is not *all* timidity. Some of it is *Democratic* beholdenness to corporate funders. No, more than "some."

True, even when Democrats speak out, it is often heard only on C-SPAN—thanks to the **so-called liberal media** (#13). But make your case boldly enough and it will *get* attention. Build it, and they will come. The public wants to elect Democrats. It's just waiting for *Democrats* to present themselves.

#44: SAMUEL "ROB" WALTON AND WAL-MART

That's right, pile on. Wal-Mart hasn't been done enough. Always low prices on trashing Wal-Mart.

Now, may we proceed? Thank you.

Wal-Mart is the world's largest retail chain and, with 1.3 million "associates," is America's largest employer (and, as we shall see, an even bigger *un*employer). Nearly $9 out of every $100 spent in U.S. retail stores is spent at Wal-Mart. On one day in 2003, it had $1.5 billion in sales. Wal-Mart operates in Canada, Mexico, Argentina, Brazil, South Korea, China, Germany, and Puerto Rico.

As a country, Wal-Mart would rank thirty-third in the world in GDP, between Ukraine and Colombia.

In 2005, Wal-Mart chairman S. Robson "Rob" Walton—son of founder Sam Walton—was ranked by *Forbes* as America's eighth richest person, with a net worth of $15 billion. In fact, Walton family members occupied spots 6 through 10 on the *Forbes* list. If alive today, Sam, who in 1998 made *Time* magazine's list of a hundred most influential people of the twentieth century, would be twice as rich as Bill Gates.

How did Sam—starting with one store in Arkansas in 1950—do it? A wide range of goods at always low prices; clean, bright, and ever-bigger stores; checkout counters at one location so customers could pay for all their purchases at once; staying open late; raiding other stores for managerial talent; adopting UPC bar codes; combining discount stores with supermarkets (Wal-Mart is now the largest grocery chain in America); threatening to stop carrying suppliers' entire product lines to obtain lower prices on specific items; eliminating smaller competitors, thereby killing business along the Main Streets of hundreds of American towns—all these were Wal-Mart innovations.

So were acting illegally to prevent unionization; closing stores to avoid employing union workers; violating environmental and labor laws; and paying the "associates" such poverty-level wages with such paltry health care benefits that many are forced to rely on public assistance, effectively making the government subsidize the company.

As of early 2005, Wal-Mart wages averaged $8.23 an hour—$2 less than standard retail industry pay. (Sam Walton argued that his company should be exempt even from the minimum wage.) Many employees can't afford the health insurance Wal-Mart offers. Part-time workers must wait two years to be eligible (50 percent of employees leave in less than a year) and can't add a spouse or children to their coverage. In Georgia, children of Wal-Mart employees are enrolled in the state children's health insurance program at a rate fourteen times that of any other employer. Wal-Mart workers' reliance on public assistance programs costs California taxpayers $86 million each year. Nationally, taxpayers pay an average of $420,750 a year in social services for each Wal-Mart store.[46]

More than one hundred charges have been lodged against Wal-Mart for such labor-law violations as firing workers who attempted to organize a union, employing child labor, locking workers into stores, and doctoring employees' time records to reduce their wages. In March 2005, Wal-Mart agreed to pay $11 million to settle a government lawsuit alleging that it knowingly hired illegal workers and underpaid them. In 2004, it was slapped with a class-action sex-discrimination lawsuit—the largest in U.S. history—alleging pay and promotion discrimination against 1.6 million current and former female employees.

Wal-Mart and the Walton Family Foundation have given generously to the antiunion National Right to Work Legal Defense Foundation. Prospective employees are shown a film about why Wal-Mart doesn't really feel unions are needed. "The company arms management with 'A Manager's Toolbox to Remaining Union Free.' Page 1 provides a hot line number under the heading: 'When union activity occurs, call. . . .' [A]n anti-union task force is on the job immediately."[47] After meat cutters at a Texas Wal-Mart voted to unionize, management switched to prepackaged meats and announced it would not use butchers at any of its stores. Soon after Wal-Mart employees in Jonquière, Quebec, voted to become the first unionized Wal-Mart staff in North America, Wal-Mart announced it would close the store.

Where Wal-Mart locates, local businesses die, unable to match its wholesale buying power. According to an Iowa State University study, in the first decade after Wal-Mart arrived in Iowa, the

46 Larry Gabriel, "Fighting Unions Always," *UAW Solidarity*, May-June 2005.
47 Ibid.

state lost 555 grocery stores, 298 hardware stores, 293 building supply stores, 161 variety stores, 158 women's apparel stores, 153 shoe stores, 116 drugstores, and 111 men's and boy's apparel stores. For every two jobs created by Wal-Mart, a community loses three that usually paid more.[48]

Not to mention the even better-paid U.S. manufacturing jobs lost because of Wal-Mart's (and competing retailers') reliance on suppliers in the world's lowest-wage labor markets. Many Wal-Mart products are manufactured in Central American maquilas by workers paid slave wages and lacking even the most basic labor and human rights. Wal-Mart imports $15 billion worth of goods a year from China (it is China's eighth largest trading partner, ahead of Russia and Britain), contributing mightily to America's huge balance-of-trade deficit and helping support China's oppressive government.

None of this bothers Wal-Mart—which does, however, impose its own "conservative" morality on customers by refusing to sell the morning-after birth-control pill in its pharmacies, or to stock the not exactly hard-core men's magazines *Maxim, FHM,* and *Stuff,* or to carry music CDs marked with the recording industry's Parental Advisory Label, which has forced record labels to release Wal-Martized versions with less offensive lyrics. Recording artists critical of Wal-Mart itself have of course been banned from the stores' shelves. Yet in 2004, Wal-Mart deemed *The Protocols of the Elders of Zion* fit to sell on its Web site, with a product description suggesting the text was genuine. Always low prices on notorious anti-Semitic forgeries.

While it purports to fight cultural pollution, Wal-Mart's basic business model is extremely polluting: store locations often destroy wetlands and other environmentally sensitive sites and necessitate increased driving. The buildings themselves and their acres of surrounding parking lot don't exactly beautify the landscape. In 2004,

48 Ibid.

Wal-Mart built a Superstore in Teotihuacan, Mexico—the most important archaeological site in all of Mesoamerica—half a mile from the Pyramid of the Sun, the largest man-made structure in the pre-Columbian New World. An ancient altar was found during excavation for the parking lot. The local community protested vigorously, to no avail. Yesterday, a unique cultural site. Today. . . .

As for the "big box store" phenomenon as a whole, you might as well complain about the increasing popularity of them there automobiles. Nevertheless, seems to me that once Staples drove every mom-and-pop stationery shop out of business, the price savings disappeared. Add to this the big-box-store "tax"—the five or ten minutes you wait in line to pay, which, based on the median U.S. salary, amounts to a surcharge of $1.75 to $3.50 on every purchase. Then there's the loss of the personal, human element in shopping. Even if you succeed in interacting with a salesperson, you'll likely never see him again, or want to: His attitude will tell you he couldn't care less whether the store sells you what you're looking for and that your presence is an unwelcome interruption of . . . whatever. But at $7 an hour and no benefits, who can blame him?

So weigh Wal-Mart's always low prices against its always nefarious effect on U.S. (and global) wages, on state and local governments' budgets, on local businesses, employment, autonomy, character, culture, and environmental health, and on the shopping experience. Do the real arithmetic.

#43: J. DENNIS HASTERT: YELLOW-MATTER CUSTARD DRIPPING FROM A DEAD DOG'S EYE

House Speaker Dennis Hastert, Republican of Illinois, may not be the entertaining devil Tom DeLay is. But he does wear a miniature gray version of the Republicans' regulation Kennedy-esque hairdo that on him looks like it's perched atop the head of a walrus. The highest-ranking officer of the House, Hastert has tended to avoid the public spotlight but more recently began to make like a proper, virulently partisan, sleazy-innuendo-dispensing Republican to whom the younger members of his party can look up with respect.

He seemed to find his voice around May 2004. After Senator John McCain argued against further tax cuts on the grounds that war is a "time of sacrifice," Hastert responded: "If you want to see sacrifice, John McCain ought to visit our young men and women at Walter Reed [Army Medical Center] and Bethesda [Naval Hospital]. There's the sacrifice in this country." What would a man who spent five years as a POW in Vietnam after being shot down on his twenty-third bombing run (while Hastert stayed out of the military) know about sacrifice? Not to mention that the issue Hastert was trying to obscure was *tax cuts*.

Hastert said of another decorated Vietnam veteran, John Kerry, that his response to a terrorist attack would be "to file a lawsuit with the World Court or something, rather than respond with troops." In September 2004, Hastert really got with the program, echoing other Republicans by saying Al Qaeda "would like to influence this election" to help Kerry by conducting an attack. (How dare anyone endanger the nation by running against **Bush**?) Hastert then answered "yes" to a reporter who helpfully asked if he thought Al Qaeda would operate with more comfort if Kerry were elected. (Reason and evidence alike suggested Al Q. preferred al W.)

Hastert was fresh from implying on **Fox News** (#28) that billionaire financier and Democratic supporter George Soros might be a drug dealer: "You know, I don't know where [he] gets his money . . . if it comes overseas or from drug groups or where it comes from." Interviewer: "You think he may be getting money from the drug cartel?" Hastert: "I'm saying we don't know." Noting that Soros' money *might* come from his hedge-fund empire, the

New Republic said that now, "if anyone asks . . . if we're saying that Dennis Hastert is overweight from eating human babies, our answer is . . . we don't know." ("Don't know." All those babies just disappeared into thin air.)

Piqued your appetite? Then chew on *these* bones of contention:

- In 2002, while Hastert's staff was working late on Bush's prescription drug bill, they enjoyed a dinner sent over by drug industry lobbyists. As Arianna Huffington put it, "the fastest way to an industry-friendly loophole or regulation is through a staffer's stomach." (How did the lobbyists know the staffers were working late, anyway? Alimentary, my dear leader: their input that night was probably not limited to food.) The following January, the first order of business for Hastert and company was to revise House ethics rules to raise the limit on the amount lobbyists can spend on meals for congressional staffers and allow lobbyists to pick up the tab for House members at charitable events such as golf outings and policy retreats held at lavish resorts. "Assume the position," wrote Huffington. "It just got a little easier for special interests to screw the public— courtesy of the public's own representatives in Washington.

- In 2003, after Rep. Nick Smith (R-MI) said GOP leaders had offered $100,000 for his son's congressional campaign in return for his "yes" vote on Bush's prescription drug bill, Hastert helped quash a House Ethics Committee investigation.

- In 2004, as 9/11 Commission members battled with Congress for a two-month extension they said they needed to finish their work, Hastert refused even to allow a vote on it.

- In a book he published in 2004, Hastert urged the replacement of the federal income tax with a flat national sales tax—a long-time GOP dream that, if realized, would mean a huge shift in the tax burden from the rich to the middle class and poor; the latter must spend a far larger percentage of their income and would thus end up in effectively higher tax brackets than the rich. As the founding fathers of the flat tax wrote in 1983, it "would be a tremendous boon to the economic elite . . . it is an obvious mathematical law that lower taxes on the successful will have to be made up by higher taxes on average people."[49] Could any words be more thrilling to Republican ears? The Repugs, by the way, already had a sales name for the sales tax: the Fair Tax. "With all due respect to Speaker Hastert," said conservative economist Bruce Bartlett, who served in the Reagan and Bush I administrations, it's "a very dumb idea." When House Republicans proposed such a plan four years earlier, Bartlett noted, they called for, effectively, a 30 percent sales tax. But Congress' Joint Committee on Taxation estimated that unless *all* goods and services were taxed, including medical care, insurance, and homes, it would require a *57 percent* sales tax to replace income tax revenues. Some estimates exceeded *100* percent.

- In September 2005, days after he questioned whether it would "make sense" for the federal government to spend money rebuilding New Orleans after Hurricane Katrina, Hastert, back in his home district, announced that the federal government would provide $1.84 million to build a road extension in the village of Annawan, Ill. "Illinois," he said, "is finally getting their fair share."

- Finally, in October 2005, in an increasingly common banana-republic-style abuse of House rules, Hastert kept open what was supposed to be a five-minute vote on a bill to provide subsidies to oil companies (business being so tough for oil companies lately) while he and DeLay "buttonholed and browbeat resistant Republicans," the *New York Times* reported. One of those, Sherwood Boehlert of New York, complained, "We're enriching people, but we are not doing anything to give the little guy a break." The bill squeaked by, 212 to 210.

---

49 Robert Hall and Alvin Rabushka, *The Flat Tax*, Hoover Institution Press, 1995.

#41 & #42: ALEX CASTELLANOS, MARK McKINNON, AND THE REST OF THE BRATS AT MAVERICK MEDIA

For lying, sleazeball, bottom-of-the-barrel political attack ads, there's no topping or bottoming the Austin, Texas–based (where else) Republican (what else) consulting firm of Maverick Media, which was founded by former (what else) country and western singer Mark McKinnon, a longtime friend and media adviser to (who else) **George W. Bush**. Every time it was thought political campaigning could get no lower, the Maverick team seemed to say, "Failure is not an option," and continued to descend, continued to explore, until they'd planted their flag at new, uncharted depths. It is the stuff National Geographic specials, Bush presidencies, and (non-**Goldberg**) 100 Screwup lists are made of.

Maverick, naturally, handled the advertising for the Bush-**Cheney** 2000 and 2004 campaigns, nearly half of whose '04 expenditures, or over $170 million, went to or through the firm.

Maverick's Alex Castellanos has been called the Father of the Modern Attack Ad, its "most notorious practitioner," "the [Republican] party's ultimate hit man," "vicious," "irresponsible," and worst of all, "effective." Castellanos, who apprenticed with **Arthur Finkelstein** (#82), has served as a media consultant to seven U.S. presidential campaigns and helped elect nine U.S. senators and six governors.

Castellanos created the infamous "White Hands" TV ad for North Carolina Senator Jesse Helms's 1990 race against an African-American. The ad showed the hands of a white worker crumpling up a job rejection notice, under the message, "they had to give [the job] to a minority because of a racial quota." Before "White Hands" aired in the campaign's closing days, Helms trailed. Helms won.

In a 1994 spot for Jeb Bush, who was challenging Florida's Democratic governor Lawton Chiles, Castellanos showed a

mother whose ten-year-old daughter had been murdered, complaining that Chiles had refused to sign the killer's death warrant
"because he's too liberal on crime." As it happened, the courts
were still hearing the killer's appeal, making rumors of a death warrant, you might say, greatly exaggerated? The ads reviews were
harsh: "A despicable lie" (*Palm Beach Post*). "Shamelessly false,
irresponsible and tasteless" (*Orlando Sun-Sentinel*). "New
depths" (*Miami Herald*). Prime scrapbook stuff for Alex.

For Jesse Helms's 1996 reelection campaign, Castellanos aired
a spot tying Democrats to racial quotas and health benefits for
homosexuals. A 1998 ad for Bob Taft, the GOP candidate for governor in Ohio, became the first gubernatorial commercial ever
cited by the Ohio Elections Commission for lying.

Castellanos is "credited" with the 2000 Republican Party ad about
prescription drugs in which the word "RATS" flashed over an image of
Al Gore before the rest of the slogan "BureaucRATS decide" appeared.
The Bush campaign denied that the "RATS" was intentional; Castellanos admitted it was. For Bush, the struggle to pronounce "sublim-
inable" [*sic*] was easily the worst part of the whole affair.

A Castellanos ad for Bush '04 displayed the words "John
Kerry's Plan" and "Weaken Fight Against Terrorists" (yup, that's
Kerry's *plan*) as a sinister-looking olive-skinned man peered into
the camera. Another showed Kerry windsurfing in order to portray him as a rich, effete playboy—presumably one who
zigzags/flip-flops and blows with the political winds. Just a week
before the election, the Bush campaign released Castellanos's
notorfamous "Wolves" ad, showing a wolf pack—the terrorists
that would devour us if Kerry were elected—under the message:
Kerry supported cuts in intelligence "so deep they would have
weakened America's defenses." Factcheck.org: "The cut Kerry
proposed in 1994 amounted to less than 4 percent, as part of a proposal to cut many programs to reduce the deficit. And in 1995 Porter
Goss, who is now Bush's CIA Director, co-sponsored a measure
that would have cut CIA personnel by 20 percent."

In 2004, Maverick's Scott Howell, a longtime GOP strategist and **Karl Rove** (#3) associate, helped elect Oklahoma Senator **Tom Coburn** (#58) by taking a page straight out of the Castellanos, uh, handbook: in an ad attacking the Democratic candidate's record on immigration, Howell showed images of dark-skinned hands receiving welfare payments. The same year, Howell helped Saxby Chambliss defeat Georgia Senator Max Cleland by using images of **Osama bin Laden** (#5) and Saddam Hussein in ads that painted Cleland, a triple-amputee Vietnam veteran, as unpatriotic.

In 2002, McKinnon told reporter Ron Suskind:

You think he [Bush]'s an idiot, don't you? . . . No, you do, all of you do, up and down the West Coast, the East Coast. . . . Let me clue you in. We don't care. You see, you're outnumbered two to one by folks in the big, wide middle of America, busy working people who don't read the *New York Times* or *Washington Post* or the *L.A. Times*. And you know what they like? They like the way he walks and the way he points, the way he exudes confidence. They have faith in him. And when you attack him for his malaprops, his jumbled syntax, it's good for us. Because you know what those folks don't like? They don't like you!

(The "you," Suskind wrote, "of course meant the entire reality-based community.")

In October 2005, Bush nominated McKinnon (congRATulations) to serve on the Broadcasting Board of Governors, which oversees Voice of America and the U.S.-funded, Arabic-language Radio Sawa and Al Hurra, which broadcast to the Middle East. The idea must be to win the war on terrorism the way they won their elections: through D&D (deception and disinformation).

After meeting with Senator John McCain (R-AZ) in June 2005, McKinnon said he would help McCain if he chooses to run for president—unless **Condoleeza Rice** (#10) or (omigod) Jeb Bush chooses to run, in which case McKinnon will reportedly "review his options." Clearly, McKinnon and his fRATernity will be screwing up America for years to come.

#39 & #40: MYRON MAGNET AND MARVIN OLASKY: BUSH'S TOUGH ~~LOVE~~ LUCK GURUS

Remember "compassionate conservatism"? It's okay, you weren't supposed to. The slogan was meant to get **George W. Bush** elected in 2000—principally by appealing to women voters and to religious conservatives who (correctly) understood it to mean increased taxpayer funding of religious groups (which would then push Jesus as the solution to poverty, drug addiction, domestic violence, teen pregnancy, bunions . . .). The slogan would also help the Bush administration maintain *the illusion* of compassion even as huge, budget-busting tax cuts were doled out to corporations and the rich and as programs to help needy Americans were slashed. Well, the leading ideologues behind these cruel and unusual policies and the authors of the key texts justifying them were Myron Magnet, editor of the right-wing Manhattan Institute's *City Journal*, and Marvin Olasky, editor of the Christian-conservative *World* magazine.

Magnet, wrote the *Texas Observer*'s Michael King, "makes his living in the most ancient clerical profession: explaining to the wealthy how profoundly they deserve their wealth." Magnet's 1993 book *The Dream and the Nightmare* blamed the creation of the underclass on 1960s-era liberal do-gooders and argued essentially that we must stop helping the poor—for their own good. Wow . . . not even Jesus was that compassionate. During the 2000 election campaign, **Karl Rove** (#3) called Magnet's book "a road map to the

Bush program" and handed out copies to those wishing to understand compassionate conservatism. Bush—who, revealingly, never
quite learned to pronounce "compassionate conservatism"—called
it the most important book he'd ever read after the Bible. (Odd
because, while the Bible *is* available in comic-book form, *The
Dream* isn't.) Magnet's ideas made their way into almost every Bush
campaign speech. Bush's "favorite campaign refrain—that his sixties generation ruined the culture and we must win it back for traditional values—is also the central message of Magnet's book,
albeit aimed most directly at those unpleasant people at the bottom
of the heap," wrote King. Bushism, you might say, *is* Magnetism. A
bipolar disorder, if you will.

Misguided 1960s idealism aimed at "making American society
more open and inclusive," wrote Magnet, gave rise to "the War on
Poverty, welfare benefit increases, court-ordered school busing,
more public housing projects, affirmative action, job-training programs, drug treatment programs, special education . . . *Roots* . . .
black studies programs, multicultural curricula . . . minority set-
asides, Martin Luther King Day," among other evils. How is it,
Magnet asks, that the underclass came into being "just as we had
passed the 1964 Civil Rights act?" Around sixteen alternate expla-
nations come to mind, including: (a) it didn't; (b) after black
workers moved north for manufacturing jobs, the jobs moved
south, and overseas.

Magnet has said "the lessons" of Victorian England "can be
applied to America and Britain [today]. You just need to say [to
the poor], 'come on fellas, shape up.' " But "happily," he writes,
"modern society isn't hierarchical, in Victorian fashion. Today's
Haves aren't the 'betters' or the 'masters' of the Have-Nots, and
today's worst-off poor are nobody's mistreated dependents or
exploited employees. . . . [T]hey don't work." I've got tens of millions of day laborers, domestics, **Wal-Mart** (#44) employees,
home health aids, and so on, who say otherwise. But Magnet's
message is that the well-to-do can rest assured they bear no

responsibility for the plight of the poor. The fault is their own. Indeed, "Victorian philanthropy isn't equal to [the Have-Nots'] plight"—in case the rich were foolishly thinking of giving any of their Bush tax savings to charity.

"Only a besotted sixties idealist," wrote King, "would condescend to notice that as [the rich] have gotten richer and richer (and richer) over the last thirty years, eighty percent of the U.S. population has seen its real wealth and income steadily decline, and that these two facts may have something to do with each other." But in Magnet's America:

> the only poor are [those who] choose not to work [and] prefer life on the streets. . . . Nowhere do relentless cutbacks in social spending, or the persistent neglect of public education, the explosion in prison construction, or the increasing militarization and corporatization of the economy, have any visible place in Magnet's Panglossian universe. On the contrary, poor people are poor and nasty because they choose to be so, and any attempt by the community at large to ameliorate their unhappy circumstances is by definition counterproductive.[50]

"If you want to help the poor," Magnet wrote in the **Wall Street Journal** (#49) in 2005, "liberate them from dependency through welfare reform." (Magnet's work, notes King, was supported by tax-deductible contributions to the Manhattan Institute: "Apparently welfare programs for conservative hacks are beyond reproach.") Fortunately, wrote Magnet, Bush's 2006 budget continued the "dismantling of antipoverty programs," such as Section 8 subsidized housing and Medicaid. So if you see what looks like a line outside a homeless shelter, they're probably just lining up to thank Bush.

50 Michael King, "Justifying the Status Quo Ante," *Texas Observer*, August 1999.

Marvin Olasky is literally the author of *Compassionate Conservatism*— the title of his 2000 book, which carried a foreword by George W. Bush. Olasky more than anyone is credited with inspiring Bush's "Faith-Based Initiatives." He advocates religion as treatment for drug addicts; forcing welfare mothers to work as a remedy for poverty; and teaching "intelligent design" (see #34) as a cure for the disease of science. Olasky is a Texas-born Jew or, rather, Jewish-born Texan and a Bush intimate who in 1972 became a Marxist and joined the Communist Party, then in the late seventies closed his heart to the workers, peasants, and rabbis and opened it to Jesus, becoming a born-again Christian. For as Kinky Freedman and the Texas Jewboys sang, *They Ain't Makin' Jews Like Jesus Anymore*. Alas, Olasky, Magnet, and Bush seem to forget what *that* jewboy sang: "Sell what you own, and give the money to the poor, and you will have treasure in heaven" (Mark 10:21).

#38: JOHN D. (FOR "DEREGULATION") GRAHAM

With apologies to Carole King: If you're down . . . in big business . . . and you need some loving care . . . and nothing, nothing is going right (or so you tell the IRS) . . . open your checkbook and think of us, and soon we will be there . . . You've got a friend: the **Bush** administration. Winter, spring, summer, or fall, if there's a health, safety, or environmental regulation you don't like, your best friend in the administration may be John D. Graham, head of the White House Office of Information and Regulatory Affairs (OIRA).

Under Graham, OIRA has become the administration's crack regulation-killing unit and chief promoter of industry-backed "sound science" (versus "junk," i.e., *independent*, science)—BushSpeak for using supposedly scientific arguments as justification for eliminating regulations that protect public health and safety but that business opposes, based on such considerations as greed and avarice, as well as rapacity. Graham has done a "better [job] than I could have done had I been there myself," a top industry lobbyist told the *Washington Post*.

Before Bush hired him in 2001, Graham headed the Harvard Center for Risk Analysis, a think tank funded by corporations and trade groups such as Dow Chemical and the Chemical Manufacturer's Association. Graham's outfit promoted the view that the costs of most health, safety, and environmental regulations outweigh the benefits. In one **auto industry** (#16)–funded analysis, Graham concluded that side air bags should not be required in cars because they would cost $400,000 for every year of life saved. Independent experts reviewing his work found—and Graham then acknowledged—that the figure was actually about $60,000. Graham published a study—funded by AT&T Wireless Communications— suggesting that there was little need to be concerned about increased accidents caused by people using cell phones while driving. He solicited tobacco industry money and worked with that industry to belittle the risks of secondhand smoke.

The "sound science" movement was in fact pioneered by the tobacco lobby, which in the early nineties "quietly formed a coalition of industries that would challenge every aspect of government science, from its studies of global warming to auto safety."[51] As one expert told the *Washington Post*, "[t]he argument that it costs too much to protect people does not sell. But what does sell is this idea that the science is not good." Another scientist called this enterprise "manufacturing uncertainty." The so-called Advancement of Sound Science Coalition was advised by future Bush Interior secretary **Gail Norton** (#18). And with the total takeover of the federal government by corporate interests under George W. Bush, the coalition's approach became the administration's.

51 Franklin Foer, "Closing of the Presidential Mind," *New Republic*, July 5, 2004.

On Bush's first day in office, the White House Office of Management and Budget (OMB), which OIRA is part of, froze more than fifty Clinton-era regulations, including at least a dozen environmental regs, on the grounds that their costs might prove unacceptable. The administration has questioned or denied global warming, the effects of particulate matter on the lungs, the safe levels of PCBs, dioxins, mercury, and arsenic, the health costs of auto emissions, and the benefits of fuel-economy standards. In fact, it has *invited* industry lobbies to challenge many health and safety standards.

Graham unveiled the administration's new "commitment to science-based quality regulation" in a draft report to Congress in March 2002, which boasted that his office had already rejected twenty significant rules on grounds of "inadequate analysis." Graham was "creating a wholesale shift away from environmental protection," a Georgetown law professor told the *Washington Post*. In 2005, Graham's office produced a "hit list" of seventy-six more regulations disliked by industry groups, offering no reasons other than the industries' own.

According to experts like Joan Claybrook, president of the watchdog group Public Citizen and former head of the National Highway Traffic Safety Administration, Graham and his office systematically inflate the costs of regulations while understating the benefits. One industry claim echoed by the Bushies is that regulations are the cause of job losses in the manufacturing sector. But few if any new regs have been added since 2000, yet job losses have skyrocketed. And regulatory costs are less than 1 percent of the cost of shipped goods. Meanwhile, every accounting report by the OMB—at least until Graham came along—"has found that regulations on the whole produce benefits that exceed costs by over threefold," Claybrook told Congress; benefits such as less illness, less loss of worker productivity, lower insurance and medical costs, even fewer traffic delays.

How can we "reduce" the "cost" of the 42,000 lives lost in

traffic crashes in the United States every year? Graham's answer: stop analyzing the benefits of new rules on the basis of *lives* saved and instead use "life-years"—the number of *years* of life saved, taking into account people's ages. Using surveys showing that younger people were willing to pay more than older people for lifesaving measures such as car air bags, Graham's office recalculated the value of the life of a person under seventy at $3.7 million; those over seventy were now worth $2.3 million a pop (or mom). Previously, all men were created equal and valued by the government at $6.1 million. The new "senior death discount" was, at Graham's own insistence, immediately pressed into service by the Environmental Protection Agency (EPA) to "lower" the benefits of clean air regulations. After news reports about Graham's devaluing of human life triggered protests, the EPA disavowed it.

Graham has also eagerly implemented the Data Quality Act (DQA), a little-known law—really just two sentences—written by an industry lobbyist and slipped into a giant appropriations bill without congressional discussion or debate during Clinton's last days in office. Supposedly intended to ensure "the quality [and] objectivity" of scientific information disseminated by federal agencies, the DQA has been used mainly by industry to challenge health and safety standards and to demand that any regulations be based on an impossible scientific *certainty*. By 2004, it had been used dozens of times by, for example, sugar interests to challenge dietary recommendations to limit sugar intake; logging groups to challenge restrictions on timber harvests; the Salt Institute to challenge the government recommendation that people cut back on salt; and the chemical industry to challenge proposed bans on toxic-chemical-treated wood used in playground equipment. "It's a tool to clobber every effort to regulate," an environmental law expert told the *Washington Post*. Using the DQA, a chemical company succeeded in blocking curbs on the use of atrazine, a major weed killer found by scientists to cause cancer and disrupt hormones in wildlife, producing creatures such as hermaphrodite

frogs and Democratic leaders with testicles. The Bush administration okayed atrazine the same day it was banned in Europe.

Graham has proposed putting the OMB in charge of reviewing
not just the economic impact but the *scientific* accuracy of any
government-issued heath, safety, or environmental warnings—for
which, said a former OMB official, "the agency is completely
lacking in the personnel, expertise, and knowledge." The move
would, however, vastly increase White House political control
over agencies like the EPA. Graham also proposed replacing gov-
ernment-funded scientists on peer-review panels with industry-
funded scientists—which, according to a Union of Concerned
Scientists report, "could ultimately destroy integrity in science as
we know it."

In 2004, more than four thousand scientists—including dozens
of Nobel laureates, university chairs and presidents, and former
federal agency directors, among them a former EPA administrator
under presidents Nixon and Ford—signed a statement accusing
the Bush administration of systematically distorting scientific find-
ings to serve political goals. No previous administration had
"engaged in such practices . . . so systematically nor on so wide a
front," said the statement, which was accompanied by thirty-seven
pages of details and examples. *That* sounds like sound science.

#37: JEFFREY HOLMSTEAD: WHEN THE POLLUTERS WRITE THE POLLUTION LAWS

From 2010 to 2020, U.S. power plants and other industrial air polluters will likely be emitting twice as much sulfur dioxide (SO_2),
50 percent more nitrogen dioxide (NO_2), and seven times as much
mercury than they would have if the Bushies had not taken over
and weakened Clean Air Act (CAA) rules. (SO_2 causes acid rain

and thousands of premature deaths from respiratory disease; NO_2 causes lung-damaging ozone smog; mercury emitted by coal-fired power plants causes brain, nerve, lung, and kidney damage, severe birth defects, and conservatism.) And no one will be more directly responsible than Jeffrey Holmstead. Except maybe **Cheney** or **Bush** or former Enron CEO and Bush buddy Kenneth Lay.

How so? In the 1990s, Holmstead was a lawyer representing electric utilities on air pollution issues. That clearly made him the incoming Bush administration's ideal choice in 2001 to head the Environmental Protection Agency (EPA)'s Office of Air and Radiation and be responsible for *regulating* major air polluters like the coal and power companies—which contributed $40 million to Republican candidates and committees from 1999 through 2003.

Who was on Bush's Energy Department transition team, which recommended appointees for top posts overseeing the energy industry? Industry-based Bush "Pioneers," or $100,000-plus fundraisers—including "Kenny Boy" Lay; the president of the Edison Electric Institute, the utilities' trade association; and the president of power giant FirstEnergy. The transition team helped secure Holmstead's spot at EPA. Power industry insiders also got the posts of deputy EPA administrator; counsel to the Office of Air and Radiation; assistant energy secretary; and assistant attorney general for environment and natural resources. The latter was put in charge of all government lawsuits against coal-fired power plants for violations of the CAA. Top energy, mining, and timber executives and lobbyists got key agency positions "overseeing" *their* own industries.

"Once in place," said a report by the government watchdog group Citizens for Sensible Safeguards, "these special-interest allies literally opened the doors of government for business. . . . And Holmstead outdid them all." Indeed, Holmstead—the power industry's chief inside man and pollution-law saboteur—epitomizes what the Bush administration is all about.

A key provision of the CAA called New Source Review (NSR) required the oldest and dirtiest power plants to install pollution-reducing equipment when the plants are expanded. For decades, many had evaded that expense. As a result, dozens of plants were spewing out pollutants far in excess of current legal limits, much of which got blown from plants in the Midwest to blue Northeast states, causing, by the EPA's own data, some *10,800 premature deaths annually*—24,000 according to the watchdog group Clear the Air—as well 5,400 cases of chronic bronchitis and five thousand hospital emergency visits for asthma.

In 2001, the EPA—as directed by Cheney's energy plan—suspended NSR enforcement and leaked its plans to scrap the rules. Soon after, it proposed lowering the CAA's reduction targets for SO_2, NO_2, and mercury and pushed back the target dates—all part of the Bushies' so-called "Clear Skies Initiative." The National Academy of Sciences has said "Clear Skies" would "weaken air quality standards . . . putting millions of Americans at greater risk from air pollution."

In July 2002, Holmstead testified before the Senate that EPA enforcement staff told him the proposed rule changes would not undermine the government's pending lawsuits—filed under Clinton—against the operators of fifty-one of the country's dirtiest plants. But in fact, the National Resources Defense Council (NRDC) reported, "other top EPA enforcement officials repeatedly told Holmstead just the opposite." Holmstead's testimony was also flatly contradicted by the Government Accountability Office, Congress's investigative arm, and by a report released by EPA's inspector general. The truth was that the owners of those plants (who were all major Bush/GOP donors *and* were among those most involved in writing Bush pollution policy) had no incentive to agree to settlements based on rules that were about to scrapped. Even the companies that had already come to agreements to install modern pollution controls now refused to sign them. "The power companies were on the verge of signing agreements . . . which would have delivered one of the greatest advances in clean air in the nation's history," reducing pollution emissions by millions of tons a year, the *New York Times Magazine* noted. "Then George W. Bush took office."

A week after the EPA issued its final rule repealing NSR in August 2003, Holmstead's chief of staff took a job as a senior executive at the utility giant Southern Co., a defendant in eight of the fifty-one NSR violation cases and a leading lobbyist for the rule change—which it had requested in writing directly to Cheney. (You smell something too? No, it's not sulfur dioxide. . . .)

That December, a federal appeals court blocked the weakened rules from taking effect after finding that they threatened irreparable harm to public health and were likely unlawful. In July 2004, only a week after the EPA solicited further public comment— which was overwhelmingly against the rule changes—Holmstead disclosed that his agency did not plan to drop any of them.

That month, the administration also proposed new standards for power plants' mercury emissions. Soon after, EPA staffers told the *Los Angeles Times* they had been told "not to undertake the normal scientific and economic studies" on mercury pollution as required under the CAA. Two staffers "said Holmstead informed them that the studies would not be conducted partly because of 'White House concern.' " Instead, the White House plan contained twelve paragraphs taken straight from a proposal submitted to it by the law firm of Latham & Watkins, which represents power utilities, and—hello—was Jeffrey Holmstead's firm. Small, polluted world!

In October 2004, BushGreenwatch.org reported that an EPA finding that 8 percent of women have blood mercury levels high enough to cause damage to unborn children was suppressed by the agency until leaked by an insider.

In February 2005, the EPA's inspector general said the White House pressured the agency to ignore twenty-one months of work by the EPA's advisory panel on mercury and to "back the approach preferred by industry." EPA scientists were given a target number preset by "Clear Skies" and told to "work backward" and "find ways to justify it," the *Washington Post* reported. It took the scientists three separate tries before the results were fully cooked. When asked by reporters, Holmstead did not deny that he or other high-level political appointees ordered this.

The White House plan—which environmental groups said would retard progress on mercury by as much as eleven years—happened to set allowable emissions just at a level that would not require the power companies to spend any money on new equipment, saving them billions of dollars. In fact, 168 of 236 Western-based power plants would not have to reduce their mercury emissions at all.

In March 2002 the Clean Air Trust named Holmstead its "clean air villain of the month." Will Holmstead go all the way to the finals for clean air villain of the century?

#36: JOHN ROBERTS AND THE AM-BUSHED SUPREME COURT

There is a widespread misconception that Chief Justice of the Supreme Court John Roberts, who was confirmed in September 2005, hasn't had enough *time* to screw up America. Throughout his confirmation, most of the media kept repeating that "little is known" about Roberts. Roberts and the White House pretended he had no opinions on any issue that might ever come up before him, and had never had any. He was nothing but a brilliant, Supremely qualified, yet oh-so-humble blank. He was a "solid conservative," the Bushites allowed, but not a "movement conservative." Moderates and liberals were to feel relieved, delighted.

But there was a bit more *there* there than met the "ayes" of the senators who voted to confirm. As a White House and Justice

Department lawyer in the Reagan and Bush I administrations (in the latter, under Solicitor General Ken Starr), in private practice from 1993 to 2003, and in his two years as a **Bush** appointee on the powerful D.C. Circuit court of appeals, Roberts:

* Urged the Supreme Court to overturn *Roe v. Wade*; won a case that stopped some doctors from even discussing abortion; and weighed in on behalf of **Operation Rescue** (#69).
* Argued in favor of officially sponsored school prayer before the Supreme Court (which rejected his argument).
* Suggested the Endangered Species Act is unconstitutional and wrote papers supporting far-right legal theories about "takings" that would make it almost impossible for the government to enforce most environmental legislation.
* Opposed clean-air rules and worked to help coal companies strip-mine mountaintops.
* Worked to keep Congress from defending parts of the Voting Rights Act.

Now the bad news. No one takes seriously Bush's pretense of caring only about his nominees' "judicial temperament," not where they stand on issues like abortion. But I have been able to get a sense of Bush's soul. And (like his soul mate Vladimir Putin) if there's one issue Bush (and, even more, **Cheney**) really cares about, it's presidential power: further strengthening the monarchy—I mean, the presidency—which is already more powerful than it has been in decades, perhaps ever—at the expense of Congress and the courts. "I have a duty to protect the executive branch from legislative encroachment," Bush has said repeatedly. What Bush and Cheney are really talking about, wrote Marisa Katz in the *New Republic*, is undoing the reforms put in place after Vietnam and Watergate in the interest of making the executive more transparent and accountable. In the Bush White House, those are fightin' words.

And this may be the real reason Cheney Bush picked Roberts. Roberts's public record, wrote Katz, "gives every indication" that he would "reposition the Court in the direction of unencumbered presidential power" and "could lead the Court to set dangerous precedents that undermine public accountability, civil liberties, and the balance of powers—the very foundations of U.S. democracy."

In the name of the "war on terrorism," the White House has assumed extraordinary powers to detain, interrogate, and prosecute terrorist suspects without regard to America's international treaty commitments or domestic legal standards. In 2004, when the Supreme Court (in *Hamdi v Rumsfeld*) rejected the administration's claim to a right to detain Americans as "enemy combatants," Sandra Day O'Connor wrote for the plurality: "We have long since made clear that a state of war is not a blank check for the president when it comes to the rights of the Nation's citizens." The White House has also "created state secrets" and classified documents at five times the rate of its predecessors. In fact, "little was known" about Roberts because the White House blocked release of a substantial portion of his papers under a Bush executive order of November 2001 that gave the president unprecedented power to withhold the records of past presidents and their aides. Most of Roberts's legal career has been spent serving presidents—Republican presidents.

That in itself could bias Roberts toward the president on issues of presidential power, Katz notes. But we know more. Roberts's memos from the Reagan era "show a young lawyer striving to defend the power of the executive." He defended Reagan's "inherent authority" to send troops to Grenada in 1983 without a declaration of war. Even after returning to private practice, Roberts, in a 1993 law journal article, defended a 1992 Supreme Court decision that held that an environmental group lacked the standing to file a lawsuit alleging a violation of the Endangered Species Act by executive branch agencies if the plaintiffs themselves did not suffer injury.

Roberts's writings suggest "he would side with **Scalia** [#11] in giving the courts, and maybe even Congress, very little say when it comes to the president's power to run the administrative state—and I think that's troubling," a law professor told Katz.

In his two years on the D.C. Circuit Court, Roberts helped deliver three big wins for the Bush administration:

- In a case involving former POWs who sought compensation from Iraq for torture they suffered during the 1991 Gulf War, Roberts argued that a 2003 antiterrorism law permitted the president to nullify such claims—and that courts should defer to statutory interpretations by the president.
- Roberts sat on the panel that agreed unanimously with the administration that it did not have to turn over records of Cheney's ~~conspi~~ meetings with energy industry executives to draft national energy policy—an extremely important precedent for increasing White House secrecy.
- In 2005, Roberts joined the three-judge panel that gave a green light to the military commissions being used to try Guantánamo detainees. "These commissions make a mockery of the U.S. justice system," wrote Katz. "They have an unusually low standard for admissible evidence, allowing hearsay and statements obtained under coercion." Roberts's nomination as chief justice portends "more kangaroo courts that shame our tradition of justice, more ad hoc policies that supplant settled domestic and international law, and more government secrets that serve political over public interests."

While praised again and again (by Republicans) for the "humility" he displayed at his confirmation hearings, Roberts's refusal to answer almost any questions directly was, wrote Lee Siegel, "an insolent reply to the existence of the hearings themselves," turning *them* into a sort of kangaroo court, and confirming his contempt for Congress.

"I come before the committee with no agenda," Roberts deadpanned.

There *is* a real void in Roberts, wrote Dahlia Lithwick in *Slate*: a concern not just for law but for *justice*. "The rule of law, in and of itself, has not always made this country fair," Lithwick noted. It would not, for example, "have read the civil rights amendments broadly, in order to level the playing field." Throughout his hearings, Roberts "presented himself as utterly neutral, without once acknowledging that judicial neutrality is a moral choice with moral consequences. . . . The problem isn't whether John Roberts can be principled and fair on a thoroughly passive court. . . . It's whether a thoroughly passive court can ever truly be principled and fair."

On the other hand, as a blogger wrote: "As much as I shudder at the thought of a Roberts Court, I can't help giggling when I imagine the look on Scalia's face when he found he wasn't inheriting Rehnquist's robe."

#35: JOHN YOO: COUNSELOR OF WAR AND TORTURE, YES-MAN EXTRAORDINAIRE TO KING GEORGE

In a review of John Yoo's 2005 book *The Powers of War and Peace*, Georgetown law professor David Cole wrote:

> Few lawyers have had more influence on President **Bush**'s legal policies in the "war on terror" than John Yoo. . . . This is a remarkable feat, because Yoo . . . was merely a mid-level attorney in the Justice Department's Office of Legal Counsel. . . . Yet by all accounts, Yoo had a hand in virtually every major legal decision involving the U.S. response to

[9/11], and at every point . . . his advice was virtually always the same—the president can do whatever the president wants.

In a memorandum written days after 9/11, Yoo argued that the government could, without obtaining warrants, use "electronic surveillance techniques and equipment that could be seen as infringements of individual liberties." In December 2005, the *New York Times* revealed that on Bush's orders, the National Security Agency (NSA)—which previously engaged only in foreign intelligence—had for three years, and without warrants, monitored the international phone calls and e-mail messages of perhaps thousands of Americans. Yoo had "worked on a classified legal opinion" on the eavesdropping program. Wild guess: he was all for it.

In an August 2002 memo, Yoo wrote that the president cannot constitutionally be barred from ordering torture in wartime—even though the United States has signed a treaty absolutely forbidding torture under all circumstances and even though Congress has passed a law that prohibits torture without any exceptions. Because the Constitution makes the president the "Commander-in-Chief," Yoo argued, no law can restrict the actions he may take in pursuit of war. "On this reasoning," wrote Cole, "the president would be entitled by the Constitution to resort to genocide if he wished."

Yoo—now back in private life, a member of the University of California at Berkeley law faculty—"seems to have few if any second thoughts about what he did, and has continued to aggressively defend his views," Cole notes. His book, for example:

> presents exactly the arguments that the president would have wanted to hear . . . that the president has unilateral authority to initiate wars without congressional approval, and to interpret, terminate, and violate international treaties at will. . . . In other words, when it comes to foreign affairs, the president

exercises unilateral authority largely unchecked by law—
constitutional or international.

Yoo professes an "originalist" approach to constitutional interpretation, whereby the Constitution must be interpreted as it was
originally understood by the Framers, the ratifiers, and the public.
"The problem for originalists who believe in a strong executive
and are cynical about international law," writes Cole, "is that the
framers held precisely the opposite views—they were intensely
wary of executive power, and . . . eager to ensure that the mutual
obligations they had negotiated with other countries would be
honored and enforced." Yoo asserts that (as Cole writes) the
Framers intended "to endow the president with power over foreign affairs virtually identical to that of the king of England." But
in fact, the Constitution embodied the colonies' rebellion against
the abuses of the British monarchy, "the prototypical example of
an unaccountable executive." At the Constitutional Convention,
the Framers decided the president was "not to be trusted" with
war-making power and that it should be left with Congress as a
way of "clogging rather than facilitating war," as one of the
Framers put it. "[T]here is as good reason today as there was
[then]" to give Congress that power, Cole writes:

As the framers accurately predicted, presidents have
proven much more eager than Congress to involve the
nation in wars. It is easier for one person to make up his
mind than for a majority of two houses of Congress to
agree on a war policy. . . . Were Congress to be eliminated
from the initial decision-making process, as Yoo would
prefer, the result would almost certainly be even more
wars, and more quagmires such as the one in Iraq.[52]

52 David Cole, "What Bush Wants to Hear," *New York Review of Books*, November
17, 2005.

#34: THE DISCOVERY INSTITUTE AND THE BLASPHEMY OF "INTELLIGENT DESIGN"

Of course, like every other man of intelligence and education I do believe in organic evolution. It surprises me that at this late date such questions should be raised.

—Woodrow Wilson, 1922

In nature, time cannot ordinarily go backward—but evolution evidently can: a species can become less intelligent. Consider *Homo americanus.* The United States is the only country in the Western world where not only is a "debate" on evolution under way but the antireality forces have had significant victories in the elections of school boards (see #75), the choice and wording of textbooks, and public opinion. According to polls, only around 40 percent of Americans believe evolution is a fact. This sets America apart from all other industrialized nations. Typically, 80 percent or more accept evolution (in Japan, it is 96 percent), and very few reject the idea outright.

The very fact that scientists are forced to waste their time debating evolution is a victory for the creationists, who get to appear on the same stage, literally and figuratively, with real scientists. That's largely the result of a shift in strategy by the creationists that followed the 1987 Supreme Court decision in *Edwards v. Aguillard,* which struck down as an unconstitutional endorsement of religion a Louisiana law giving creationism equal teaching time with evolution. The decision led the creationists to, well, evolve—to dress up creationism as science. Voilà, "intelligent design" (ID): the proposition that nature—especially in the structure of proteins and amino acids in cells—is so complex that it can only have resulted from intelligent, conscious design. (Actually, the "blind," Darwinian evolution of cellular processes has been understood and proven for decades.) Implicit in "design," of course, is a mighty Designer, and a purpose: to make life—God-fearing, heterosexual, Republican life—possible.

"Masquerading as a science," wrote Michelle Goldberg in *Salon*, ID "aims to convince the public that evolution is a theory under fire within the scientific community and doesn't deserve its preeminent place in the biology curriculum." As a biologist told Goldberg, the idea that there is "a powerful upwelling of controversy within the scientific community" over evolution "is absolute nonsense." Nonetheless, wrote Goldberg, the ID proponents have "created the terms that now dominate the debate from the halls of Congress to local school boards. They're the reason that, after a decade when the consensus on evolution in education seemed secure, Darwin's enemies are on the move."

Quietly leading the movement is the Center for Science and Culture (CSC), which is part of the Seattle-based Discovery Institute. Founded in 1991 by former Reagan official Bruce Chapman, the institute's leading funder is Christian Reconstructionist and billionaire banking heir Howard Ahmanson, who also funds a magazine that has called for homosexuals to be stoned and a think tank, the Claremont Institute, that praises "the God-fearing Caucasian middle class." Ahmanson "makes the biblical argument for no minimum wage, no right to healthcare, and no requirement for compassion towards the poor."[53] The CSC just happens to also support, along with ID, "tort reform," lower taxes, and less government regulation—good social-Darwinist policies like those.

CSC, wrote Goldberg, "provides the 'scientific' and philosophical arguments to bolster the opponents of evolution in local political struggles. . . . At times, though, it's refreshingly candid about its true goal—a grandiose scheme to undermine the secular legacy of the Enlightenment and rebuild society on religious foundations."

53 Max Blumenthal, "Avenging Angel of the Religious Right," *Salon*, January 6, 2004.

CSC's program adviser, Phillip E. Johnson—no, not the architect, but the architect of CSC's "Wedge" and "Teach the Controversy" strategies—has written: "This isn't really, and never has been a debate about science. It's about religion and philosophy."

"Our strategy has been to change the subject a bit so that we can get [ID], which really means the reality of God . . . into the schools," wrote Johnson, a UC Berkeley ~~Biology~~ law professor known as the "father of the ID movement." "The Wedge Strategy"—the actual title of a 1999 CSC fund-raising proposal—said ID's scientific-sounding arguments were merely a wedge to promote "Christian and theistic convictions"; CSC "seeks nothing less than the overthrow of [scientific] materialism and its cultural legacies." In the nineteenth century,

> [T]he bedrock [Western] principle [that] human beings are created in the image of God . . . came under wholesale attack by intellectuals drawing on the discoveries of modern science. . . . thinkers such as Charles Darwin, Karl Marx, and Sigmund Freud portrayed humans not as moral and spiritual beings, but as animals or machines . . . whose behavior and very thoughts were dictated by the unbending forces of biology, chemistry, and environment. This materialistic conception of reality eventually infected virtually every area of our culture, from politics and economics to literature and art.

True—and not true: the distinction between "material" and "spiritual" is simplistic and artificial. There's very little that's *material* in modern physics's view of *matter* itself. Marx was surprisingly "spiritual" in his social ideals. Freud abandoned his biologism early on. Darwin was trained as a clergyman.

At any rate, no *solid*, durable, stain-resistant spirituality or religion can be built except on what is actually known—not on denial of it. But then, the ID folks don't *dispute* modern science (note the, uh, Freudian slip in the preceding quote: "the *discoveries* of modern science") so much as *dislike* its cultural consequences. (The crusading Argentine-Jewish newspaper editor Jacobo Timerman, who was imprisoned by the right-wing Argentine military regime in the 1970s, later quoted his chief torturer as saying: "Marx destroyed the Christian idea of society, Freud, the Christian idea of the family, and Einstein, the Christian idea of time and space." Now, that *is* an un-Christian axis of intellectual evil.)

As of 2005, Wikipedia noted, "none of the [CSC's] fellows has yet produced the original scientific research" promised. Instead, the institute "has promoted ID politically," mainly through books and op-ed and magazine articles by ID proponents, appearances in venues like **James Dobson** (#15)'s radio program, and support from allies like Senator **Rick Santorum** (#23).

This is, indeed, the ID movement's dirty little secret. It shares with the left-wing postmodernists of the recent past the relativistic view that, as Noam Scheiber put it in the *New Republic*, "truth follows from power and not from its intrinsic rightness," that science, like history, is "written" by the political victors and therefore the way to win intellectually is to win politically. Or as Bruce Chapman himself has said: "All ideas that achieve a sort of uniform acceptance ultimately fall apart . . . after a few people keep knocking away at it." (The germ theory of disease? The round earth?) There's your IDer's respect for science: centuries of painstaking scientific progress can be canceled if we just do enough PR and elect the right people. These "religious" folks have no respect whatsoever for God's creation, if you will. It's as that Bush aide, who disparaged non-Bushists as the "reality-based community," blasphemed: "We create our own reality." The scientist—recognizing that the fundamentals of nature are a certain way, not another, and that humans cannot decide them, only discover them—is infinitely more religious.

#33: JAMES "ONE OF THE DUMBEST MEMBERS OF CONGRESS" INHOFE

His middle name is actually Mountain. But what mountain? A mountain of what? The **so-called liberal media** (#13) have shown no interest in the issue.

Global warming, he says, is "the second-largest hoax ever played on the American people, after the separation of church and state."[54] (For the *seven* largest, I'd nominate the 2000 and 2004 presidential elections, the Iraq War, the 1994, 1996, and 2002 elections that put and kept Inhofe in the U.S. Senate, and a certain infamous, Inhofe-less *100 People* book.) Inhofe, Republican of Oklahoma, will forever be remembered for his contribution to the extremist partisan poisoning and the extreme dumbing down of that once august body, the Senate.

In 1967, Inhofe, then a Tulsa real estate developer, made his first trip to Washington to testify against Lady Bird Johnson's highway beautification project. In 1972, as an Oklahoma state senator, he recommended that Jane Fonda and Senator George McGovern be hanged for treason for opposing the Vietnam War. In 1993, then-Representative Inhofe vowed never to hire gay staffers because they could be "disruptive in terms of unit cohesion." (No gays in *this* man's army.) He cheerfully described his own 1994 campaign platform as "God, gays, and guns." The day after Timothy McVeigh's 1995 terrorist bombing of a federal office building in Oklahoma City—in Inhofe's state—Inhofe saw fit to attack lazy bureaucrats: "We are not sure how many federal employees are missing because we don't know how many were playing hooky." In 1996, Inhofe was the only senator to vote with his party *every* time. That year he led the fight for a gay-marriage ban and in 1997 he blocked President Clinton's nomination of James Hormel, the

---

54 "Bush Plans Pollution Rules by March, Disappointing Utilities," Bloomberg.com, January 21, 2005.

first openly gay ambassadorial nominee, calling him "a gay activist who puts his agenda ahead of the agenda of America." When a propeller fell off a small plane Inhofe was flying in 1999, he hinted that someone in the Clinton administration had sabotaged it.[55]

Surveying Oklahoma's congressional delegation in 1998 (also see #58) David Plotz wrote in *Slate*: "They accomplish nothing. . . . Most of them don't know how to compromise or draft legislation that others will vote for, and they are too principled—or too dumb—to learn how." But in today's GOP, "their ideological purity and troublemaking have made them power brokers."

In 2003, after Senator Trent Lott of Mississippi apologized for saying that if the racial segregationist Strom Thurmond had succeeded in his 1948 presidential run, "we wouldn't have had all these problems over all these years," Inhofe said, "I think that is a stupid statement." Meaning, of course, Lott's *apology*. Inhofe called Thurmond "a great man"; said of Lott's apology for having opposed a national Martin Luther King, Jr., holiday, "I would have voted the same way"; and blamed the "liberal" media for Lott's fall from Senate majority leader.

In the first days after 9/11, Inhofe tried to cram a measure to permit oil and gas drilling in Alaska's Arctic National Wildlife Refuge into an emergency defense-spending bill. In 2002, Inhofe, perhaps the most fanatically anti-environmental senator in Senate history—he once compared the Environmental Protection Agency (EPA) to the Gestapo and called its then-chief, Carol Browner, "Tokyo Rose"—was, logically enough, made chairman of the Environment and Public Works Committee. Aware that GOP anti-environmentalism could be politically damaging, the White House got Inhofe to shut up for a little while. "Right now the administration is sitting below the radar and is just ripping EPA to shreds," and "working hard to make sure [Inhofe] doesn't

55 Editorial, "Tortured Logic," *The New Republic*, May 24, 2004.

disrupt" the dismantling of the regulatory system, a former Clinton official told the *New Republic*'s Michael Crowley. At the same time, wrote Crowley, "a fire-breathing Inhofe" may be "just what **Bush** wants, a foil against which he can cast himself as a moderate." At any rate, Inhofe was just "a briefly dormant volcano." In 2005, he vowed that regulation of carbon dioxide emissions, the main human cause of global warming, "certainly will not be part of" Bush's Clear Skies plan (see #37), a weakening of pollution rules that Inhofe had just reintroduced in the Senate.

Inhofe is also, well, Inhofe on foreign affairs. As a high-ranking GOP member of the Armed Services Committee, he said "the spiritual door was opened" for the 9/11 attacks by the U.S. policy of "pressur[ing]" Israel not to retaliate for terrorist attacks. When photographs emerged in May 2004 of prisoners at Abu Ghraib prison in Iraq hooded and attached to electrodes or lying naked on the floor, forced into mock-sexual positions by grinning U.S. soldiers—soon followed by reports from Guantánamo of prisoners shocked with electric guns, strangled, burned, forced to masturbate while wearing panties over their heads, sodomized with toilet plungers, deprived of food or water, and/or chained to the ceiling and kicked and beaten for days, sometimes to death—Inhofe declared that he was "more outraged by the outrage" over the "treatment" than by the "treatment" itself. He also called the Red Cross—which found that 70 to 90 percent of Abu Ghraib prisoners had committed no crime—a "bleeding heart." The bleeding idiot.

Inhofe, the *New Republic* commented, "has managed to cement his reputation as not only one of the most vulgar members of Congress . . . but also one of the stupidest." *Slate*'s Plotz confirmed that Inhofe is "[w]idely considered one of the dumbest members of Congress." Which, nowadays especially, sets a pretty high standard.

#32: ANN COULTER: FASCIST FLIRT

One really *doesn't* want to give Coulter—the far-right comedienne, commentator, and author of such bestsellers as *Slander: Liberal Lies about the American Right* and *Treason: Liberal Treachery from the Cold War to the War on Terrorism*—more of what she wants, needs, and lives on: Attention, quotes, the delighted shrieks of her mostly young, male, conservative fans, and the gasps of liberals at her wildly Wildean inversions of liberal common sense (her main gimmick). (Have her quotes been issued yet in *Little Red Book* form? *The Vituperation and Venom of Ann Coulter? Coulter's Guide for College Maledictorians?*) But what is a poor masochist, who needs to be tied up and Coultered because he's been a very naughty liberal, to do?

But if we must do this abominatrix—and of course, we must—let's just do some sample quotes and get it over with as quickly as possible:

- "There are a lot of bad Republicans; there are no good Democrats."
- "[Liberals] adore pornography and the mechanization of sex."
- "Liberals hate America . . . they hate all religions except Islam, post 9/11. Even Islamic terrorists don't hate America like liberals do."
- "We need to execute people like ['American Taliban'] John Walker [Lindh] in order to physically intimidate liberals, by making them realize that they can be killed, too. Otherwise, they will turn out to be outright traitors." Why wait? After all:
- "The presumption of innocence only means you don't go right to jail."
- "We should invade [Muslims'] countries, kill their leaders and convert them to Christianity. We weren't punctilious about locating and punishing only Hitler and his top officers. We

carpet-bombed German cities; we killed civilians." And that's what we need more of.

- "Being nice to people is, in fact, one of the incidental tenets of Christianity (as opposed to other religions whose tenets are more along the lines of 'kill everyone who doesn't smell bad and doesn't answer to the name Mohammed')."
- "Bumper sticker idea for liberals: News magazines don't kill people, Muslims do."
- "When we were fighting communism, OK, they had mass murderers and gulags, but they were white men and they were sane. Now we're up against absolutely insane savages."
- "Not all Muslims may be terrorists, but all terrorists are Muslims."
- "Press passes can't be that hard to come by if the White House allows that old Arab Helen Thomas to sit within yards of the president."
- "The only standard journalists respect is: Will this story promote the left-wing agenda?"
- "Would that it were so! . . . That the American military were targeting journalists."
- "My only regret with Timothy McVeigh is he did not go to the *New York Times* building."
- "It would be a much better country if women did not vote [because] in every presidential election since 1950—except Goldwater in '64—the Republican would have won, if only the men had voted."
- "[Women] should not vote [because they] have no capacity to understand how money is earned. They have a lot of ideas on how to spend it . . . it's always more money on education . . . child care . . . day care."
- "I have to say I'm all for public flogging."
- "Frankly, I'm not a big fan of the First Amendment [free speech]." (And when Coulter speaks, neither am I.)
- "I think we had enough laws about the turn of the [nineteenth/twentieth] century." Would she repeal laws back to

the Emancipation Proclamation? "That would be a good start."

* "God said . . . Go forth, be fruitful, multiply, and rape the planet—it's yours. That's our job: drilling, mining and stripping. . . . Big gas-guzzling cars with phones and CD players and wet bars—that's the Biblical view." And if we fuck this planet up, God'll just give us another one.
* "My libertarian friends . . . never appreciate the benefits of local fascism."
* On a high school shooting in Kentucky: "If those kids had been carrying guns they would have gunned down this one [teenage] gunman."
* "[T]here are . . . 39 million greedy geezers collecting Social Security."
* "[A] cruise missile is more important than Head Start." I agree—depending on whom it targets.

#31: THE ABOR-ING, ABHORENT, ABWHORENT DAVID HOROWITZ

It has been said (though *not* by Winston Churchill) that if you're not a leftist when you're twenty, you're a fool; if you're still a leftist when you're forty, you're a fool. Whoever said it was, of course, half-wrong. But David Horowitz has been wrong *all* his life, both as a strict Marxist ideologue in his youth, when he edited the radical magazine *Ramparts* and worked with the Black Panthers, and as a fanatical, well-funded, highly influential *right-wing* ideologue since his extreme overcorrection in the late 1970s.

Two quotations may serve to describe the political . . . maturation of this writer, activist, and commentator:

* From a 1969 essay: "Liberation is [not] merely a national

concern. The dimension of the struggle, as Lenin and the Bolsheviks so clearly saw, is international: its road is the socialist revolution."

• January 2001: "What about the debt blacks owe to America—to white America—for liberating them from slavery?" At the same time, Horowitz managed to claim that blacks *benefited* from slavery and to accuse a black historian of racism for questioning his claims.[56]

Two more:

• From his 1999 article "Guns Don't Kill Black People, Other Blacks Do": "If blacks are oppressed in America, why isn't there a black exodus?" And if conservatives are oppressed in America, as Horowitz pretends (see below), why isn't there—*please*—a conservative exodus?

• In Nicaragua in 1987, where he had been sent (by Assistant Secretary of State and later indicted Iran-Contra figure Elliott Abrams) to advise anti-Sandinistas: "I can't wait for the contras to march into this town and liberate it from these fucking Sandinistas!" The CIA, Contra leaders, and other witnesses informed congressional committees that the Contras "raped, tortured and killed unarmed civilians, including children" and that "groups of civilians, including women and children, were burned, dismembered, blinded and beheaded."[57] In 1982-84 alone, Oxfam reported, over 7,000 civilians were killed by the Contras.

Horowitz edits the online magazine FrontPage (FrontPageMag.com) and has authored such books as *Hating Whitey*

56 "Academic Freedom under Attack," AmericanProgress.org, February 16, 2005.

57 William Blum, *Killing Hope: US Military and CIA Interventions Since World War II*, Common Courage Press, 2003, p. 293

and Other Progressive Causes; *Liberal Racism*; *The Feminist Assault on the Military*; *Noam Chomsky's Jihad against America*; *How the Left Undermined America's Security*; *Unholy Alliance: Radical Islam and the American Left*; and in 2000, *The Art of Political War: How Republicans Can Fight to Win*, endorsed and distributed by **Karl Rove** (#3), **Tom DeLay** (#6), and the **Heritage Foundation** (#8).

With millions of dollars in funding from the Bradley, Olin, **Scaife** (#21), and other right-wing billionaires' foundations, Horowitz pursues a multitude of exciting projects. A top target is the campaign for reparations for slavery, a campaign Horowitz calls "racist." Horowitz's legal arm, the Individual Rights Foundation (IRF), represents professionals who see themselves as victims of affirmative-action policies. In 1998, IRF sued the University of California on behalf of the aptly named right-wing radio ranter Michael Savage (whom even **Bernard Goldberg** [#73] includes in his *100 People*), who was turned down for the position of dean of the UC-Berkeley Journalism School (in favor of Orville Schell, a China expert and author of twelve books and 206 articles). Horowitz's DiscoverTheNetworks.org Web site is dedicated to finding and exposing "leftists" wherever they may be hiding and conspiring, and, as the site explains, "also the institutions that fund and sustain [the left, and] the paths through which the left exerts its influence on the larger body politic." (What you thought the *right* was in power?)

Since 9/11, Horowitz has been specially busy smearing liberals as traitors. The antiwar marchers in Washington, D.C., in October 2002 were "100,000 Communists" "dedicated to America's destruction," "a movement of, by and for America's enemies within," whose agenda is to "weaken America's defenses" and "force America's defeat in the war with terror." (On the weakening of the military and the pre-9/11 neglect of terrorism, see, for example, **Rumsfeld**, **Cheney**, and **Rice**.) As Kurt Nimmo wrote in CounterPunch.org, "Because David Horowitz wanted to destroy his country when he was a Marxist some thirty odd years ago does not mean all progressives desire to do the same now." Well, neocon patriarch Irving Kristol famously defined a "neoconservative" as "a liberal who's been mugged," so maybe head injuries have something to do with it.

In 2003, Horowitz began his struggle to rid college campuses, or as he says, "the PC gulag," of the tyranny of liberal and "leftist" faculties and hiring committees. Campuses, he claimed, are a "hostile environment" for conservatives; professors push a political agenda and peddle "propaganda not facts." (Unlike Horowitz himself, who—as his views on slavery suggest—is refreshingly free of academic credentials.) Horowitz's remedy was to draft an "Academic Bill of Rights" (ABOR) that would restrict what professors could say in their classrooms, bar them from "persistently" discussing controversial issues, allow students who think their beliefs are being dissed to sue, and halt liberal "pollution" on campus.

By early 2005, versions of Horowitz's bill had been introduced by conservatives in the House of Representatives, six or seven state legislatures, and university systems in at least twenty states. The sponsor of an ABOR in Ohio, state Senator Larry Mumper, explained that "80 percent or so" of professors are "anti-American" "Democrats, liberals or socialists or card-carrying Communists" who bully and attempt to indoctrinate students. (How did Mumper know about this liberal reign of terror? He had heard of a student who said she was discriminated against because she supported **Bush**.) The Republican sponsor of an ABOR in Florida (where there are no issues like poverty to attend to) said students should sue if a professor says evolution is a fact and refuses to discuss "intelligent design" (#34). In the name of "academic" or "intellectual diversity" (suddenly the right wants "diversity"), Horowitz's bill implies that *all* academic questions must be left open or reopened: whether slavery was really bad, whether evolution is real. . . . If that's "diversity," give me liberal tyranny.

Supporters of "academic freedom" have made it clear that what they really want to institute are affirmative-action programs for hiring conservative professors. Horowitz—doubtless an avid supporter of African-American, women's, and Chicano studies—has suggested starting departments of "Conservative Studies."

Actually, not only do most colleges already have rules ensuring free expression, but it's increasingly the conservative movement that sets the academic agenda. "A dozen right-wing institutions now spend $38 million annually pushing their agenda to students," the Center for American Progress noted. The ultraconservative Leadership Institute claims to have trained more than forty thousand college students to become "conservative leaders." Horowitz's own Students for Academic Freedom has chapters on 150 campuses. Such groups have no progressive counterpart.

Apostates from communism, wrote journalist-historian Isaac Deutscher in 1950, continue "to see the world in white and black," but with the pattern reversed; and many end up doing "the most vicious things." But according to a contemporary who knew Horowitz in the sixties, Fred Gardner, Horowitz and his longtime collaborator Peter Collier "were never radicals for a minute." Horowitz's disillusion with the Soviet Union, the Panthers, and so on, would lead a real radical "to call for a movement that's serious about establishing equality," Gardner wrote. Horowitz's and Collier's goal "was and is personal success. It's no coincidence that they were 'left' in the '60s and 'right' in the '80s,"[58] and the oh-oh's ('00s).

---

58 Fred Gardner, "Hollywood Confidential: Part I," *Viet Nam Generation Journal & Newsletter*, November 1991.

#30: SEAN "FAIR AND BALANCED," "GOD IS A REPUBLICAN" HANNITY

The titles of two books by Sean Hannity, syndicated ABC radio host and star of (#28) **Fox News'** *Hannity and Colmes*, should tell you all you need to know about him and his style of fairness and balance (f&b): *Deliver Us from Evil: Defeating Terrorism, Despotism, and Liberalism*, and *Let Freedom Ring: Winning the War of Liberty against Liberalism* (both published by Regan Books, which, along with Fox, is owned by #14, **Rupert Murdoch's** News Corp.). Is Hannity biased? Sure. Against *terrorism, despotism, and liberalism*. Aren't you?

But get into your hazmat suit and let's descend a bit further into the strange, one-sided world of Sean Hannity. (Expect to experience some disorientation at first as you adjust to the relativistic distortion of space, time, and politics.) Let the insanity begin:

- During the 2000 Florida recount battle, Hannity—staying, you know, objective, f&b—bellowed repeatedly that the Democrats were trying to "steal the election" and that Gore, "because of his blind ambition has brought us to the brink of a constitutional crisis." Having more votes yet trying to steal the election? Trying to ensure a fair outcome? That *is* terrorism and despotism.

- In June 2004, when Hannity's guest Reverend **Franklin Graham** (#84) said, "I don't think **God** [#77] is a Republican or a Democrat," Hannity, evidently fresh from a face-to-Face, corrected him: "He's no Democrat, Reverend." (Socialist Worker's Party?)

- In August 2005 on his radio show, Hannity read excerpts of an article describing a protest at the funeral in Indianapolis of a soldier killed in Iraq. The protesters were members of a Topeka, Kansas, church who claim that American deaths in

Iraq are God's punishment of America for accepting gays and lesbians. But Hannity didn't mention that. He said, "I guess this is just another example of how the antiwar left supports our brave troops." (Don't bother him with details . . . there's a war on!)

* In August 2005, Hannity attacked leading Democratic senators as "a bunch of hard-liberal extremists" for presuming—as the Constitution mandates—to seek information on **Bush** Supreme Court nominee **John Roberts** (#36)'s background and philosophy before voting to approve him. "They want an abortion litmus test and a religious litmus test," Hannity charged. Roberts, of course, was nominated *because* he passed the *Republicans'* religious and ideological litmus test.

* Then it was reported that Roberts provided pro bono help to gay-rights activists in the landmark *Romer v. Evans* case, in which those raving liberals on the U.S. Supreme Court struck down a Colorado law that would have prevented any local government in the state from acting to protect gays from discrimination. Hannity now told his audience he was "concerned" by Roberts's involvement on "the wrong side" of the case and that he "certainly want[s] to know more." He urged his listeners to "look at whatever information becomes available" and demanded "good questions" from the senators interviewing Roberts.

* In 2004, Hannity said "Tony, I think you're right" when guest Tony Blankley, editorial page editor of **Sun Myung Moon** (#54)'s *Washington Times*, called pro-Democratic financier and philanthropist George Soros "a Jew who figured out a way to survive the Holocaust" (sneaky bastard!) as well as a "left-wing crank" (who has spent millions promoting freedom in former communist countries), "self-admitted atheist" (a hanging offense right there), "robber baron," and "pirate capitalist" who's "spending [his money] on trying to influence the American public in an election." (Now, why didn't Enron's Ken

Lay or Exxon's **Lee Raymond** [#12] or MBNA's **Charles Cawley** [#86] think of doing that?)

Hannity's personal Web site features (along with links to #27, **Rush Limbaugh**'s show, and #22, the **NRA**) a dating service called "Hannidate" that matches conservative-minded singles—presumably to discourage polluting the conservative gene pool through intermarriage with liberals.

#29: BILL O'REILLY
AND THE "OH, REALLY" FACTOR

At the start of each *O'Reilly Factor* show on **Fox News** (#28), Bill O'Reilly announces: "Caution: you are about to enter a no spin zone." Caution: *you* are about to enter a wildly spinning zone, usually resulting in a complete loss of balance (as in "fairness and").

With the most-watched cable news program in America, averaging 3 million viewers, a syndicated radio show and newspaper column, and five best-selling books, including the number-one best-selling *O'Reilly Factor* book, O'Reilly—the third most popular U.S. TV personality, behind Oprah Winfrey and David Letterman, and *the* most popular among Republicans, according to one poll—calls himself "a forlorn and misunderstood journalist."

O'Reilly "poses nightly as an outraged common man speaking out against the corruption of the liberal elites who run the country from Hollywood and Washington," wrote Seth Ackerman and Peter Hart of Fairness and Accuracy in Reporting (FAIR). "We're the only show from a working-class point of view," O'Reilly—who earns $10 million a year from Fox alone—told the *Washington Post*. "I understand working-class Americans. I'm as lower-middle-class as they come." In fact, the *Post* noted, O'Reilly's father's $35,000 salary—around $92,000 in current dollars—was more than enough to send Bill to a private college without financial aid. And according to his mother, he grew up not in working-class Levittown, Long Island, as he claims, but in nearby middle-class Westbury. "Why fake a humble background?" mused columnist Michael Kinsley. "Partly for business reasons: Joe Six-pack vs. the elitists is a good posture for any talk show host, especially one on Fox."

O'Reilly denies being *conservative*. (Okay. Reactionary? Fascist?) "See, I don't want to fit any of those labels." He calls himself an "independent." In January 2005, talking about reports that a CBS *60 Minutes* producer may have got leads from Kerry campaign people for a story questioning **Bush**'s National Guard service, he said: "news organizations and reporters can never ally themselves with party politics. That is against the rules."

No mention by O'Reilly that he was a registered Republican until December 2000—four years after his first Fox show premiered—when the *Washington Post* found out and was about to print the fact. O'Reilly then pleaded clerical error: someone else checked "Republican" on his form. (The *Post* also noted that the "independent's" office doormat had an image of Hillary Clinton's face.)

No mention by O'Reilly of conservative columnist Armstrong Williams, whom the Bush administration had paid for over a year to plug its education policies, or of Maggie Gallagher and Michael McManus, conservative journalists who touted Bush's plans to spend $300 million of public money to promote marriage in their columns without disclosing that they were on the Bush payroll to help develop the program. (O'Reilly, by the way, interviewed two disgruntled ex–CBS news reporters for the segment. That made it three–zero, with no one to speak for CBS.)

As Chris Mooney noted in the *American Prospect*, O'Reilly will refer to someone like former Clinton Labor Secretary Robert Reich as a "communist" but "apply no political qualifier whatsoever to the conservative columnist Michelle Malkin" (see #71).

A few more utterly spinless, utterly *"Pravda"* (true/truth) O'Reillyisms:

- In 2000: "Now for the top story tonight: Is Al Gore running for president on a quasi-socialistic platform?"[59] (Compare and contrast with McCarthy's—I mean, O'Reilly's—comment on Bush: "[He] ran on the slogan 'reformer with results.' That sounds good to me.")
- "How on earth could 38 Democratic senators vote against" Bush's $1.7 trillion 2001 tax cut—the biggest in U.S. history? "This is not a big tax cut. A tax cut that puts money in the pockets of all working Americans is a good thing, period." (The richest 1 percent of "working Americans" got about twice as much as the bottom 60 percent combined. Their children and grandchildren got the biggest deficits and debt in U.S. history. Homeland security, troops in Iraq, health care, education, and infrastructure got stiffed.)
- "That's my advice to all homosexuals. . . . Shut up, don't tell anybody what you do, your life will be a lot easier."
- "And if Al Qaeda comes in here and blows you up, we're not going to do anything about it. . . . We're going to say, 'Look, every other place in America is off limits to you, except San Francisco. You want to blow up the Coit Tower? Go ahead.' "
- About his daughter: "She's 20 months old . . . same age as Jesse Jackson's. Only she's legitimate." From 1998 through mid-2001 alone, O'Reilly did fifty-six *Factor* segments about Jackson and his "moral failures." You could cover O'Reilly's in fewer than that.
- "I don't understand why in the year 2000 . . . a certain segment of the African-American community does not understand that they must aggressively pursue their child's welfare. That is, they have to stop drinking, they have to stop taking drugs and

boozing, and—and whites do it, too! Whites do it, too!" (So . . . *what does it have to do with race?*)

- O'Reilly the environmentalist: "I believe there is global warming. I know that's controversial. For every scientist who says there is, there's one that says there isn't." (The "controversy" runs more like ten thousand to one.)
- Guest: Drilling in the Arctic National Wildlife Refuge would only yield six to nine months of oil. O'Reilly: "That's your opinion!" Guest: Certain Israeli settlements are illegal. O'Reilly: "That's your opinion!" Guest: Marijuana impairs driving less than alcohol does. "Well, that's your opinion!"
- Referring to the woman who accused Bill Clinton of raping her: "[The *Los Angeles Times*] never mentioned Juanita Broaddrick's name, ever." Actual number of *Times* mentions up till then: twenty-one.

Which brings to mind former *O'Reilly Factor* producer Andrea Mackris, who sued O'Reilly in October 2004 for allegedly making sexually inappropriate comments to her and attempting to engage in phone sex. O'Reilly's lawyers did not deny that sexually explicit conversations took place. The cases were settled out of court, with the terms remaining private.

These terms, however, *were* previously made public by O'Reilly: On Bill Clinton: "[U]nder the federal guidelines, as you know, if you have more power than a subordinate . . . it's sexual harassment for you to have even a consensual affair with that person." After photos of an Ohio TV anchor participating in a wet T-shirt contest were posted on the Internet: "[I]n every newscaster's contract, there's a moral clause that says, if you embarrass the station publicly in any way, they can let you go." On a survey about sex in the workplace: "I have to explain to the audience that there is no sex allowed at Fox on the job. . . . But MSNBC apparently have lots of sex over there, which is why we beat them in the ratings. Because as we're working to give you programs, they're all having sex." (No sex on the job at Fox? Maybe *that* explains all the craziness.)

"I try to force Bill to be more fair," Fox CEO **Roger Ailes** (#28) told the *New Yorker*'s Ken Auletta. Keep trying, Roger.

#28: ROGER AILES AND AL-JAFOX

"Who would be the most likely to cheat at cards—Bill Clinton or Al Gore?"

—Fox News poll, May 2000

What ails America, besides corny, obvious wordplay? Right-wing media ownership and bias. Who or what epitomizes right-wing bias, compounding the sin with the cynical, barefaced lie of a slogan "Fair and Balanced"? The Fox News Channel. Who's the cat that won't cop out when there's danger all about? Shaft. Who heads Fox—aka the Republican News Channel, the White House News Channel, GOP TV, and Faux News? Chairman and CEO Roger Ailes.

They say this cat Ailes is a baaad mother. Well, we can prove it.

Ailes began his career in political chicanery with the 1968 Richard Nixon campaign, when the then-twenty-seven-year-old media adviser had Nixon field questions from what looked like a wide range of citizens but was in fact a prescreened audience. The campaign paid for TV stations to broadcast the events, which were made to appear as news. Hey, the **Bush** crew might want to try . . . oh, have they?

As media consultant for the 1988 George H. W. Bush campaign, Ailes helped plan the racism-exploiting Willie Horton TV ads highlighting Democratic candidate Michael Dukakis's support for a Massachusetts weekend furlough program that allowed Horton, a convicted rapist and murderer who is black, to escape and commit a rape and armed robbery. (Dukakis had abolished the furlough program—which was enacted by a Republican governor —long before the campaign.) "The only question is whether we depict Willie Horton with a knife in his hand or without it," said Ailes. Ailes "has two speeds," Bush campaign manager Lee Atwater marveled: "Attack and destroy."

So, when **Rupert Murdoch** (#14) started Fox News in 1996 as a right-wing rival to CNN, hiring this Republican hit man (who had also coached Ronald Reagan and produced **Rush Limbaugh** [#27]'s TV show) to run it was no more than a way to ensure fairness and balance. Really.

NBC's CEO Bob Wright told Ken Auletta in the *New Yorker*: "What Fox did was say, 'We're going to grab this pent-up anger— shouting—that we're seeing on talk radio and put it onto television.'" That, "and below-the-belt political campaigning [were what] Ailes brought with him to Fox," wrote Seth Ackerman of Fairness and Accuracy in Reporting (FAIR). Friends warned Ailes he would be accused of blatantly promoting right-wing viewpoints. "Good!" He said. "That'll drive my ratings up!" By 2002, Fox had overtaken CNN as the leader in cable news ratings.

Fox, wrote Tim Rutten in the *Los Angeles Times*, is "the most blatantly biased major American news organization since the era of yellow journalism." From the network that also claims "We report, you decide" comes a ceaseless flow of pro-Republican propaganda and attacks on liberals, moderates, Democrats, and Fox rivals. Asked by *Advertising Age* whether a more accurate tag line for Fox might be "We report. *We* decide," Fox host **Bill O'Reilly** (#29) gave a rare "no-spin" reply: "Well, you're probably right."

Three stories really put Fox on the map. Ailes launched *The O'Reilly Factor*, which became its top-rated show, the very day the Clinton–Monica Lewinsky story broke in early 1998. It was Fox's "perfect story," wrote Auletta. While it lasted, "that story probably led [Fox's "news" reports] nine out of ten times," a former Fox staffer told *The Nation.* "It was OK to run a Newt Gingrich soundbite [on the story] by itself," another recalled. "But if you ran a soundbite by a Democrat you also had to run a soundbite by a Republican."

Throughout the 2000 election and Florida recount battle, Fox served as a full-time PR machine for Bush. And after 9/11, wrote Auletta, "Fox, far more than any other television enterprise, went to war." Naturally, Ailes "accused CNN of being overly solicitous to America's enemies," insinuating, Auletta noted, "that journalistic independence—reporting, say, on Afghan civilian deaths or military mistakes—was somehow unpatriotic."

Fox's lineup of contributors is dominated by right-wing pundits like Fred Barnes, John Podhoretz, and John Fund and former Nixon, Reagan, and Bush staffers like Monica Crowley and Jim Pinkerton. A few middle-of-the-road guests and cohosts are offered as the "liberals" to "balance" ultraconservatives—"liberals" like Mara Liasson, who, according to a Fox insider quoted by *New York* magazine, assured Ailes before being hired that she was a Republican; Mort Kondrake, a self-described "Democrat who is disgusted with the Democratic Party"; and Juan Williams, who "was so outraged over attacks on his friend **Clarence Thomas** [#11]," Ackerman noted, "that he declared that 'liberals have become monsters.' "

According to a count by the watchdog group Media Matters, Republican and conservative commentators on Fox outnumber Democrats and progressives by a ratio of nineteen to seven. On *Special Report with Brit Hume,* FAIR found an eight to one imbalance. The guest list was also 91 percent male and 93 percent white. Liberal guests are attacked aggressively by O'Reilly, **Sean Hannity** (#30), et al., while conservatives are thrown softballs, then allowed to hold forth without interruption.

Fox, wrote Ackerman, is "a central hub of the conservative movement's well-oiled media machine . . . a highly effective right-wing echo chamber where GOP-friendly news stories can be promoted, repeated and amplified." As Al Gore told the *New York Observer*, a story "will start at the Republican National Committee [and] explode the next day on Fox News. . . . And pretty soon they'll start baiting the mainstream media for allegedly ignoring the story they've pushed into the zeitgeist."

Perhaps these stool samples of Foxism will bear out Ailes et al.'s insistence that Fox is in fact the only *un*biased network:

- On election night 2000, Fox was the first network to prematurely call Florida for Bush, establishing the false impression that Bush was the rightful winner. Heading Fox's election team was Bush's first cousin, John Ellis. ("Jeb," as in the First Brother, is short for John Ellis Bush.) Ellis had recently written, "I am loyal to my cousin, Governor George Bush of Texas. I put that loyalty ahead of my loyalty to anyone else outside my immediate family." That obviously includes— *ex*cludes, rather—any journalistic responsibility to the public.

- After Bush was officially declared the winner, anchor Tony Snow—a former speechwriter for Bush Sr.—asked Bush Chief of Staff **Andrew Card** (#17): "Now, the President-elect says that he wants to reach across the partisan divide, and a lot of people are interpreting that as meaning that he has got to water down his views to appease liberal Republicans and Democrats. Is that what he's going to do?" (*Appeasement?* God forbid. There must be no negotiation with, as Hannity would say, terrorists and liberals!)

- In March 2001, anchor Brit Hume bombarded **Dick Cheney** with tough questions about Bush's proposed tax cut, antichoice views, failure to address the California energy crisis, opposition to campaign finance reform. . . . Just kidding. Hume asked: "Do you sense in some of the opposition to [attorney general nominee John Ashcroft] anti-Christian bigotry?"

- In 2003, anchor (not *commentator*, mind you) John Gibson described a war protest as composed of "knuckleheads."

Gibson is more recently the dumbass author of *The War on Christmas: How the Liberal Plot to Ban the Sacred Christian Holiday Is Worse Than You Thought.*

- When some members of Congress favored loosening immigration rules for such cases as families of 9/11 victims, Fox morning anchor Steve Doocy raved: "Guess who's giving sympathy to illegal immigrants linked to terrorists? You're looking at her." Photo of Senator Hillary Clinton.

- After France and Germany opposed a UN resolution for war against Iraq, the phrase "axis of weasels," coined by Murdoch's *New York Post*, became a refrain on Fox and often appeared in a banner at the bottom of the screen.

- When a correspondent warned that "the Arab street" was angry over what it saw as "an American war of occupation," Fox anchor David Asman commented, "There's a certain ridiculousness to that point of view."

- After MSNBC's Peter Arnett let himself be interviewed by Iraqi television before the fall of Baghdad, Fox ran an ad saying: "He spoke out against America's armed forces. He said America's war against terrorism had failed. He even vilified America's leadership. And he worked for MSNBC." So what if the only true part was "he worked for MSNBC"? Stop being so reality-based.

- Anchor Neil Cavuto ended an interview with the not-yet-indicted **Tom DeLay** (#6) thus: "You know, a lot of your loyal fans, Mr. Majority Leader, say, That has a nice ring to it, but they like 'President DeLay.' You interested?"

- During 2004, up to Election Day, Sean Hannity ended his show by saying, "Only [blank] days until George Bush is elected president." (Before the studly Hannity selected the goofy-looking Alan Colmes as his opposite for the *Hannity & Colmes* show, Fox called it "Hannity & Liberal to Be Determined." The show, wrote Seth Ackerman, resembles "a Harlem Globetrotters game in which everyone knows which side is supposed to win.")

- For two days in 2003—in repayment for "putting us down," said Ailes—the Fox morning show insisted CNN's Aaron Brown was really a dentist who just worked nights at CNN. Ailes called the Fox-CNN rivalry a "holy war." "Ailes requires enemies the way a tank requires fuel," Auletta wrote. "I don't ignore anything," Ailes told him. "Somebody gets in my face, I get in their face."

Okay, face this—a University of Maryland study in 2004 found that Americans who got most of their news from Fox were three times more likely than viewers of any other network to hold mistaken beliefs such as: WMDs and/or a significant WMD program had been found in Iraq (this even after the U.S. weapons inspectors had conclusively said otherwise); Iraq was involved in 9/11 (for which the 9/11 Commission had concluded there was no evidence); and there was broad international support for the Iraq War. In fact, the study found, one would have done better on the survey by receiving no news and simply guessing than by watching Faux.

The Ailes effect has poisoned the other cable networks. Trying (unsuccessfully) to compete by imitating Fox, CNN introduced more talk shows; CNN correspondents complained that it was harder to get airtime for actual news. MSNBC, the most desperate Fox wannabe, hired right-wing hosts Joe Scarborough and the too-crazy-even-for-**Bernie-Goldberg** Michael Savage; hired former GOP House Majority Leader Dick Armey—he who called gay congressman Barney Frank "Barney fag"—as a commentator; killed its most liberal and top-rated show, *[Phil] Donahue*; and duplicated Fox's display of an American flag in a corner of its screen during what both networks obediently called "Operation Iraqi Freedom."

But Fox's greatest influence, media scholar Todd Gitlin told Auletta, is "felt in Washington" where "it emboldens the right wing" to feel that its policies have wide support.

So all hail Ailes for helping destroy fairness and balance in our TV news, and our politics.

#27: RUSH LIMBAUGH IS A BIG FAT *FASCIST* IDIOT

Why "fascist"? Not to try to one-up Al Franken, our thirty-seventh greatest American and author of the 1996 masterpiece *Rush Limbaugh Is a Big Fat Idiot*, but because bigotry, sexism, homophobia, xenophobia, constant demonization of liberals as enemies of the state, hatred of intellectuals, glorification of war, obsessive emphasis on law and order (with regard to minorities and the poor, not businessmen or conservative politicians), and a high level of idiocy are all characteristics of fascism.

Why "big fat"? Because while Limbaugh, who topped out at 325 pounds, has lost around a third of his obesity, he has lost none of the *obscenity* that led him to describe thirteen-year-old Chelsea Clinton as "the White House dog" on his former TV show and to put up a picture of Clinton Labor Secretary Robert Reich—who is four feet, ten and a half inches tall as a result of a childhood bone disease—that showed him from the forehead up. (Irony: X-rays of Limbaugh from the forehead up show solid bone. Whence "dittohead," from Greek *dittocephalos* = bonehead.)

Limbaugh is the right-wing host of the most popular talk-radio show in America; broadcast on some six hundred stations, it reaches 13–20 million listeners weekly. Limbaugh is "credited" with the takeover of AM radio by right-wing talk. Former GOP congressman Vin Weber said of the Republicans' sweep of the 1994 congressional elections (which was before the advent of #28, **Fox News**) that Limbaugh was "really as responsible . . . as any other person." He surely deserves a generous portion of blame for **George W. Bush** as well.

Limbaugh's career took off after the Federal Communications Commission repealed the Fairness Doctrine in 1987, thus freeing radio stations from having to air opposing points of view. ("I don't need to be balanced with equal time, because *I am equal time!*" Limbaugh likes to say.) Beginning in 1988, his show was syndicated nationally by a network owned by **Clear Channel** (#50). The rest is idiocy and mendacity history. The masochistic reader is referred to a book from Fairness and Accuracy In Reporting (FAIR) titled *The Way Things Aren't: Rush Limbaugh's Reign of Error: Over 100 Outrageously False and Foolish Statements from America's Most Powerful Radio and TV Commentator.* Or to Franken's *Idiot.* Or to the watchdog group Media Matters for America, which monitored the *Rush Limbaugh Show* for around six weeks in the spring of 2004.[60]

During those six weeks, the "mainstream conservative"—as the *Washington Post's* Howard Kurtz all too accurately called Limbaugh—used the term "feminazis" (which he coined) eight times; suggested women want to be sexually harassed; repeatedly said Democrats "hate this country" and side with terrorists; twice resurrected long-discredited right-wing claims that Clinton aide Vince Foster was murdered, hinting at the Clintons' involvement; repeatedly called Senator John Kerry a "gigolo," environmentalists "total wackos," and Howard Dean "a very sick man"; and said, "I'm proud to be a member of the lying crook Republican attack machine."

Descend with me now into Limbo to collect a few more soil samples. Many of the following Limbaughisms come from just the short period that Media Matters monitored:

- "We had an attack in Weird-zakistan or whatever—one of these Zakstan places. Uzbekistan, yes, whatever it is. They're all Weird-zakistan to me, but—how many Zakistans are there over

---

60 "Meet the New Rush, Same as the Old Rush," MediaMatters.org.

there? Seems like a new one pops up every day. You can't keep
track of them. I'm a geography expert and I've never heard of
some of these . . . there was one the other day that I—that I—
Kazakistan, Kazikstan, oh, I've heard of those."—George W.
Limbaugh. (Ahh, what's the difference? A stan's a stan. Just
nuke 'em all.)

- "[T]here's some little strife going on in Venezuela with that
  wacko, Cesar Chavez, down there. Hugo. Hugo, Cesar—whatever. A Chavez is a Chavez. We've always had problems with
  them." César Chávez was the Mexican-American founder of
  the United Farm Workers union.

- Abu Ghraib "is no different than what happens at the Skull and
  Bones [Yale student's society] initiation. . . . I'm talking about
  people [the Abu Ghraib guards] having a good time . . . it looks
  just like anything you'd see Madonna or Britney Spears do on
  stage." Oh, to "initiate" Rush . . .

- "Some of these babes, I'm telling you, like the sexual harassment crowd: They're out there protesting what they actually
  wish would happen to them sometimes."

- "We're not sexists, we're chauvinists—we're male chauvinist
  pigs, and we're happy to be because we think that's what men
  were destined to be. We think that's what women want." I've
  asked women: 93.8 percent agreed strongly with the statement, "I'd like to remove Rush Limbaugh's tiny testicles to
  ensure he never procreates"; 3.6 percent said "Not sure."

- "Feminism was established to allow unattractive women
  access to the mainstream."

- "What if [Fidel] Castro shows up and says I endorse Kerry? The
  Black Caucus would like that." "Castro's the kind of guy that
  Kerry would probably lionize." In the December 2004 issue of
  Cigar Aficionado, Limbaugh lionized Cuban cigars, whose
  flavor the French-loving, Castro-economy-supporting, East-
  Coast elitist compared to Bordeaux grapes.

- "The answer is to go out and find [drug users], convict them, and send them up the river." "All of us who accept the responsibilities of life and don't destroy our lives on drugs, we'll pay for whatever messes you [drug addicts] get into." All this was before Limbaugh admitted he was addicted to opioid painkillers—which he allegedly purchased illegally—and that he had spent a month at a drug rehab facility. "There's no hypocrisy" in his previous remarks, he said.

- Democrats "don't like God," "hate this Constitution," "hate freedom," and "hate this country."
- "You don't hear the Democrats being critical of terrorists." Democrats "celebrate privately" the terrorists bombing Madrid in March 2004. "[W]hat's good for Al Qaeda is good for the Democratic Party [and] for John Kerry." "[W]e know what [Al Qaeda] want: they want Kerry, they want the Democrats in power." An apparent Al Qaeda letter that surfaced in March 2004 said it was not possible to find a leader "more foolish than [Bush], who deals with matters by force rather than with wisdom," whereas "Kerry will kill our nation while it sleeps because he and the Democrats have the cunning to embellish blasphemy and present it to the Arab and Muslim nation as civilization. . . . Because of this we desire you [Bush] to be elected."
- "Who do you think the terrorists enjoy watching more on TV? Aljazeera or the [9/11] Commission coverage . . . ? I say it's a toss-up." I say they prefer listening to Limbaugh; it assures them America is inhabited by morons and must soon collapse.
- On John Kerry's marriage: "Well, there aren't too many . . . little heiresses running around that are single, have 500 million [dollars] that some guy can marry into."
- "I'm almost going to come out in favor of war every 10 years so that we always have a group of people in this country that know what it's like. It's not healthy to go without a war for all these many years." Limbaugh did not serve in Vietnam and told ABC News in 1992, "I did not want to go."

- "When a gay person turns his back on you, it's anything but an insult—it's an invitation." You wish, maybe.
- "One of the things I want to do before I die is conduct the Homeless Olympics. The 10-meter Shopping Cart Relay, the Dumpster Dig, and the Hop, Skip, and Trip."
- "I mean, let's face it, we didn't have slavery in this country for over 100 years because it was a bad thing. Quite the opposite: slavery built the South. I'm not saying we should bring it back; I'm just saying it had its merits. For one thing, the streets were safer after dark."
- "You know who deserves a posthumous Medal of Honor? James Earl Ray [the confessed assassin of Martin Luther King]. We miss you, James. Godspeed."

Drug addiction must do terrible things to the mind. So must listening to Limbaugh.

#26: MICHAEL LEDEEN: IMPROVING ON MUSSOLINI

Ledeen has been called the driving philosophical force behind the neoconservative movement and (by me, right here) "the most influential and unabashed warmonger of our time." A resident scholar at the **American Enterprise Institute** (#7), contributing editor at *National Review*, and former Pentagon, State Department, and White House consultant under Reagan (when his Israeli intelligence contacts were used to help broker the illegal Iran-Contra affair), Ledeen is often quoted by top **Bush** officials, including **Cheney**, **Rumsfeld**, and former Under Secretary of Defense Paul Wolfowitz.

But they don't quote quotes like these—at least not in public: in March 2003, Ledeen, a leading and longtime proponent of the invasion of Iraq—*and* of Iran, Syria, and no doubt other countries yet to be named—told a forum that "the level of casualties [in Iraq] is secondary" because "we are a warlike people . . . we love war." In his 2000 book *Machiavelli on Modern Leadership: Why Machiavelli's Iron Rules Are as Timely and Important Today as Five Centuries Ago,* he wrote that "Change—above all violent change—is the essence of human history"; "the only way to achieve peace is through total war"; and "The sparing of civilian lives cannot be the total war's first priority. . . . The purpose of total war is to permanently force your will onto another people." He was quoted approvingly by National Review Online editor Jonah Goldberg as saying: "Every ten years or so, the United States needs to pick up some small crappy little country and throw it against the wall, just to show the world we mean business." "We can lead by the force of high moral example," Ledeen wrote, "[but] fear is much more reliable, and lasts longer. Once we show that we are capable of dealing out terrible punishment to our enemies"—who need a fresher reminder than Hiroshima and Nagasaki?—"our power will be far greater."

In April 2003—one month into the Iraq War—Ledeen gave an address titled "Time to Focus on Iran," and declared, "the time for diplomacy is at an end." Ledeen's attacks on Iran, even when Iran was assisting the U.S., "helped keep the Bush administration from seeking any rapprochement with Tehran," wrote William Beeman of the Pacific News Service in 2003. "Were it in Ledeen's hands, we would invade Iran today."

Most Americans have never heard of Michael Ledeen, Beeman noted, but if the U.S. "ends up in an extended shooting war throughout the Middle East, it will be largely due to his inspiration."

Ledeen has made clear that he regrets that the U.S. won the Cold War without a shot being fired. Critics of Bush's foreign policy like to say you can't impose democracy through the barrel of a gun. That, Ledeen preaches, is the *only* way. His sin is not just some benign *miscalculation* of the costs, risks, and necessity of military actions. It is his constant and vociferous *preference* for, his Nietzschean *glorification* of, war over diplomacy. In a 2003 book, he characterized America as follows:

> Creative destruction is our middle name, both within our own society and abroad. We tear down the old order every day, from business to science, literature, art, architecture, and cinema to politics and the law. Our enemies have always hated this whirlwind of energy and creativity, which menaces their traditions (whatever they may be) and shames them for their inability to keep pace. Seeing America undo traditional societies, they fear us, for they do not wish to be undone. . . . They must attack us in order to survive, just as we must destroy them to advance our historic mission.

(Perhaps it was Ledeen's love of "creative destruction" that moved him, within four days of Hurricane Katrina striking New Orleans in August 2005, to declare the city "dead.")

If those thoughts remind you of fascism, it's because, wrote John Laughland in the *American Conservative*, that is where Ledeen's "personal political odyssey" began. In 1977, Ledeen devoted "an enthusiastic biography" to "the high priest of fascism," Gabriele d'Annunzio. In Ledeen's 1972 book *Universal Fascism* (the title refers to the dream of some fascists, extolled by Ledeen, of exporting Italian fascism to the whole world), he wrote that the fascist movement was driven by "a desire to renew": "the old ruling class had to be swept away so that newer, more dynamic elements—capable of effecting fundamental changes—could come to power." (As the author of a 1932 fascist manifesto wrote, the choice was between "old Europe or young Europe." Familiar?) The problem with Mussolini, wrote Ledeen, was that "He never had enough confidence in the Italian people to permit them a genuine participation in fascism." Therefore, Mussolini's was "a failed revolution."

The right, Ledeen insists, must reclaim its "revolutionary tradition." Writes Laughland: "The purest ideologues of fascism . . . wanted something very similar to that which Ledeen himself wants now, namely a 'worldwide mass movement' enabling the peoples of the world, 'liberated' by American militarism, to participate in the "greatest experiment in human freedom." In his 1996 book *Freedom Betrayed,* Ledeen wrote, "The people yearn for the real thing—revolution."

Don't you know that you can count me out? Then again, I look good in brown.

#25: THE FEDERALIST SOCIETY: THE LONG, FAR-RIGHT ARM OF THE LAW

In a speech before the Federalist Society in November 2005, **Karl Rove** (#3) mockingly compared criticism of the group to conspiracy theories about "the Bavarian Illuminati . . . the Knights Templar . . . the Trilateralists, the Bilderbergers or the neocons." With all due respect to Rove's conspiratorial expertise, *those* (except of course the neocons) were *imaginary* conspiracies. The Washington, D.C.–based Federalist Society for Law and Public Policy Studies, a powerful, right-wing lawyers' group, is, alas, as real as the **Bush** administration, in which Federalist Society membership is virtually a prerequisite for a high-level legal or judicial appointment. "You have thoroughly infiltrated the ranks of the White House," Rove congratulated the members.

Formed in 1982, the forty-thousand-member society aims to bring about a radical transformation of the American legal system. It wages war against a wide range of civil rights, women's rights, and environmental, health, and safety regulations and *for* the rights of corporations, and advocates for federal funding of religious groups and for teaching creationism and distributing religious materials in public schools. Richly funded by right-wing foundations for its advocacy, litigation, publications, Web sites, and conferences, the organization targets the courts, the American Bar Association, and federal judicial appointments and recruits tomorrow's shock troops through its Student Division, which has more than five thousand members at 145 law schools.

Society members including **John Yoo** (#35) and D.C. chapter president Theodore Olson were instrumental in winning the White House for Bush. During the 2000 Florida recount battle, Olson argued Bush's case before the U.S. Supreme Court in *Bush v. Gore.* As the Institute for Democratic Studies put it in 2001, the society "changed the course of American politics" and was now "poised to transform the landscape of American law and society."

In the 1990s, Olson allegedly took part in the Arkansas Project —a five-year effort backed by billionaire **Richard Scaife** (#21) to dig up dirt on President Clinton—and was a close associate of arch–Clinton hunter and fellow Federalist Ken Starr. He also represented plaintiffs in a successful challenge to the University of Texas affirmative-action program. Bush appointed Olson as solicitor general, who represents the administration before the Supreme Court, where Olsen would stand before fellow Federalists **Antonin Scalia** and **Clarence Thomas** (#11). Several other justices have served the society in an advisory capacity or spoken under its auspices.

Society members were instrumental in securing the nomination of John Ashcroft as attorney general. Other members tapped by President Rovebush included Interior Secretary **Gale Norton** (#18) (once named the society's Young Lawyer of the Year); first-term Energy Secretary Spencer Abraham, one of the society's three cofounders; first-term Labor Solicitor Eugene Scalia (Antonin's son); Deputy Attorney General Larry Thompson; Assistant Attorney General Viet Dinh; and Assistant Attorney General for Environment and Natural Resources Thomas Sansonetti. Another Society cofounder, Lee Liberman Otis, played a key role in setting up the administration's judicial selection process, as she had under Bush I—examining "all candidates for federal judgeships for ideological purity," a U.S. Court of Appeals judge wrote in 1992. "It is well known that no federal judicial appointment is made without her imprimatur." She herself boasted openly that no one who was not a Federalist member had received a judicial appointment from old man Bush, as she didn't call him.

Society members insist the Constitution should be interpreted according to their own dubious claims about the Framers' intentions. In practice, this gives conservative judges a rationale for enforcing the undemocratic social and moral values of a bygone era of gross economic, social, and racial inequality, radical, unfettered capitalism, and men in wigs and stockings.

Radically challenging Congress's authority to legislate, the society advocates severely limiting the regulatory power of the Environmental Protection Agency and the Occupational Safety and Health Administration and abolishing outright the Securities and Exchange Commission—which would mean no regulatory oversight whatsoever of the financial dealings of corporations. Society publications and speakers target federal civil- and labor-rights laws, including desegregation orders, voting rights, and gender- and age-discrimination and sexual-harassment laws, even the Americans with Disabilities Act. There you have the Bush deregulatory agenda: Give free reign to the Enrons and Arthur Andersens and polluters of the world while attacking the legal protections of workers, women, minorities, the aged, and the handicapped.

The society's leaders have included some of the most sinister—I mean, influential—figures on the right, such as Reagan's attorney general, Edwin Meese III; former federal judge and Supreme Court nominee Robert Bork; former Christian Coalition president Donald Hodel; Bush I White House counsel C. Boyden Gray; former Senate Judiciary Committee chair Orrin Hatch; **Linda Chavez** (#87); and **American Enterprise Institute** (#7) fellow Charles Murray, a promoter of the idea that blacks are genetically inferior.

Despite all this, the society assiduously portrays itself as—are you ready?—nonpartisan. In his keynote address at its 1999 convention, for example, Justice Clarence Thomas commended the society "for maintaining the wall of separation between law and politics." I *knew* he had a better joke in him than the can-of-Coke line.

#24: THE RED MENACE OF GROVER NORQUIST

It might surprise you to know that one of the most powerful players in Republican politics over the past ten years is said to be an admirer of Lenin and to have a portrait of him prominently displayed in his home. But after all, Norquist—like his close comrades Newt Gingrich (eighty-four ethics charges against him while House Speaker), indicted GOP House leader **Tom DeLay** (#6), indicted lobbyist Jack Abramoff, and not-yet-indicted copresident **Karl Rove** (#3)—proudly refers to himself as a "revolutionary." Indeed, if Lenin were alive, he might well have a portrait of Grovimir Glennisovich Norquistov on *his* wall, in admiration of the right-wing activist's Bolshevik zeal, ruthlessness, and strategic wiles.

Norquist is the president of Americans for Tax Reform (ATR), which lobbies for tax cuts, a flat tax rate, and "tort reform" (limiting the rights of victims of corporate or medical negligence or malfeasance to sue) and against abortion, gun control (Norquist is an **NRA** [#22] board member), and any communistic restrictions on corporations and wealthy individuals sheltering their assets in offshore tax havens.

Like a female **Ann Coulter** (#32), Norquist revels in the shock and awe his remarks induce in liberals and moderates. Conservative commentator **Tucker Carlson** (#93) (admiringly?): "Norquist is a mean-spirited, humorless, dishonest little creep . . . an embarrassing anomaly, the leering, drunken uncle everyone else wishes would stay home. Norquist is repulsive, granted." But no anomaly: He is at the very center—is indeed a chief architect—of the Republican political machine and the GOP–K Street axis of corruption and evil.

Norquist's goals are simple enough: (a) essentially kill the "Democrat" Party; (b) eliminate three quarters of the federal government by 2050—from the Internal Revenue Service and the Education Department to the Food and Drug Administration. (Why should the *government* regulate drug safety? Trial and error—individual risk-taking *that's* the American way.) His most famous remark is: "I don't want to abolish government. I simply want to reduce it to the size where I can . . . drown it in the bathtub." He has equated taxes, especially the estate tax (which affects only the richest 2 percent of households), with the Holocaust.

In the early 1990s, Norquist began hosting the "Wednesday Meeting" of his so-called Leave Us Alone Coalition, a loose collection of groups opposed to government restrictions on free markets, private property rights, gun ownership, and so on (but not, of course, on private medical or sexual choices). Since even before 2000, **Bush** and **Cheney** aides have attended every week. The meeting enables the White House to hear and respond quickly to conservatives' complaints and "is the political equivalent of one-stop shopping: By making a single pitch, the administration can generate pressure on members of Congress, calls to radio talk shows, and political buzz from dozens of grassroots organizations."[61]

Norquist has helped orchestrate the administration's stealth stepwise elimination of the progressive tax system through elimination of taxes on dividends, capital gains, estates—all income

[61] "Grover Norquist," Wikipedia.org.

derived from *wealth* rather than *work*—and its replacement with a flat tax, which would shift the tax burden onto the middle class and working poor.

The Norqueviks seek to reduce the Democrats to a small minority party of blacks, Jews, and a few "left-wingers." Thus Norquist said of conservative Democratic Rep. Charlie Stenholm that under DeLay's illegally engineered Texas congressional redistricting plan, "it is exactly the Stenholms of the world who will disappear . . . the moderate Democrats. They will go so that no Texan need grow up thinking that being a Democrat is acceptable behavior." (The redistricting in fact cost Stenholm and four other Texas Democrats their seats in 2004.)

Norquist prevails on state legislators to put his agenda ahead of their oaths of allegiance to the people of their states by signing "the Norquist pledge" never, under any circumstances, to vote to raise taxes. In 2003, Norquist told the *Denver Post*, "We are trying to change the tones in the state capitals—and turn them toward bitter nastiness and partisanship. Bipartisanship is another name for date rape."

Norquist's, well, rapaciousness goes back to his college years. He first teamed up with Abramoff in 1980 to organize college campuses for Reagan-Bush, then to take command of the College Republicans. "They owed their bond to a shared affinity for bomb-throwing, hardcore conservatism," wrote Franklin Foer in the *New Republic*. The two "instructed organizers to memorize a speech from the movie *Patton*, [but to] replace references to Nazis with references to Democrats. As in, 'The Democrats are the enemy. Wade into them! Spill their blood! Shoot them in the belly!' "

In the 1980s and early nineties, Norquist promoted U.S. support for and served as an economic adviser to Angolan rebel leader Jonas Savimbi (who was backed by the Reagan adminstration, the **Heritage Foundation** [#8], and South Africa's apartheid regime) and was registered with the Justice Department as a foreign agent of Angola. Conservative columnist David Brooks has written: "Folks like Norquist and [Jack] Abramoff were talking up the virtues of international sons of liberty like . . . Savimbi and Congo's dictator Mobutu Sese Seko—all while receiving compensation from these upstanding gentlemen . . . [notwithstanding] Savimbi's little cannibalism problem."

In 1994, Norquist worked with Gingrich and the Heritage Foundation to draft the GOP's "Contract with America," to which the Republicans credited their winning control of the House of Representatives in the 1994 election. In 1995, Norquist and DeLay, then House Republican Whip, began to organize the "K Street Project," whose purpose was to cleanse the lobbying community (centered on Washington's K Street) of Democrats and ensure that all top lobbying jobs and all corporate political contributions would go to Republicans or allied organizations. "We will hunt [these liberal groups] down one by one and extinguish their funding sources," Norquist explained. It was made clear that firms could not do business with, contribute to, or employ Democrats if they hoped to advance their agendas in the newly GOP-controlled House. The operation has continued to this day, with weekly meetings presided over by Sen. **Rick Santorum** (#23) and Rep. Roy Blunt (R-OK) to fill top lobbying jobs with party loyalists.

As a result, K Street has been steadily transformed into an arm of the GOP. Like the urban Democratic machines of yore, wrote Nicholas Confessore in *Washington Monthly*, the new Republican political machine is built upon patronage and contracts—but *outside* of government, among Washington's thousands of trade associations and corporate offices. Through K Street, "Republican leaders can now marshal armies of lobbyists, lawyers, and public relations experts—not to mention enormous amounts of money— to meet the party's goals." In return, major public programs are turned "into a form of private political spoils." This—not popular support for Bush or his policies—has been the secret to Bush's legislative success.

Norquist has helped promote Bush's Social Security privatization scheme, which would divert trillions of dollars in (former) Social Security revenues to the financial services firms that would manage the new private accounts. They would in return contribute to Republicans and back their initiatives. Think of it as a huge scheme for looting and laundering public funds and dividing them between the GOP and its corporate partners. Bush's Medicare bill of 2003 was likewise designed to move people from Medicare into the "private" sector—for under the plan, Confessore explains, "the medical insurance industry would gradually become a captive of Washington, living off the business steered to it by the government"—like the defense sector, "a revolving door for Republican officials, and vastly supportive, politically and financially, of the GOP."

The aim? One-party government, dummy. Republicans control more and more K Street jobs; reap more and more K Street money; win larger and larger majorities on the Hill. "The larger the Republican majority, the less reason K Street has to . . . contribute to the campaigns of Democratic politicians, slowly starving them of the means by which to challenge GOP rule."[62]

But are the wheels coming off? In 2002, Norquist was accused of using his organization to launder money for right-wing Oregon activist Bill Sizemore, whom a jury in a civil lawsuit found guilty of racketeering. In 2005, DeLay and Abramoff were indicted, and Norquist's ties to Abramoff came under federal investigation. Abramoff had teamed up with **Ralph Reed** (#56) to charge a Louisiana Indian tribe millions to organize a "Christian" crusade against gambling in order to shut down a rival tribe's casino—then charged the rival tribe $4.2 million to lobby lawmakers to reopen it! E-mails released by federal investigators suggested that Norquist facilitated the scheme.

62 Nicholas Confessore, "Welcome to the Machine: How the GOP Disciplined K Street and Made Bush Supreme," *Washington Monthly*, July/August 2003.

The investigators also subpoenaed the Council of Republicans for Environmental Advocacy (CREA), to which Abramoff's Indian-tribes clients gave money on his recommendation. According to Republicans for Environmental Protection, CREA, which was created in 1997 by Norquist and future Bush Interior Secretary **Gail Norton** (#18), is a "greenscam" front group for the mining, logging, chemical, and coal industries, from which it gets funding while supporting Bush's "environmental" policies.

Two more Norquist projects demand attention. Some time in the late 1990s, Norquist decided that getting Jews to vote Republican was too difficult, and turned instead to the fast-growing American Muslim community, figuring, according to a Norquist aide, "that he could turn Muslims into the obvious counterweight to the relationship between the Jews and Dems." Norquist credited his "Muslim strategy" for Bush's win in 2000.

In 2003, right-wing activist **David Horowitz** (#31)—"with a heavy heart"—published a long exposé by former Reagan official Frank Gaffney in his FrontPage online magazine on, in Horowitz's words, "Norquist's activities in behalf of the Islamist Fifth Column." Norquist, wrote Horowitz, "has formed alliances with prominent Islamic radicals who have ties to the Saudis and to Libya and to Palestine Islamic Jihad, and who are now under indictment by U.S. authorities." Norquist's Islamic Institute, a lobby group he founded in 1998, was initially financed by Abdurahman Alamoudi, a self-declared supporter of Hamas and Hezbollah and of the terrorism- and slavery-harboring Sudanese government. Alamoudi told the Annual Convention of the Islamic Association of Palestine in 1996, "If we are outside this country we can say 'Oh, Allah destroy America.' "

Norquist appointed Alamoudi's deputy, Khaled Saffuri, to head the Islamic Institute. Together, Horowitz wrote, "they gained access to the White House for Alamoudi . . . and others with similar agendas." With Norquist's help, Saffuri became the Bush 2000 campaign's National Advisor on Arab and Muslim Affairs, and

Institute board member Suhail Khan became the Bush administration's adviser on Muslim outreach. Two weeks after 9/11, Bush appeared at the White House with Islamic leaders reportedly vouched for by Norquist. They included the president of the American Muslim Council, whose leaders had repeatedly called Hamas "freedom fighters"; the head of the Muslim Public Affairs Council, who on the afternoon of 9/11 told a radio audience that "we should put the State of Israel on the suspect list"; and, sitting right next to Bush, the president of the Islamic Society of North America, who had told a Washington crowd chanting pro-Hezbollah slogans, "America has to learn if you remain on the side of injustice, the wrath of God will come." Another of Norquist's clients, the **Council on American-Islamic Relations (CAIR)** (#74), has been accused by both federal law enforcement officials and by some Muslim organizations of extremism and terrorist connections. Norquist responded to critics of his Muslim "outreach" effort by accusing them of racism.

Last and least, Norquist heads the Ronald Reagan Legacy Project, which seeks to replace Alexander Hamilton's portrait with (no, not Lenin's) Reagan's on the $10 bill and to add Reagan's head to Mount Rushmore. Takes gutzon to propose such a thing. Now, *Norquist's* head on display. . . .

#23: RICK SANTORUM
(HEY, GOOGLE "SANTORUM")

Pennsylvania senator Rick Santorum, wrote Michael Crowley in the *New Republic*, is one of that new breed of Republican senators that disdain the institution's "traditions of earnest debate, bipartisan friendship, and staid decorum" and who have turned the Senate "into the sort of embittered, partisan battlefield that the House has become." Santorum came to the Senate in 1995 "with all the subtlety of an air-raid siren" and soon earned "a reputation for obnoxious ambition that he has spent years trying to repair."

Indeed? Consider a few of his "repair" efforts.

Since 2001, Santorum has headed up the Senate side of the notorious K Street Project, a grand scheme set up in the nineties by **Tom DeLay** (#6) and **Grover Norquist** (#24) to convert the corporate lobbying community into a Republican political patronage/money machine and starve the Democrats of money and power. Santorum has held weekly meetings with top Republican lobbyists to ensure that top lobbying positions—and the money and congressional influence they wield—go to party loyalists.

Santorum tried to insert language crafted by the **Discovery Institute** (#34) into Bush's No Child Left Behind education bill that would have required the teaching in public school science classes of creationism and "intelligent design," which scientists regard as pure santorum. (Google it. Go ahead.)

In a 2003 interview with the Associated Press, Santorum equated private homosexual sex between consenting adults with bigamy, polygamy, "man on child" and "man on dog." In the ensuing furor, Republicans and conservative commentators rallied to his support. (**George W. Bush**: "The senator is an inclusive man." Inclusive of raging bigotry.) Meanwhile, in the same interview, Santorum minimized the Roman Catholic Church sex abuse scandal—which was about the abuse of *children*—by saying it involved "post-pubescent men" in "a basic homosexual relationship." He added and later repeated that it was "no surprise" the scandal was centered in "Boston, a seat of academic, political and cultural liberalism." He had previously defended the priests as victims of a "sick culture." These conservatives. No belief in personal responsibility. The priests were helpless under the influence of those secular liberal pederasts. Guess who else is a victim here? Santorum, who, in response to criticism of his remarks, said he was being targeted by the Democratic Senatorial Campaign Committee. (One would hope so.)

In the same interview, Santorum said he believed (contrary to the Supreme Court in *Lawrence v. Texas*, 2003) that consenting adults do not have a constitutional right to privacy, even within marriage, with respect to sexual acts that "undermine society and the family." (He must know of some humdinger sexual acts.) He denies the right of married couples to buy and use birth control (contrary to the Supreme Court's 1965 decision in *Griswold v. Connecticut*). In 2004, he said "defending marriage" was the "ultimate homeland security." Picture Department of Family Security agents storming bedrooms in midnight raids while the bomb makers next door ply their trade. And since Santorum has not ruled out a run for president in 2008, *keep* picturing that.

But on privacy, you see, it all *depends*. In July 2005, when Santorum's director of communication confirmed speculation that he was gay—describing himself as an "out gay man"—Santorum said: "It is entirely unacceptable that my staffs' personal lives are considered fair game by partisans" who committed "this rude and mean-spirited invasion of [his aide's] personal life."

Two months earlier, Santorum played a key role in shepherding through the Senate the special Terri Schiavo legislation that would have forced the severely brain-damaged Florida woman to be kept "alive," contrary to her husband's wishes and, according to him, her own.

But it's back to "private good, public bad" when it comes to business—again, *depending* on whether government serves corporate interests or those of the public. Santorum, of course, supports Bush's Social Security privatization plan, which would line the pockets of Wall Street financial services firms. In July 2005, the Senate passed a bill cosponsored by Santorum—and, in effect, the **NRA** (#22)—that would shield gun manufacturers, dealers, and importers from lawsuits brought by victims of gun crimes, including those involving illegally sold guns, and of accidents involving defective guns.

During the May 2005 battle over Bush judicial nominees (see

#61–#64), Santorum called Senate Democrats' efforts to retain the two-hundred-year-old filibuster rule, which allows a forty-vote minority to keep debate going, "the equivalent of Adolf Hitler" occupying Paris. (Santorum had previously compared the *New York Times* to Nazis, Communists, and Baathists. Pick one crazy slur and stick to it, damn it.) The Democrats, he demanded, must not block Bush's nominees—the way *he* voted to block a number of Clinton's.

In September 2005, a few days after Hurricane Katrina and President Bush left hundreds dead and thousands stranded in New Orleans, Santorum remarked: "There may be a need to look at tougher penalties on those who *decide to ride it out*" (emphasis added. Stiffer penalties on those who decide to be poor should also be considered. Done? Oh, right). He also tried to excuse the Bush administration of "any major errors" by claiming, "the weather service gave no warning, or not sufficient warning." His Republican colleague, Senator Jim DeMint: "After reviewing the actions taken by the National Weather Service, I am convinced that this was one of the most accurate hurricane predictions we have ever seen."

Pro–Iraq War? Of course. What does being fanatically "pro-life" have to do with opposing the needless, criminal waste of tens of thousands of lives in a politically and personally motivated war?

Does it get any more "pro-life" than this? In 1996, when Rick's and his wife Karen's son Gabriel was born prematurely and lived for only two hours, the couple refused to let the hospital take the body to the morgue, but instead remained in bed with it overnight, then brought it home to let their other children cuddle.[63] Karen Santorum wrote a book about the experience. If I'm not mistaken, the message was, an unborn child is a person. It's just everyone else that Santorum doesn't seem so sure about.

---

63 Michael Sokolove, "The Believer," *New York Times Magazine*, May 22, 2005.

#22: WAYNE LAPIERRE AND THE NATIONAL RAVING-LUNATIC ASSOCIATION (NRA)

Perhaps no bullet points can penetrate the Kevlar skulls of gun control opponents, but the facts are:

* More than 30,000 people a year in the U.S. are killed by guns— roughly the number of Americans killed in the Korean War.
* There are around 192 million privately owned firearms, including 65 million handguns.
* Over half of family murders are caused by guns. Around 1,400 children and teenagers kill themselves each year and 1,600 kill someone else with a gun.
* Of the roughly thirty thousand suicides a year, 57 percent are accomplished with a gun.
* A gun kept in the home triples the risk of homicide, increases the risk of suicide fivefold, and is twenty-two times more likely to be used in an unintentional shooting, criminal assault, homicide, or suicide than in self-defense.
* Handguns are used in roughly nine thousand murders a year— compared to fifteen in Japan, thirty in Britain, and one hundred in Canada.
* Gun violence costs over $100 billion a year in medical, legal, judicial, and other such costs.
* U.S. gun shows are Al Qaeda–recommended outlets for terrorists looking for top brands at competitive prices and without troublesome background checks, thanks to the gun lobby, led by the National Rifle Association (NRA), probably the most powerful political lobby in America.

The 4-*million*-member NRA is well armed with arguments designed to refute or, rather, muddy all of these facts, whose import is obvious to anyone not suffering from, well, lead poisoning. But who are you going to believe—the American Bar Association, Children's Defense Fund, National Association of Police Organizations, National Coalition of Public Safety Officers, International Brotherhood of Police Officers, and the hundreds of other organizations that support stricter gun control—or people who say things like:

- Gun control advocates are "fakes, frauds and liars . . . a shadowy network of extremist social guerillas."—Wayne LaPierre, NRA executive vice president and chief executive officer since 1991. (NRA's president—previously Charlton Heston—serves mainly as the group's chief spokesperson.)
- "[T]he consensus is that no more than five to ten people in a hundred who die by gunfire in Los Angeles are any loss to society." As for the others, "It would seem a valid social service to keep them well-supplied with ammunition."— Jeff Cooper, NRA board member. More: "[T]he proper solution to our inner city problem might be the mass drowning of street punks. Every month in a different big city we should sew up a thousand of them in a huge sack and dump it into the Mississippi." "If we grant [liberty] to too diverse a population, order disappears." Los Angeles is a "Third World metropolis formerly occupied by Americans." Also suggested calling black South Africans from Gauteng province "Orang-gautengs." (The NRA calls itself "this nation's oldest civil rights organization.")
- "Apartheid isn't that cut and dry. All men are not created equal. [Black South Africans] still put bones in their noses, they still walk around naked, they wipe their butts with their hands. . . . You give 'em toothpaste, they fucking eat it."—Ted Nugent, rock guitarist, NRA board member since 1995, and prospective candidate for governor of Michigan, in a 1990 interview. Also: "I use the word nigger a lot because I hang around with a lot of niggers."
- "If we win [the 2000 presidential election], we'll have a Supreme Court that will back us to the hilt . . . [and] a president

where we work out of their office."—Kayne Robinson, former
NRA president.

That last remark wasn't just braggadocio. The NRA's heavy
campaigning in Tennessee and Arkansas—where it warned
people that Al Gore would "take their guns"—has been "credited"
with costing Al Gore those states, either of which would have
given him the election. In the 1994 election, the NRA claimed to
have defeated nineteen of the twenty-four House members on its
hit list and could rightly claim to have made Newt Gingrich House
speaker. One NRA victim, Rep. Jack Brooks of Texas, was a lifelong NRA member *and* had led the fight in the House against the
assault weapons ban enacted that year, but then voted for a major
crime bill after the ban was put into it. Did he think he could get
away with that?

With its gun to the head of U.S. politics, what else does the
NRA demand, and, especially lately, receive?

- In 1999, a month after the killing of twelve students and a
  teacher at Columbine High School by two students using guns
  bought from unlicensed dealers at gun shows, NRA pressure—and senator and NRA board member Larry Craig (R-ID)—
  succeeded in killing a federal bill to require background
  checks before such purchases are completed.
- At the NRA's behest, a measure was buried in a budget bill
  passed by the House in January 2004 requiring the FBI to erase
  records of gun sales within twenty-four hours of the purchase
  instead of the previous ninety days—you know, to make it
  harder to trace illegal sales to wanted criminals or, say, foil a
  terrorist plot. The measure also freed gun shops and dealers
  from the requirement to conduct regular inventories and
  report missing weapons. This would allow dealers to cover up
  illegal sales, as may have been the case with the gun used by
  the D.C.-area snipers Muhammad and Malvo in 2003. See, it's

not just about opposing *additional* gun laws, as the NRA
claims, but also about weakening those we have.

* In 2004, the ten-year ban on military-style, rapid-fire assault
weapons such as AK-47s expired and was not renewed, thanks
to the NRA/Republican-controlled Congress and **George W.
Bush**. (That year, the gun lobby gave 88 percent of its campaign contributions to Republicans.) If you're planning a
commando assault on a deer or need to protect your turf from
rival drug gangs, these are the weapons for you. Now available
at gun shops everywhere.

* In July 2005, the Senate passed the so-called Gun Industry
Immunity Bill—sponsored by Senator Larry Craig (R-NRA)—
shielding gun manufacturers, dealers, and importers from lawsuits brought by victims of gun crimes. Did you know the NRA
represents "gun consumers," not the gun *industry*? So it
insists.

How about a legal right to shoot anyone you feel threatens
you? Sure. In October 2005, the so-called "Shoot First" law (or as
the legislators called it, the "Stand Your Ground" law) pushed by
the NRA went into effect in Florida over the protests of law
enforcement officials. Previously, Floridians, if threatened in a
public place, were required first to try to withdraw. Now they're
free to "shoot first," immune from criminal or civil charges. Governor Jeb Bush said "shame on" the Brady Campaign to Prevent
Gun Violence for distributing leaflets at Miami International Airport advising visitors on how to avoid provoking potentially hostile locals.

The NRA also wants to make it legal everywhere to carry concealed handguns into schools, bars, churches, and sports sta-
diums; repeal safety training requirements for concealed weapon
permit holders; repeal permit requirements for concealed handguns; and prohibit sheriffs from considering the mental illness of
an applicant when issuing a concealed weapon permit. (The NRA

would feel threatened by *that*.) The only gun owners the NRA seems hostile to are law enforcement officers.

What is the NRA's real concern? The Constitution? "Freedom"? Another answer is suggested by NRA leaders' well-documented contacts and cross-memberships with right-wing extremist militia groups. Nugent shoots with and praises members of the Michigan Militia. Another NRA board member belonged to the Illinois Militia. Another, Robert K. Brown, publishes *Soldier of Fortune* magazine, which advertises militia and conspiracy materials, military equipment and training, and Nazi memorabilia. Another, referring to the 1993 storming of the Branch Davidian compound in Waco, Texas, called government agents "jackbooted, baby burning bushwhackers," said BATF (Bureau of Alcohol, Tobacco and Firearms) stands for "Burn All Toddlers First," and wrote: "The time has come for us to openly discuss something that up to this time we have mainly whispered about. The purpose of the 2nd Amendment [right to bear arms] is to *threaten* the government" (emphasis added).

In response to the 1992 L.A. riots, NRA board member T. J. Johnston organized the Orange County Corps, which he claimed has one thousand armed members, including three hundred people grouped into a ready response team, "armed and ready to meet any challenge at a moment's notice," in case "the rioters come south."[64] LaPierre, more subtly, encourages NRA members to "join together to build and protect their families and communities."

Come on. As though the gun nuts' central vision isn't of white folks besieged on one side by hordes of marauding blacks and on the other by (at least before Bush) a "liberal"- and "Zionist"-controlled federal government trying to take away white Christians' right to defend themselves from the looters and rapists closing in around them.

---

64 Josh Sugarmann and Kristen Rand, "NRA Family Values," Violence Policy Center, June 1996.

They're insane. They own a large portion of our government. **Bernard Goldberg** apparently has no problem with that.

#21: RICHARD MELLON SCAIFE: BANKROLLER OF THE VAST RIGHT-WING CONSPIRACY

One profile describes the secretive Scaife, heir to a slice of the Mellon oil and banking fortune, as the man who "has bankrolled the modern conservative movement." Scaife's personal fortune was estimated by *Forbes* in 2005 at a pathetic $1.2 billion, making him only the 283rd richest American. He does, however, control the three main Scaife family foundations—the largest source of conservative-foundation giving. "By concentrating his giving on a specific ideological objective for nearly 40 years," said the *Washington Post* in 1999, Scaife "has had a disproportionate impact on the rise of the right." And by extension, on the rise of **George W. Bush**, and all that *that* implies. Credit Scaife, too, some say, with giving the conservative movement its distinctively vicious, hateful, and paranoid character.

Scaife-funded right-wing organizations include the **Heritage Foundation** (#8), the **American Enterprise Institute** (#7), the **Federalist Society** (#25), the Hoover Institution on War, Revolution and Peace (But Mainly War), *American Spectator* magazine, the Hudson Institute, the Committee for the Free (Enterprise) World, the Committee on the Present (Communist) Danger, the Center for (Anti-)Immigration Studies, the Independent Women's Forum (don't let the name fool you), the Institute on (Mixing) Religion and Public Life . . . in all, some *150* centers, institutes, committees, roundtables, and cabals.

They include think tanks that promote Scaife's favorite causes—private property rights, lower taxes, and fewer regulations;

"public interest" law firms that oppose affirmative action; academic institutions that hire and promote conservative intellectuals; conservative campus groups and publications; watchdog groups that critique and harass media organizations. Together, said the *Washington Post*, "these groups constitute a conservative intellectual infrastructure that . . . helped Ronald Reagan initiate a new Republican era in 1980, and helped Newt Gingrich initiate another one in 1994." Thanks to Scaife, "conservative ideas once dismissed as flaky or extreme moved into the mainstream . . . [and] 'the long-standing conservative crusade to discredit government as a vehicle for societal progress has come to fruition as never before.'"[65]

It was Scaife whom the Clintonites pointed to as the central figure in, as Hillary Clinton put it, a "vast right-wing conspiracy" (VRWC) that "has been conspiring against my husband since the day he announced for president," and whom James Carville called "the archconservative godfather." At the time, Carville's boss, President Clinton, was the target of the Arkansas Project—a Scaife-funded campaign to uncover Clinton's secret life of crime and mayhem.

Scaife himself is notoriously prone to conspiracy theories. He told a magazine publisher: "Listen, [Clinton] can order people done away with at his will. . . . God, there must be 60 people [associated with Clinton] who have died mysteriously." In 1994, Scaife reportedly declared, "We're going to get Clinton," and made it clear he meant get him out of the White House. Scaife's involvement in the Arkansas Project—only one of numerous anti-Clinton efforts he helped fund, including Paula Jones's sexual harassment suit—resulted in his being subpoenaed for allegedly tampering with a federal witness. But by tainting Al Gore by association, it also arguably resulted in President Bush.

65 Robert G. Kaiser and Ira Chinoy, "Scaife: Funding Father of the Right," *Washington Post*, May 2, 1999.

Scaife also owns and publishes his hometown *Pittsburgh Tri-bune-Review* (because freedom of the press is famously limited to those who own one). The story is told by Fairness and Accuracy in Reporting (FAIR) that in the final days of the 2000 presidential campaign—in which Pennsylvania was considered *the* battleground state—Scaife ordered all photographs and prominent mentions of Al Gore removed from the front page. "As a result, the paper's pre-election Sunday edition had a front page featuring George W. Bush in every campaign-related headline and photograph."

According to the eminent historian Al Franken, the very tone of right wingers like **Bill O'Reilly** (#29) and **Ann Coulter** (#32) can be traced back to Scaife and in particular to a famous episode in 1981 when a reporter asked Scaife about his funding of conservative groups; he thoughtfully replied, "You fucking communist cunt, get out of here." According to Franken, Scaife "went on to tell her that she was ugly and that her teeth were 'terrible' " and that her mother, who was not present, was "ugly, too."

"If you're not my friend, you're my enemy—he lives by that kind of code," the former editor of the then-Scaife-owned *Sacramento Union* told the *Washington Post*. "In general he sees certain villains in American life and thinks he should do everything he can to attack them and bring them down." But although Scaife is fond of conspiracy theories, he has been described as incapable of managing any sort of conspiracy himself. Conservative activists "remember Scaife as someone who had little to say, and little to contribute when he did speak," the *Post* reported. Well, as Thomas Mellon, founder of the family fortune, observed in 1885: "The normal condition of man is hard work, self-denial, acquisition and accumulation; as soon as his descendants are freed from the necessity of such exertion they begin to degenerate sooner or later in both body and mind."

Scaife is known "as a man who bears grudges," the *Post* also noted. "People are really afraid of him," said one charity director.

A former aide described his history of "hurting people . . . who he gets at cross [purposes] with."

So it's been very nice knowing you all.

#20: PHYLLIS SCHLAFLY: MOTHER OF ALL RIGHT-WING CRAZIES

It might seem ungentlemanly to attack a lady in her eighties, especially one who has been fighting the good fight against feminism and liberalism and moderate conservatism for decades. Perhaps I should let someone else do it. Alan Wolfe, in the not-exactly-left-wing *New Republic*:

> Schlafly has to be regarded as one of the two or three most important Americans of the last half of the twentieth century. . . . Had she never been born, the Constitution would now include an Equal Rights Amendment [ERA]. . . . [S]he played an instrumental role in driving moderates out of the Republican Party and replacing them with the hard-right politicians who currently dominate Congress. **Tom DeLay** [#6] owes more to Phyllis Schlafly than she owes to him. Let it be said of Phyllis Schlafly that every idea she had was scatter-brained, dangerous, and hateful. The more influential she became, the worse off America became. The ugliness of American politics today can be directly traced back to Schlafly's vituperative, apocalyptic, character-assassinating campaign against the ERA . . . . **Karl Rove** [#3] only perfected what Phyllis Schlafly invented. And the wild, filthy rhetoric of [**Ann**] **Coulter** [#32] and some of her screaming reactionary colleagues owes a great deal to Schlafly.

Schlafly's formative milieu, Midwestern America in the 1940s, "was honeycombed with people who denounced Franklin Delano Roosevelt, saw no role for the United States in the struggle against European fascism, and hated east-coast elites for their cosmopolitanism," Wolfe writes. The world that Phyllis idealized "had no place for labor unions, cities, racial minorities, Jews, or liberated women." Her old-right crowd was remarkably uninterested in taking on Hitler while he was killing all those European Jews but "became obsessed with the evils of communism in the years after World War II. . . . Joe McCarthy they trusted and admired completely."

In the 1950s, Schlafly cowrote "screeds which, if anyone had taken them seriously, would have brought the United States into a full-scale nuclear war with the Soviet Union."[66] She opposed any ban on nuclear weapons testing and any arms talks with the Soviets and supported the Bricker Amendment, which would have effectively prevented the president from negotiating international treaties—period. But while advocating huge military budgets, Schlafly opposed the taxes needed to pay for them. (Sounds oddly familiar.) In 1960, Robert Welch, the founder of the far-right-wing John Birch Society (which regarded liberals as "secret communist traitors" and Dwight Eisenhower as a "willing agent of the Soviet Union"), called Schlafly "one of our most loyal members."

Schlafly first gained national attention by helping Barry Goldwater win the GOP presidential nomination in 1964. Goldwater had voted against the 1964 Civil Rights Act, and conservatives like Schlafly loved him for it. During the 1970s, Schlafly often attacked Nixon for negotiating a strategic arms limitation and missile treaties with the Russians and wrote a book condemning Henry Kissinger as a liberal. The conservatives, wrote Wolfe, "were,

66 Alan Wolfe, "Mrs. America," *The New Republic*, October 3, 2005.

almost all of them . . . capable of saying anything and doing anything, no matter how damaging to their country . . . and Schlafly personified [their] irresponsibility."

According to a worshipful biographer, Schlafly believed that "America faced an enemy within that threatened the traditional order of a Christian-based society." (*There's* a two-thousand-year-old theme. . . .) She was convinced, according to Wolfe, "that a cabal of media executives [and] international bankers ran the world."

Defeating the ERA in 1980 was Schlafly's signature achievement. She argued that the proposed constitutional amendment— which would have guaranteed equal rights under law to persons of all genders—would lead to abortion on demand, women in combat, and homosexual marriage. Before her "Stop ERA" movement swung into action, the amendment was passed by the Senate 84 to 8, by the House 354 to 23, and by thirty-five of the thirty-eight state legislatures necessary for ratification. This was the kind of "elitist," "out-of-touch" "liberalism" against which Schlafly styled herself a populist champion. The ERA was supported by such dangerous radicals as Betty Ford—"but by the time Schlafly had gotten her hands on the issue," Wolfe wrote, "it was transformed into a subversive move to destroy motherhood, harm children, and wipe out the nuclear family."

Schlafly knows no dirtier word than "feminist." America is under assault by "feminist professors," "feminist lawyers," even "feminist mathematicians." Beware the feminist "agenda" and "game plan."

In the 1950s and 1960s, Schlafly writes, women "didn't need Zoloft or Prozac"—in part, apparently, because "women's magazines were helpful and hopeful." (Yes. So were the *tranquilizers* that doctors prescribed to millions of women diagnosed with "housewife's fatigue," who could see no reason to get out of bed and who popped the pills like cough drops.) Women benefited from a "Christian tradition of chivalry" wherein men (Christian ones only, apparently) worked to support their families.

Feminists have made life a stress-filled hell for women by mocking and shaming them out of their proper place, the home—"a pleasanter and more fulfilling work environment than the office"—into the workplace. (In case you thought *economic need* did that.) How Schlafly proposes to make one income sufficient again—even as American jobs become increasingly insecure and poorly paid—is unclear. Or did jobs become insecure and poorly paid *because* women entered the workplace? And could they have been drafted into it by *business*—not *feminism*—for that very purpose?

Yet, at the same time, Schlafly writes that "American women today live longer, healthier lives than ever, filled with a multitude of opportunities for education, travel and employment" (no thanks to feminism?)—while it is feminists who "are all busy selling American women . . . the attitude that women's lives are full of misery and threats." Go figure.

According to Schlafly, Title IX, the 1972 law requiring that schools and colleges receiving federal funds not discriminate on the basis of sex, is "a feminist weapon to harm men and anything masculine." Thanks to "feminist lawsuits," it has led to the promotion of women's collegiate athletics "at the cost of a savage attack on men's sports," because "men on sports teams act like men, and the feminists are hostile to the male culture." Women don't even *want* to play sports. Feminism is only "pushing girls into higher risks of injury and hormonal-changing drugs." ("Torn anterior cruciate ligaments [ACLs] are crippling women athletes at an alarming rate.") "While football players are known to date cheerleaders"—*there's* your place, girls—"women collegiate athletes are not known to chase quarterbacks"! Hmm . . . is that because women who like sports are all . . . you know . . . ?

Thankfully, "according to an Australian-Chinese study" (*another* one?), Schlafly writes, "moderate exercise such as housework decreases the risk of ovarian cancer" and breast cancer. She recommends "walking behind a vacuum cleaner."

These right-wingers have some odd ideas about "family values." Schlafly opposes federal funding for day care and family leave and at a conference in 2005 on "Remedies to Judicial Tyranny" suggested that Supreme Court Justice Anthony Kennedy's opinion forbidding capital punishment for juveniles "is a good ground of impeachment." At least she didn't, like another speaker at the conference, hint that Kennedy should be assassinated (the right's knee-jerk response to any Kennedy, it seems).

Schlafly is of course—despite having a gay son—a vigorous opponent of gay rights. She believes people may demand "restrictions on homosexuals for public health reasons" because of AIDS, and in 2004 she was a pivotal force for including a constitutional ban on gay marriage in the GOP platform.

Schlafly "succeeded so well," Wolfe writes, "that she rendered herself superfluous. . . . [H]er work is done, and **George W. Bush**'s America is the result."

#19: ALBERTO GONZALES: "WHAT COULD BE WORSE THAN ASHCROFT?"

That was the widespread feeling among liberals and Democrats (and any surviving moderate Republicans) when **George W. Bush** picked Alberto Gonzales in November 2004 to replace outgoing Attorney General John Ashcroft. But many may look back wistfully at Ashcroft as an incompetent boob who at least gave them things to both laugh and cry about.

With Gonzales—the highest-ranking Hispanic in U.S. government history and a potential Bush nominee to the Supreme Court—tears of mirth are few. The tears of innocent detainees and torture victims, on the other hand . . .

From 1982 until 1994, Gonzales was an attorney and partner with the Houston law firm Vinson and Elkins, which specializes in "oil and gas matters" and was the late Enron's law firm. From 1994 to 2001, Gonzales served under then–Texas governor Bush as general counsel, Texas secretary of state, and justice of the Texas Supreme Court.

Under Bush and Gonzales—who as the governor's counsel reviewed all clemency requests—Texas executed 152 people, far more people than any other state—indeed, more than other *country* over the same period. According to *Atlantic Monthly*, Gonzales "gave insufficient counsel, failed to take into consideration a wide array of factors, and actively worked against clemency in a number of borderline cases."

The most conspicuous theme of Gonzales's service under President Bush has been: anything to enhance the president's power, increase White House secrecy, and reduce accountability to Congress or the public.

As first-term White House counsel, Gonzales in November 2001 drafted a Bush executive order that placed limitations on the Freedom of Information Act to allow the sitting president to block release of records of former presidents, and allow former presidents or vice presidents or their families to block release of documents against the will of a sitting president. Bush and **Cheney** had privatized history, giving themselves and their families permanent control over their records going back to the beginning of the Reagan administration—including, perhaps, such embarrassing matters as U.S. support for and arming of S. Hussein and (indirectly) **O. bin Laden** (#5).

In a January 2002 memo, Gonzales advised Bush that Al Qaeda and Taliban suspects could be exempted from the Third Geneva Convention's ban on torture and coercion, parts of which Gonzales described as "obsolete" and "quaint." As critics noted, enemies might adopt similar policies, label *our* soldiers "unlawful combatants" or even "terrorists," and exempt *them* from Geneva protections. The move, wrote then-Secretary of State Colin Powell in a countermemo, "will reverse over a century of U.S.

policy and practice"; have "immediate adverse consequences for our conduct of foreign policy"; "undermine public support among critical allies, making military cooperation more difficult to sustain; [and cause] legal problems with extradition" of terror suspects to the United States (which is just what has happened). Of course, Gonzales's advice, not Powell's, prevailed.

In July 2002, Gonzales and other government lawyers met to discuss what interrogation techniques the U.S. might get away with. Among those discussed were mock burials and "waterboarding," or making a suspect think he's drowning. The lawyers "discussed in great detail how to legally justify such methods."[67]

An August 2002 Justice Department memo, drafted under Gonzales's supervision, advised Bush that the president's powers "were so expansive that he and his surrogates were not bound by congressional laws or international treaties proscribing torture," *Newsweek* reported. The memo said torture "may be justified" and that only "the pain accompanying serious physical injury, such as organ failure, impairment of bodily function, or even death" constitutes torture—mere "cruel, inhuman or degrading" treatment does not. The memo shocked military lawyers (judge advocates general, or JAGs). "Every flag JAG lodged complaints," a senior Pentagon official told the *Washington Post*. "It's really unprecedented," one JAG said. "Once you start telling people it's okay to break the law, there's no telling where they might stop." Indeed, the memo—which Gonzales reaffirmed his agreement with in 2005—became the basis for new Pentagon guidelines that permitted "exceptional interrogations" and that said domestic and international prohibitions against torture were "inapplicable" to interrogations undertaken at Guantánamo or, under the president's authority, anywhere else.

Even after the White House promised a no-tolerance policy on torture in the wake of Abu Ghraib, Gonzales signed off on memos

67 "The Torture Meeting," AmericanProgress.org, December 20, 2004.

that said CIA officers and other nonmilitary personnel "fall outside the bounds of a 2002 directive issued by President Bush that pledged the humane treatment of prisoners in American custody" and that a separate congressional ban on cruel, unusual, and inhumane treatment had "a limited reach." As the *New York Times* noted, Gonzales's order regarding the CIA "is significant because the intelligence agency has carried out some of the government's most aggressive and controversial interrogation tactics." Gonzales also authored the presidential order that authorized the use of military tribunals to try terrorist suspects and (not to spare the civil liberties of ordinary Americans) was an early advocate of the USA Patriot Act.

Gonzales led the White House's legal fight against Congress to keep Cheney's energy task force documents secret. And he helped Bush avoid giving the 9/11 Commission documents about the pre-9/11 terrorism warnings Bush had received. The panel asked to see 360 of the President's Daily Briefings (PDBs). After a long battle, Gonzales agreed to let them see twenty-four; insisted the White House be allowed to "edit" them and decide which portions were "relevant"; limited their viewing to four of the panel members, who could then write brief summaries for the others; then objected to the wording of the summaries and refused to let the other commissioners see them. Most galling to some commissioners was Gonzales's claim to be protecting the principles of executive privilege and confidential advice—after the White House had selectively shared some of the PDBs with Bob Woodward for his flattering book *Bush at War*.

Gonzales has been regarded as moderate compared to Ashcroft. In the past, he has not opposed abortion or affirmative action. But the policies he has helped to draft and defend have aborted human rights and civil liberties and created an affirmative-action program that rewards arrogance and secrecy in the White House and empowers torturers in the military and intelligence services.

#18: GAIL A. NORTON, INDUSTRY'S INSIDE MAN AT INTERIOR

Interior Secretary Norton's previous career as a lawyer and mining and chemical industry lobbyist was devoted to *fighting* the Interior Department on behalf of industries that wanted to exploit public lands. She championed industries' "right to pollute" and called for the abolition of the Interior Department's Bureau of Land Management (BLM) and "the transfer to private ownership of federally held, so-called public lands." She was a protégé of Ronald Reagan's far-right-wing Interior secretary James Watt (who ordered the buffalo on the Interior Department seal turned to face right instead of left): "James Watt in a skirt," said a Sierra Club spokesman. But Watt's proclivities are not our concern. The Natural Resources Defense Council called Norton "an ideological extremist who has worked for more than two decades to systematically dismantle our nation's environmental protections. The direct beneficiaries of her views on enforcement are mining, grazing, timber, oil and other multinational corporations."

She was, in short, the perfect choice in 2001 to become **George W. Bush**'s Secretary of the Interior, in charge of 436 millions acres of public land—around one fifth of America's land area, including many of the most beautiful and environmentally sensitive areas in the West and much of the country's water resources.

Although more than 90 percent of this land, which is managed by the BLM, was already open for energy leasing and development, under Norton, BLM managers sent field personnel memos describing oil and gas leases and drilling permits as "their No. 1 priority" and directing them to speed up environmental reviews. Millions of new acres have been opened for oil, gas, and coal exploitation as a result.

Norton has long been associated with the Wise Use Movement, which aims to open public lands and wilderness areas for commercial uses and whose founder in the 1980s, Ron Arnold, said his goal was to "destroy the environmental movement." From 1979 to 1983, Norton was senior attorney for the Mountain States Legal Foundation, which supports oil, mining, development, and timber interests in attacking environmental protections. She has also worked for the Hoover Institution, a right-wing think tank, and served on the advisory boards of two other right-wing groups, Defenders of Property Rights and the Washington Legal Foundation. From 1984 to 1990, Norton served in the Reagan and Bush I administrations, where she sought to open the Arctic National Wildlife Reserve to oil drilling.

As Colorado's attorney general during the 1990s, Norton was a strong advocate of the state's innovative "self-audit" law, which lets companies decide for themselves whether they are complying with environmental requirements and gives them immunity from litigation and fines for violations. While Norton was "enforcing" this policy, one company dumped so much toxic waste into a Colorado river that it killed every living thing in a seventeen-mile stretch. When the federal government challenged "self-audit" laws, Norton spoke of "free markets" versus "communism." Norton also led the defense of Colorado's Amendment 2, an antigay ballot initiative that was struck down by the U.S. Supreme Court in 1996.

From 1999 to 2001, Norton was a lobbyist for a number of companies that had political interests before the Interior Department. One of her clients, NL Industries, formerly National Lead Company, a lead-paint manufacturer, was facing numerous lawsuits involving seventy-five toxic-waste sites and the poisoning of children by lead paint.

In 1998, Norton and **Grover Norquist** (#24) founded the Council of Republicans for Environmental Advocacy (CREA), which is funded by such groups as the National Mining Association, the National Coal Council, the Chemical Manufacturers Association, the American Forest Paper Association, **Ford** (#16), BP Amoco, and **Coors** Brewing (#53). CREA has been identified even by the rival Republicans for Environmental Protection as a

"greenscam" group designed "to fool voters" and obscure the anti-
environmental records of Republicans. In 2005, CREA was subpoenaed by federal investigators in connection with indicted GOP
superlobbyist Jack Abramoff, who got Indian tribes whose gambling interests he was ripping off—I mean, *representing*—to contribute money to CREA. The Interior Department has authority
over Indian gaming. CREA—whose president was a former
Norton campaign worker in Colorado—had "communicated" with
Norton aides at Interior about Abramoff's Indian gaming interests
and with Norton herself, the *Washington Post* reported.

As Interior secretary, Norton appointed a host of other oil, gas,
and coal industry lobbyists to important department jobs. The
most infamorious (I've used up "infamous" and "notorious") was
Deputy Secretary Stephen Griles, whom Friends of the Earth
called "the poster child of the corporate influence on this administration." After agreeing "to avoid any actual or apparent conflicts of interest" while serving at Interior, Griles intervened
repeatedly with the Environmental Protection Agency (EPA) on
behalf of his "former" energy industry clients to "try to expedite,"
in his words, drilling of up to seventy thousand coal-bed methane
natural-gas wells across vast, scenic, and environmentally sensitive areas of Wyoming and Montana. These wells contaminate
streams, would in total waste enough groundwater to flood a large
city beneath 140 feet of water, and would leave behind more than
25,000 miles of new roads and 5,300 miles of utility lines. Rather
than paying for any of this, the drilling companies were to be subsidized for it—meanwhile paying only a few dollars per acre for
drilling rights on public land while reaping windfalls on the gas.
Under Norton and Griles, Interior gave the green light to more
than fifty thousand such wells. It also:

- Reversed a Clinton regulation that gave federal officials power
  to block mining operations on public land that could cause
  "substantial and irreparable harm." Forty percent of Western
  watersheds were already polluted by mining.

- Pushed back the planned phaseout of **snowmobiles** (see #83) in Yellowstone and Grand Teton national parks.
- Gutted the "roadless rule," a key regulation protecting 60 million acres of national forest from road building and logging (for which the timber industry is federally subsidized).

But if you prefer, you can, like **Bernard Goldberg** (#73), get worked up about *Edward* Norton and Cameron Diaz and all those other Hollywood liberals who are screwing up America.

#17: ANDREW CARD, WHITE HOUSE CHIEF OF DOG-WAGGING STAFF

If you still think it was right to invade Iraq, read no further. There's no space here to argue the basic issue. (Yes there is: It was illegal, politically motivated falsely advertized and harmful to national security!) But if not, you ought to know about the role played by this innocuous, "uncontroversial" figure.

First, ask yourself—and be brutally honest: Is it likely the White House chief of staff was *not* in on the White House conspiracy— repeat, *conspiracy*—to mislead America into war?

Second: Know, oh ignorant one, that in September 2002, when the White House was beginning its disinformation campaign to prepare the public for the war it had planned long before 9/11—and people like conservative CNN senior political analyst Bill Schneider were asking, "Why now? Why, more than 11 years after the Gulf War, is it suddenly so urgent for the U.S. to go after Saddam Hussein now?" and wondering if it had anything to do with wanting to make the Republicans look strong and the Dems weak and wishy-washy on the "war on terrorism" heading into the November 2002 elections—it was Card who told the *New York Times*: "From a marketing point of view, you don't introduce new products in August."

Third, consider, briefly, the "product" and whether *you* would approve it were *you* head of the Food, Drug, and Deception Administration (FDDA). Here is how Joseph Cirincione summarized it in the Bulletin of the Atomic Scientists:

> As **George W. Bush** and **Dick Cheney** lower their hands after being sworn in for their second terms, they will be smiling. And with good reason. They will have gotten away with the greatest con in the history of the American presidency. They willfully and systematically misled the American people and our closest allies on the most crucial question any government faces: Must we go to war? . . . Not one of the dozens of claims they made about Iraq's alleged stockpiles of chemical and biological weapons, missiles, unmanned drones, or most importantly, Iraq's nuclear weapons and ties to Al Qaeda, were true. Not one. . . . We now know with absolute certainty, as Cheney likes to say, that during the buildup to the 2003 Iraq War Saddam Hussein did not have any of these weapons, did not have production programs for manufacturing these weapons, and did not have plans to restart programs for these weapons. . . . The weapons were not destroyed shortly before the war, nor were they moved to Syria, as some still claim. They never existed. . . . [T]he weapons and facilities had been destroyed by the United Nations inspectors and U.S. bombing strikes in the 1990s. . . . In short, administration officials "hoodwinked" America.

In summer 2002, the Bushies' politically, ideologically, and personally motivated drive for war ran into serious opposition from respected Republican moderates, such as retired general Brent Scowcroft, who warned that an invasion of Iraq "could turn the whole region into a cauldron and, thus, destroy the war on terrorism." The administration's response "was to craft a scheme to convince America and the world that war with Iraq was necessary and urgent"—a scheme "that required patently untrue public statements and egregious manipulations of intelligence."[68]

And so, in August, Card secretly set up a special White House Iraq Group (WHIG) that was chaired by **Karl Rove** (#3) and included **Condoleezza Rice** (#10), her deputy, Stephen Hadley (who later took "responsibility" for the Sixteen Words about "uranium from Africa" in Bush's January 2003 State of the Union address but who nevertheless succeeded Rice in 2005 as National Security Advisor), Cheney, chief of staff (and Valerie Plame identity leaker) I. Lewis "Scooter" Libby, and White House spinmeisters Karen Hughes and Mary Matalin. WHIG's mission: to coordinate "all the executive branch elements in the new campaign"—or, to put it less nicely, the *lies* that took the country into what Lt. Gen. William Odom, Reagan's National Security Agency director, has called "the greatest strategic disaster in United States history."

Next to corruption on *that* scale, it seems almost superfluous to mention that from 1993 to 1998, Card headed the American Automobile Manufacturers Association and from 1999 to 2001 served as General Motors's chief lobbyist. Yet perhaps it *is* worth mentioning in light of the Bush administration's iron resolve to protect the auto industry from any increases in vehicle fuel efficiency standards, the auto industry's top political priority. Which translates into the need for more oil. Why, by Michael (as in Moore)! It all seems to fit together somehow.

Card resigned in March 2006, apparently in response to widespread calls for a shakeup in the Bush team. (His replacement: "outsider" Joshua Bolten. Correction—that's failed White House OMB director and longtime Bush lackey, Joshua Bolten.)

---

68 Joseph Cirincione, "Not One Claim Was True," *Bulletin of the Atomic Scientists*, January/February 2005.

#16: BILL FORD, JR., AND THE U.S. AUTO INDUSTRY

In 2004, *Men's Fitness* magazine ranked Detroit as the nation's most obese city. The same year, for the first time since the mid-1970s, the average new car or light-duty truck (**SUV**, #67) sold in the United States weighed in at more than two tons. "The fattening of the nation's automobiles is a principal reason that average fuel economy has stopped improving and the nation's consumption of crude oil has been swelling," noted the *New York Times*. Not to mention the additional toxic pollutants and global-warming greenhouse gases released by burning more fuel. (Passenger vehicles consume 40 percent of all the oil used in the U.S.)

That same year, the Bush administration, responding to lobbying by the auto industry and conservative groups, proposed new fuel economy regulations that would pave the way for even heavier vehicles.

With the possible exception of **George W. Bush**, no one has done more to encourage these trends than Ford Motor Chairman and CEO William Ford, Jr. Ford has distinguished himself even among his industry co-conspirators by reneging on his pledge to significantly increase SUVs' fuel economy, personally lobbying Congress against raising fuel standards, introducing the industry's biggest, most gas-guzzling SUV models, and producing its least fuel-efficient and most polluting fleet of vehicles every year from 2000 to 2005 and for fifteen of the twenty-five years before that. Today's Fords get fewer miles per gallon (mpg) on average than the 1920s Model T.

New vehicles are actually even heavier than statistics indicate, because the largest SUVs, including Hummers and Ford Excursions, are not classed as light-duty and so are not counted in average weight calculations *or* covered by fuel economy rules for passenger vehicles. The manufacturers, whose most profitable products are SUVs and minivans, have fought to preserve this loophole.

The largest SUVs are also exempt from many safety standards. "Government studies say these giant vehicles are increasing the overall number of deaths in accidents, mainly because of the threat they pose to people in cars they hit in collisions," the *Times* reported. But the auto industry and its conservative shills (Bush Chief of Staff **Andrew Card**, #17, was formerly the top lobbyist for the auto industry) not only claim—falsely—that SUVs are safer but that, as the Alliance of Automobile Manufacturers said, "If all vehicles were made heavier, it would have a positive impact on safety." In fact, after a decade and a half of ever-heavier vehicles, U.S. traffic deaths have risen to their highest levels since 1990.

Although soaring fuel costs (partly the *result* of soaring vehicle size) have slowed sales of SUVs, the industry, just as in the 1970s, is once again resisting consumer demand for more fuel-efficient vehicles, thereby losing market share and costing the U.S. more manufacturing jobs. (In May 2005, Ford announced layoffs of 5 percent of its U.S. salaried workforce, due in part to slumping SUV sales.) But instead of raising fuel standards as part of its energy plan, the Bush administration created a $100,000 tax write-off for Hummer purchasers.

It didn't stop there. In 2002, the Bushies struck a major blow in the war on energy conservation by suing the state of California for requiring a fuel efficiency standard higher than the federal one. ("For those keeping score," wrote Arianna Huffington, "the Bush administration is in favor of states' rights when the states want to weaken federal safety standards of any kind, and against states' rights when the states want stronger measures.") Bill Ford himself lobbied against California's plan to allow cars that get 45 mpg to use car pool lanes even without passengers. Because only Toyota and Honda hybrids can meet this standard, Ford likened the proposal to a "Buy Japanese" campaign.

In 2004, John Kerry called for increasing average fuel-economy from 24 to 36 mpg by 2015. Not surprisingly, Ford executives contributed eleven times as much to Bush's presidential campaign as to Kerry's. In the crucial swing state of Michigan, the Bush 2004 campaign portrayed Kerry as dangerous for the state (which had lost nearly 185,000 jobs under Bush).

Bill Ford, Jr., Henry Ford's great-grandson, became Ford's chairman in 1999 and CEO in 2001. His corporate bio describes him as "a lifelong environmentalist." Ford "led efforts to build a new, environmentally friendly stadium" for the Detroit Lions and literally "greened" Ford's Rouge River plant (grass grows on the roof). He drove an electric Ford Ranger. And in 2000, he promised a 25 percent reduction in SUV fuel consumption by 2005. Within days, General Motors and Daimler Chrysler made identical commitments, "creating the appearance of an environmental race between the 'Big Three' that helped to undermine a Senate measure that would have nearly doubled the fuel economy requirement for light-duty trucks" by 2015.[69]

Ford withdrew its pledge in April of 2003, and again the other manufacturers quickly followed suit. End result: no mandatory *or* voluntary efficiency increase.

In the meantime, Bill Ford had introduced the Ford Expedition (14 mpg city, 17 highway, and rated close to "worst" on greenhouse emissions) and the 9,200-pound, 19-foot Excursion (11 mpg city, 15 highway), which earned Ford the Sierra Club's "Exxon Valdez Environmental Achievement Award." Ford did not introduce the Excursion at the Detroit Auto Show; as a Ford insider told *Business Week*, "The Excursion isn't a thing you want to roll out with trumpets and brass bands."

Unlike Ford's latest "environmental" ad campaign. Launched in 2004, the "Greening of the Blue Oval" campaign touted the new Ford Escape hybrid, of which Ford planned to produce all of twenty thousand—which would raise the Ford fleet's average fuel

---

69 "Ford Motors Threatens To Sue Over Pinocchio Ads," Bluewater Network, February 27, 2004

economy by 0.04 mpg. "Escape" seems a fitting name. It evokes not only escape to the great outdoors but escape from environmental and economic reality, escape from corporate responsibility, escape from the hole Ford is digging for itself.

#15: JAMES DOBSON: FOCUS ON THE FLIM-FLAM

The purpose of separation of church and state is to keep forever from these shores the ceaseless strife that has soaked the soil of Europe with blood for centuries.

—James Madison, 1803

The purpose of James Dobson is to end forever the separation of church and state that has guaranteed freedom of belief and expression in America for over two centuries; effect a takeover by the evangelical Christian minority of society's most important institutions, from the government, courts, and public schools to the media; control and censor television and textbooks; banish the teaching of evolution—and perhaps the theory of the round earth; abolish potentially lifesaving stem-cell research (which Dobson compared to Nazi medical experiments on concentration camp inmates), abortion (obviously), birth control, and all but abstinence-only sex education; and make war on women's rights (Dobson: "women are merely waiting for their husbands to assume leadership") and on gays and lesbians in the name of "family values." "Not even the war on terror eclipses" the "defense of the family" in importance, Dobson has written.

Dobson, the chairman of Focus on the Family (FOF, pronounced *eff-off*), "is now America's most influential evangelical leader, with a following reportedly greater than that of either Falwell or **Robertson** [#55] at his peak," wrote Michael Crowley in *Slate*. Dobson's daily *Focus on the Family* radio program is heard by more than 200 million people in 164 countries. His TV program is broadcast on some eighty U.S. stations. FOF publishes more than a dozen periodicals, as well as weekly bulletins inserted in Sunday church service programs, and runs seminars to train evangelical Christians for political activism. The Family Research Council, FOF's lobbying arm on Capitol Hill, was spun off from FOF in 1992 in order to preserve FOF's tax-exempt status, to which lobby groups are not entitled.

Dobson—without, of course, *lobbying*—never lets up the pressure on political leaders to pass legislation backed by FOF and other far-right groups. In the mid-1990s, pressure from Dobson led to the creation of the Values Action Team, which brought together Christian-right lobbyists and right-wing members of Congress to coordinate legislative strategy. In 1998, Dobson, unhappy with the ~~progress~~ regress against abortion and gay rights, threatened to leave the GOP and "take as many people with me as possible." In 2004, he organized huge stadium rallies for Bush and used his radio program to warn his 7 million U.S. listeners that not to vote would be a sin. He played an important role in the defeat of then–Senate Minority Leader Tom Daschle and may have delivered Bush his election-deciding victories in Ohio and Florida.

Dobson, wrote Crowley in November 2004, is "already leveraging his new power."

When a thank-you call came from the White House, Dobson issued the staffer a blunt warning that **Bush** "needs to be more aggressive" about pressing the religious right's pro-life, anti-gay rights agenda, or [the GOP] would "pay a price in four years." And when the pro-choice Pennsylvania Sen. Arlen Specter made conciliatory noises about appointing moderates to the Supreme Court, Dobson launched a fevered campaign to prevent him from assuming the chairmanship of the Senate Judiciary Committee. . . . Dobson is now a Republican kingmaker.

Dobson, who holds a Ph.D. in child development, first gained notoriety through his 1970 book *Dare to Discipline* (one of seventeen books by him), which recommended the spanking of children, beginning at the age of eighteen months (or younger if the infant shows signs of homosexuality or liberalism). "It is not necessary to beat the child into submission," he cautions. "However, the spanking should be of sufficient magnitude to cause the child to cry genuinely."

Now on to the punishment of gays. In 1991, FOF helped pass Colorado's Amendment 2, which prohibits local governments from enacting laws to protect gay rights. Dobson contends that "tolerance and diversity" are "buzzwords" used by proponents and agents of the "gay agenda" (GA) to promote homosexuality. In 2005, Dobson was falsely and viciously accused of attacking the TV cartoon character SpongeBob Squarepants—a humanoid kitchen sponge—for being an agent of the GA because he occasionally holds hands with his sidekick Patrick Starfish and likes to watch the imaginary yet dangerous TV show *The Adventures of Mermaid Man and Barnacle Boy.* Actually, FOF was attacking the We Are Family Foundation (WAFF), which used SpongeBob and other popular cartoon characters in what Dobson called a "pro-homosexual video" to promote tolerance and diversity among children. In fact, neither the video not its accompanying materials referred to sexual identity. A WAFF spokesman said anyone who thought the video promoted homosexuality "needs to visit their doctor and get their medication increased." Alas, there is no known cure for hatred or stupidity. "Faith" doesn't appear to work.

#14: RUPERT MURDOCH: "THE DIRTY DIGGER"

There's no room here to describe the growth of Rupert Murdoch's company, News Corp., into the world's largest media empire, including some 175 newspapers, the **Fox News** network (#28), a couple of cable TV and satellite networks, and other businesses on sixteen continents—except to quote this: "Despite [Murdoch's] personal conservatism, he allowed his editors (particularly in Britain) to exploit the selling power of soft-core erotica in the form of topless page three girls . . . to increase circulation. As a result, Auberon Waugh of *Private Eye* dubbed him The Dirty Digger, a name that has endured."[70]

Nor is there room to even mention how, for example, Margaret Thatcher helped Murdoch break Britain's printers' unions; how, by using offshore tax havens, Murdoch's main British holding company paid no net corporation tax from at least 1988 through 1999 despite profits of $2.1 billion; how Murdoch eliminated the BBC from his Hong Kong–based Star Satellite news service because the communist Chinese government didn't appreciate BBC's criticisms of it, and how his publishing house, Harper-Collins, canceled publication of the memoirs of the former British governor of Hong Kong, which were critical of the Chinese regime, allegedly because Murdoch was trying to break into the Chinese TV market.

While those moves tell us much about Murdoch, our focus must remain on Screwing Up America, where News Corp.—of which Murdoch is chairman, CEO, and controlling shareholder— owns the Fox network; thirty-five TV stations; a controlling share of DirecTV, the largest U.S. satellite TV service; the *New York Post*, one of the world's most influential tabloids, which Murdoch turned from New York's most liberal paper into one of the most

70 Wikipedia.org.

conservative in the United States; the conservative *Weekly Standard* magazine; HarperCollins; and the 20th Century Fox movie studio, which, since Murdoch's takeover in 1984, "has backed away from its reputation for literary adaptations and adult themes to concentrate on 'popcorn' movies."[71]

If Murdoch had given America *only* Fox News, it would have more than earned him this tribute. (Fox's right-wing politics flow directly from Murdoch's. As Daphne Eviatar wrote in *The Nation*, "Fox management's far heavier hand than at other networks [reflects] the fact that Murdoch owns 30 percent of the stock of News Corporation.") But, having paid our respects to Fox in other sections, let us peruse a randomly selected issue of the *New York Post*—October 13, 2005.

Page 3: full-page-length photo of "supermodel" Gisele Bundchen modeling the Victoria's Secret Fantasy Bra—but that doesn't make up for a story about "teen starlet" Lindsay Lohan's "bad-boy dad." Big page 4 headline: "7 More Perverts Confined." It's better than the *Onion*. Page 7: "Marlene Dietrich's *Un*sexy Secret." Page 9: Investigative report on how "the L Line Is New York's Love Train, Sizzling with More Romantic Heat than Any Other Pickup Spot in the City." *That's* community service. However, pages 10, 11, and 14 are all celebrity gossip. Pages 16–17: Lurid crime stories. Opinion section: Editorial attacking Kofi Annan; letters attacking Hillary Clinton; an excerpt from the right-wing *National Review* magazine—a regular feature; and today's syndicated opinion columnists—right-wingers Robert Novak and George F. Will and the more moderate but pro–Iraq War Jim Hoagland. On other days, the *Post* offers right-wingers John Podhoretz, Rich Lowrie, Maggie secretly-funded-by-the-White-House Gallagher, Michelle internment-of-Japanese-Americans-was-right Malkin, **Linda Chavez** (#87), and **Bill O'Really** (#29). Liberals basically need not apply.

71 Wikipedia.org.

But best of all was the front page. That day, the rival *Daily News*'s lead story was "Terror Tip for Rich": Through "close connections to Homeland Security and other federal officials," went the story, "the city's rich and well-connected were tipped off to last week's subway terror threat days before average New Yorkers." The *Post*'s main front page story? "Screwball: Mel [NY Yankees pitching coach Mel Stottlemyre] Blasts Boss [George Steinbrenner] And Quits." (Rest of the front page: "iPod TV: $299 gadget to play top shows." A *news story*, not an ad.) The *Post* does not criticize Republican leaders such as New York mayor Michael Bloomberg, Governor George Pataki, or the other **George**; it attacks their critics.

In November 2003, as the 9/11 Commission was battling the Bush administration for more time to complete its work, which it needed because the Bush administration was refusing to turn over documents and witnesses, a *Post* editorial attacked Republican commission chairman Thomas Kean's "run-amok," "bizarre," "emperor"-like behavior.

When photos of prisoner "abuse" at Abu Ghraib came to light in 2004, *Post* editor Col Allan said he wouldn't run them because "a handful of U.S. soldiers" shouldn't be allowed to "reflect poorly" on the rest (see #4 for more about the "handful"). A November 2005 *Post* editorial, posing as a Veterans Day salute, attacked "craven politicians" for "questioning the integrity" of "Operation Iraqi Freedom." No more of that *questioning*. (The same issue, however, included some hard-hitting war reporting— about the unveiling of a Stella McCartney clothing line at H&M stores in Manhattan. The quintessentially *Post* headline: "H&M Hordes 'Rack' Havoc with War Cry: 'Back Off My Dress, Bitch!' ") All 175 Murdoch-owned newspapers worldwide editorialized in favor of the Iraq War. "Compared with Murdoch," *The Nation* commented, "Mao Zedong, who said, 'Let a hundred flowers bloom,' was a free-speech fanatic."

Murdoch was a friend and supporter of Ronald Reagan and

said of **Pat** "the Democrats and the homosexuals want to destroy the Christians" **Robertson**'s 1988 presidential bid: "He's right on all the issues."

Nonetheless, wrote James Fallows in the *Atlantic Monthly*: "The real difference between Murdoch and an activist like [**Richard**] **Scaife** [#21] is that Murdoch seems to be most interested in the political connections that will help his business." All of News Corp.'s "programming, positions, and alliances . . . are consistent with . . . corporate advantage. . . . [Murdoch] makes his political points when convenient as an adjunct to making money." Of all big media owners, Eviatar wrote, "Murdoch may be the most blatant . . . about putting profits above principles."

Murdoch, who moved News Corp.'s headquarters to the U.S. to protest Australia's media ownership rules and took U.S. citizenship in order to legally own U.S. TV stations, is a powerful opponent of ownership restrictions—such as the rule that, in theory only, prevents News Corp. from owning both the *New York Post* and New York's Fox 5 channel. That's the channel that in 2005 refused to air a campaign ad for a gay Democratic candidate for Manhattan borough president because the ad took a swipe at George W. Bush (and/or because the candidate introduced his partner in the spot). In another instance, two award-winning reporters at a Fox-owned station in Florida, Jane Akre and Steve Wilson, claimed their contract was canceled because they refused to soft-pedal an investigative story about the effect of bovine growth hormone (BGH) on the state's milk supply after BGH producer Monsanto complained to Fox CEO **Roger Ailes** (#28). They sued, and Akre won her case. (Wilson lost his.)

But hey, isn't the right to own and censor all the media in a given city—or country, or planet—a matter of free speech and freedom of the press? Here Murdoch's support for Bush seems to have paid off. In January 2004, the White House got a last-minute amendment snuck into a vital spending bill that overrode the federal rule that a single network could own local TV stations that collectively reach no more than 35 percent of the national viewership. Congress had voted to keep the rule. "The practical effect of the changes demanded by the White House," wrote Sen. Diane Feinstein (D-CA), "is to protect [Fox] and CBS-Viacom from having to comply" with the lower cap. And, she might have added, to help keep Americans safe from alternative viewpoints that challenge government and corporate policies.

#13: THE SO-CALLED LIBERAL MEDIA

In exit polls on Election Day, 2004, the largest number of voters—a whopping 22 percent—picked "moral values" as the most important issue. This was spun by almost all of the so-called liberal media (SCLM) to show that the country had swung to the right on the most heartfelt and defining issues. Few reports stressed that 78 percent named other priorities. Few bothered to mention that 22 percent was the same proportion as in 1996—or to question what people meant by "moral values" (gay marriage, or the morality of lying about Iraq, failing to armor the troops, and cutting veterans' benefits while running up huge budget deficits to give tax cuts to the rich?), *or* to note that if "Iraq" and "terrorism" were grouped together as "war issues," 34 percent of voters felt *those* were the most important issues, while "economy and jobs," "taxes," and "health care," if combined as "economic issues," would have come in at 33 percent.

Bush's 2.5 percent popular vote win was the narrowest of any sitting president in U.S. history, while his Electoral College win was the narrowest since Woodrow Wilson's in 1916. Voters identified themselves as 37 percent Republicans, 37 percent Democrats, and 26 percent independents, while an awe-inspiring 34 percent self-identified as conservative—again, the same level as in 1996. Only 29.5 percent of eligible voters voted for Bush.

But never mind any of *that*. The media's story was that Bush's smashing, 50.8-to-48.3 percent popular vote win represented . . . well, let the SCLM speak for themselves:

> *Boston Globe*: "[A] clear mandate to advance a conservative agenda."
> Renee Montague of National Public Radio: "By any definition I think you could call this a mandate."
> CNN's Wolf Blitzer: "[H]e's got a mandate from the American people . . . by all accounts."
> MSNBC's Chris Matthews: "To me the big story is the president's mandate."
> *USA Today*: "Clear mandate."
> *Dallas Morning News*: A "newly minted mandate."
> *Los Angeles Times*: "Bush can claim a solid mandate of 51 percent of the vote"!
> *New York Times* (the alleged headquarters of the liberal media conspiracy): "[H]e has the real thing."

As Eric Boehlert wrote in *Slate*, the *press* gave Bush his "mandate," "falling to its knees in record time."

It was much the same in 2000, following the selection of Bush by the conservative majority on the Supreme Court: the media as a whole instantly dropped the trivial subject of who really won the election. The NORC Ballots Project, whose results, published in November 2001, showed that a full recount of Florida votes would have made Gore the winner, was virtually ignored by media organizations—even those, such as the *New York Times* and *Washington Post*, that sponsored the study. After 9/11, the media substituted flag-waving and cheerleading for journalism and suspended all questioning or criticism of the Bush administration, as though Bush was somehow the *hero* of the moment rather than the president on whose watch the worst terrorist attack ever on U.S. soil had occurred. Stories about the pre-9/11 warnings the administration had failed to act upon quickly came and went—and it was back to wall-to-wall coverage of celebrity murderers and child molesters.

We know what to expect from the *blatantly* right-wing media (see #15, #29, #50, #51). The more unforgivable failure to fulfill the responsibilities of journalism—by, for example, calling the Bush administration to account on issues including 9/11, Iraq, the environment, Plamegate, Halliburtongate, FEMAgate, budget-busting-Bush-tax-cuts-for-the-rich-gate—has been that of the SCLM, by which I mean mainly the three broadcast TV networks (owned by those great liberal corporations, General Electric, Disney, and Viacom, which spun off CBS in January 2006), the major "liberal" and centrist newspapers, and the more "liberal" of the major weekly newsmagazines—most of which can be trusted to put their own business interests and those of their generally conservative corporate advertisers ahead of their responsibility to report.

Republican Party chair Rich Bond admitted back in 1992 that the constant complaints of "liberal media bias" by the right were part of "a strategy" of keeping pressure up on the media to lean rightward, akin to sports coaches "working the refs" for every advantage. And this "great little racket," as a conservative editor called it, has been highly successful "in convincing reporters that they are somehow out of step with the lives and values of 'ordinary' Americans," wrote Eric Alterman. Under relentless pressure from right-wing activists and talk show hosts, the *New York Times*'s editors have begun to "bend over backward to coddle conservatives." Op-ed columnist Nicholas Kristof has written that the paper suffers from a "failure to hire more red state evangelicals." One editor suggested an affirmative-action program for conservatives. Executive editor Bill Keller sent the staff a memo urging reporters and editors to "stretch beyond our predominantly urban, culturally liberal orientation."

Ironically, Alterman noted, right-wing critics "happen to have a point" about the media being out of touch with Americans' values:

"Those values are a great deal more liberal than either the media or their right-wing minders imagine."

In a Pew Research poll conducted in May 2005, 65 percent favored providing health insurance to all Americans, even if it means increasing taxes; 86 percent said that they favor raising the minimum wage; 77 percent said the country "should do whatever it takes to protect the environment"; liberal views prevail on a host of other issues. But most people don't know that most people hold these views because most of the SCLM play along with the story of America's supposed shift rightward.

Having to debate about the real bias of the SCLM is almost as absurd as having to debate about the reality of evolution. Examples are endless:

- Up to three quarters of news reporters, editors, and executives say they have avoided, softened, or played up stories to benefit their media company's and advertisers' interests (Fairness and Accuracy In Reporting [FAIR] has catalogued hundreds of examples), which tends to translate into friendly treatment of the conservative politicians and policies that most media owners and corporate advertisers support.

- A study by the Project for Excellence in Journalism found that in the last weeks of the 2000 presidential campaign, Bush was twice as likely to receive positive coverage as Gore. "More than three-quarters of the campaign coverage included discussion that Gore lies and exaggerates or is tainted by scandal, while the most common theme about Bush was that he is a 'different kind of Republican,'" noted Daphne Eviatar in *The Nation*.

- Throughout the lead-up to the invasion of Iraq and afterwards, the "liberal" *New York Times* ran story after story about Iraq's dreadful WMDs by reporter Judith Miller, who relied on such sources as **Dick Cheney** and exiled Iraqi businessman and would-be Iraqi leader Ahmed Chalabi.

- In 2004, CBS News—known as the most "liberal" of the three broadcast networks—withheld the story and photographs of "abuse" at the Abu Ghraib prison in Iraq for two weeks at the Pentagon's request, releasing them only when it learned the *New Yorker* was about to print an exposé.

- In a November 2004 segment about Bush's Social Security privatization scheme on CNN's *Wolf Blitzer Reports*, "Only two experts were interviewed on camera—one from the conservative **American Enterprise Institute** [AEI, #7] and one from the very conservative **Heritage Foundation** [#8]. Both enthusiastically supported Bush's unprecedented plan," Eric Boehlert noted. CNN is popularly known around the right-wing blogosphere as the Communist News Network—even though CNN's senior political analyst, Bill Schneider, billed by CNN as a nonpartisan political analyst, was previously a resident scholar at the AEI.

- The watchdog group Media Matters for America inventoried all guests who appeared on **Fox,** CNN, and MSNBC during their January 20, 2005, inauguration coverage and reported that Republican and conservative commentators outnumbered Democrats and progressives nineteen to seven on Fox, thirteen to two on MSNBC, and ten to one on CNN. Moreover, the rare Democrat or progressive usually appeared opposite conservatives, whereas most Republican and conservative guests appeared solo or alongside fellow conservatives.

- I could write a book *per day* on conservative bias and cheerleading for Bush at CNBC, which gets news content and analysis from the *Wall Street Journal* (WSJ, #49). Examples? Chief commentator Bill Seidman, 2004: "I don't want to help John Kerry any more than I have to"; every single appearance by CNBC Washington bureau chief and WSJ contributing editor Alan Murray.

- On "liberal" PBS (see #48), liberal *Now* is outnumbered by shows like *Journal Editorial Report,* hosted entirely by the WSJ editorial board, and *The McLaughlin Group,* with a panel of three conservatives (including host John McLaughlin), one moderate, and one liberal. Longest-running show in PBS history? William F. Buckley's *Firing Line.* PBS's *News Hour* is primarily funded by Archer Daniels Midland—and it shows.

- Someday, wrote media critic Todd Gitlin, historians will note with astonishment how the so-called Swift Boat Veterans for Truth (SBVT), "many of its members inveterate liars . . . succeeded in hijacking the presidential campaign for the better part of the month of August" with their smears on John Kerry's war record, while "journalists performed as accomplices . . . thereby buying them piles of publicity that money couldn't have bought. . . . Whatever Kerry said about health care, Iraq, and jobs instantly became Topics B, C, and D." SBVT leader John O'Neill "stated his views again and again without being called on them—not by George Stephanopoulos on ABC's *This Week,* nor by [CNN's] Wolf Blitzer. . . . CBS and NBC barely disputed the Swifties' accusations." Story after story noted that veterans disagreed on the accusations without mentioning that no documents nor any of Kerry's crewmates supported them. A *New York Times* editor told *Editor & Publisher:* "Now that we're yelled at so much by Fox News and **Limbaugh**, the error is to bend on the side of the [SBVT] charges."

There you have the so-called liberal media in a nutshell: neutrality, at best, in the face of outright lies by the right. (As *New York Times* columnist Paul Krugman once wrote, "If President Bush said that the Earth was flat, news headlines would read, 'Opinions Differ on Shape of the Earth.' ") With "balance" like that, who needs Fox's "fairness"?

#12: LEE RAYMOND, EXXONMOBIL, AND THE AMERICAN PETROLEUM INSTITUTE

Isn't it bad enough to produce the stuff that produces the carbon dioxide that produces global warming, without also producing a mass disinformation campaign to deny it all and lobbying massively to block regulation of greenhouse emissions? Isn't it enough to sell a dwindling and polluting resource that keeps America embroiled in the world's most perilous regions, without also blocking measures to reduce oil dependence?

Under chairman and CEO Lee Raymond, ExxonMobil, the world's largest oil company, is in the forefront of industry efforts to mislead the public on these issues. Forty public policy groups and think tanks "have this in common," *Mother Jones* magazine reported in 2005. "They seek to undermine the scientific consensus that humans are causing the earth to overheat"—not in peer-reviewed scientific journals but in press releases and opinion pieces—"and they all get money from ExxonMobil."[72]

In 2003, a University of California science historian reviewed nearly a thousand scientific papers on global climate change published in the previous ten years and could not find one that disagreed with the consensus view that greenhouse gases emitted by human activity are contributing to global warming. But conservative Exxon-funded think tanks "are trying to undermine this conclusion with a disinformation campaign" employing "reports" dressed up as science and "skeptic propaganda masquerading as journalism," wrote Chris Mooney in *Mother Jones*. The think tanks provide ammunition for policy-makers like Senator **James Inhofe** (#33), the chair of the Environment and Public Works Committee, who calls global warming "a hoax" (and who received nearly $290,000 from oil and gas companies for his 2002 reelection campaign).

72 Chris Mooney, "Some Like It Hot," *Mother Jones*, May/June 2005.

The think tanks Mooney identified received more than $8 million from Exxon between 2000 and 2003. A drop in the barrel of the more than $55 million Exxon spent on lobbying from 1999 to 2005 (and its $25.3 *billion* in net earnings in 2004); but as one Exxon-funded flack said when advising corporations to fund think tanks: "You will be amazed at how much they do with so little." Exxon has filled the tanks of the **Heritage Foundation** (#8); the **American Enterprise Institute** (AEI, #7)—whose vice chairman of the board is Lee Raymond; the Competitive Enterprise Institute (CEI), which twice sued to block a federal report showing the impact of climate change; and the Committee for a Constructive Tomorrow (CCT), where senior fellow Paul Driessen, "who is white, has made it his mission to portray Kyoto-style emissions regulations as an attack on people of color," Mooney noted. Exxon's efforts on global warming have even included funding for religious and civil-rights groups. "No company appears to be working harder to support those who debunk global warming," wrote Mooney.

Indeed, as the scientific consensus on global warming solidified, other oil companies backed off. Shell, Texaco, and British Petroleum, as well as the Big Three U.S. automobile manufacturers, abandoned the Global Climate Coalition (GCC), an industry group that was formed in the late 1980s to deny global warming. After a report in 2001 by the Intergovernmental Panel on Climate Change (IPCC) concluded that greenhouse emissions could raise global temperatures by more than 10 degrees Fahrenheit by 2100, which would have catastrophic effects, the GCC closed up shop. "Consensus as strong as the one that has developed around this topic is rare in science," the editor-in-chief of *Science* magazine wrote at the time. Nonetheless, a whole cottage industry has sprung up to criticize the IPCC analysis, much of it linked to Exxon-funded think tanks. Exxon and the main oil industry trade group, the American Petroleum Institute (API)—which Lee Raymond has twice served as chairman—carry on the fight.

In 1998, the *New York Times* exposed an API memo outlining a strategy to invest millions to "maximize the impact of scientific views consistent with ours with Congress, the media and other key audiences." The document stated: "Victory will be achieved when . . . recognition of uncertainty becomes part of the 'conventional wisdom' "—rather like a famous tobacco company memo from the late 1960s, which said: "Doubt is our product since it is the best means of competing with the 'body of fact' . . . [and] of establishing a controversy."

Among the API plotters were executives of the aforementioned CEI and CCT and Exxon lobbyist Randy Randol, who, less than a month after **George W. Bush** took office in 2001, sent a memo to the White House asking whether IPCC chairman Robert Watson, a leading atmospheric scientist, could "be replaced now at the request of the U.S.?" And behold, he was. Randol's memo also singled out Clinton-appointed government climate experts, asking whether they had been "removed from their positions of influence."

Meanwhile, more than thirty former energy-industry executives, lobbyists, and lawyers got high-level jobs in the new ~~Exxon~~ Bush administration—beginning, of course, with Bush and **Cheney.** Cheney met with Lee Raymond within three weeks of taking office. Exxon officials met repeatedly with Cheney's energy task force, which plotted an industry-friendly energy policy with industry insiders behind closed doors. Former API economist and AEI fellow Diana Furchtgott-Roth became chief of staff of the White House Council of Economic Advisers. The Randy Randol–recommended Harlan Watson became the State Department's "senior climate negotiator." A former Exxon lobbyist on "climate change," Larisa Dobriansky, became head of the Energy Department's Office of Climate Change Policy. Her sister, Paula Dobriansky, within months of being appointed under secretary of state for global affairs, met with Randol and the GCC, whom she assured that Bush "rejected [the] Kyoto [accord on global warming] in part, based on input from you." She met with Exxon executives to discuss climate policy just days after 9/11— which the Bush administration exploited to push for industry wishes like oil drilling in Alaska's Arctic National Wildlife Refuge.

Philip Cooney, an attorney who had formerly headed API's "climate team" and its fight against the Kyoto accord, was appointed chief of staff of the Bush White House Council on Environmental Quality (CEQ). Cooney resigned in June 2005 after leaked documents revealed that this ~~scientist~~ lawyer had repeatedly doctored government reports to play down the link between greenhouse emissions and global warming. Five days later, ExxonMobil announced that he was joining the firm.

The Exxon/Big Oil propaganda machine relies heavily on the right-wing-media echo-chamber effect. When the Arctic Climate Impact Assessment (ACIA), a landmark international study combining the work of some three hundred scientists, warned in November 2004 that the Arctic is warming "at almost twice the rate as that of the rest of the world," it was attacked first on **FoxNews**.com by columnist Steven Milloy of the libertarian Cato Institute (another Exxon grantee). His column (which cited a single paragraph from a 146-page overview of the twelve-hundred-plus-page ACIA report) was reprinted two days later by **Sun Myung Moon** (#54)'s *Washington Times*. Neither outlet disclosed that Milloy also runs two cozy "think tanks" registered to his home address which had jointly received at least $90,000 from Exxon. Milloy was quickly echoed by the Web site TechCentral-Station and the conservative George C. Marshall Institute—both Exxon grantees. *Those* "critiques" were then cited by Senator Inhofe and by the CEI, which put out a press release stating that the ACIA "has already generated analysis pointing out numerous flaws and distortions."

The industry does not address "climate change" alone. The Cato Institute, which also receives grants from Chevron and Unocal, issues reports claiming that "fossil-fuel resources are becoming more abundant, not scarcer." Experts are becoming more certain every year that the opposite is true. "Similarly, the Chevron-Exxon-Mobil-Shell–backed Heritage Foundation issues talking points actually saying cars 'clean our air,' " noted David Sirota in the *American Prospect.* "But with the White House headed by two oilmen, industry nonsense substitutes for public policy."

Exxon should have no trouble continuing to fund such efforts. In July 2005, Bush signed an energy bill consisting mostly of $9 billion in tax breaks and incentives for oil, gas, coal, and electricity producers. The day before, Exxon reported a 32 percent jump in profits—and that was for the year *before* oil prices soared to over $60 a barrel.

#11: ANTONIN SCALIA AND CLARENCE THOMAS: SUPREME INJUSTICES

In 2000, screwer-upper #2 said he wanted to nominate Supreme Court justices "in the mold of Justice Scalia or Justice Thomas"—the Court's two most right-wing justices. Analyzing every one of their opinions, People for the American Way concluded that under a ScaThomas majority (Thomas almost invariably votes with Scalia, his mentor), "*Roe v. Wade* would of course be reversed, but so would more than 100 other precedents covering privacy rights, religious liberty, environmental protection, worker safety and health, civil rights, and a host of other important issues." In 1989, when Scalia explicitly stated that *Roe* should be overturned, Justice Harry Blackmun noted: "To overturn a constitutional decision that secured a fundamental personal liberty to millions of persons would be unprecedented in our 200 years of constitutional history."

Federalist Society (#25) members Scalia and Thomas, wrote lawyer and author Adam Cohen in the *New York Times*, "are judicial activists, eager to use the fast-expanding federalism doctrine [which challenges Congress's authority to legislate] to strike down laws that protect people's rights," as well as air-pollution laws, campaign-finance laws, and more. Cohen described a ScaThologized America:

> Abortion might be a crime in most states. Gay people could be thrown in prison for having sex in their homes. States might be free to become mini-theocracies, endorsing Christianity and using tax money to help spread the gospel. The Constitution might no longer protect inmates from being brutalized by prison guards. Family and medical leave and environmental protections could disappear.[73]

Hysteria? Hyperbole? Hardly. Harken to these hard, cold facts. ScaThomas:

- Dissented when the Court, in *Lawrence v. Texas* (2003), ruled that the police violated the liberty of a gay Texas man when they raided his home and arrested him for having sex there. The ruling struck down Texas's "Homosexual Conduct" law.
- Dissented when the court ruled that the beating of a Louisiana inmate violated the Eighth Amendment prohibition of cruel and unusual punishment. While a supervisor looked on, two guards shackled the inmate, then punched and kicked him, leaving him with a swollen face, loosened teeth, and a cracked dental plate. ScaThomas called the harm "insignificant."
- Dissented when the court ruled that a poor mother of two from Mississippi had a right to appeal after the state terminated her parental rights because she could not afford a $2,300 court fee. If she didn't have the money, ScaThomas insisted, her children would have to be put up for adoption.

73 Adam Cohen, "Imagining America if George Bush Chose the Supreme Court," *New York Times*, October 18, 2004.

- Dissented when the court ruled that Tennessee violated the Americans With Disabilities Act by not providing a wheelchair-accessible courtroom. The case involved a wheelchair-bound man who refused to drag himself or be carried up two flights of stairs for a court appearance.
- Dissented from the court's ruling upholding the University of Michigan's affirmative-action program. Scalia was also the sole dissenter when the court required the state-supported Virginia Military Academy to admit women. (Thomas did not take part.) ScaThomas "appear eager to dismantle a wide array of diversity programs."
- Argued against basic rights of criminal suspects such as the Miranda warning about the right to remain silent.
- Dissented when the court upheld the Family and Medical Leave Act.
- Suggested that the First Amendment prohibition on establishing a religion may not apply to the states—in which case, states could adopt particular religions and use tax money to proselytize for them.
- Voted to strip the EPA of its authority to prevent air pollution by industries when state agencies improperly fail to do so.
- Were the only dissenters when the Court, in 2004, overturned the Texas death sentence of a nineteen-year-old with an IQ of 78, in which the Texas appeals court's errors were so clear to the majority that it decided the case on the basis of the briefs without even hearing arguments. (Texas's clemency procedures are an international scandal. Since 1976, Texas has executed more people than the next six states combined and more than any other *country* outside the United States.)
- Suddenly abandoned their long-standing commitment to states' rights when they ruled in 2000 in *Bush v. Gore* that Florida had violated the Constitution's Equal Protection Clause—a ruling that astounded most legal experts with its barefaced partisanship.

In 2000, ScaThomas voted to strike down the Violence Against Women Act (which permitted victims of rape, domestic violence, and other crimes to sue their attackers in federal court) as beyond congressional authority. They advocate preventing the federal government from requiring state legislatures to enact laws, for example, to protect the public against environmental damage or against terrorism. And in ScaThomas's view, free speech means protection for almost any commercial advertising claims—for example, by the drug industry—and for unlimited political campaign contributions. As for *political* speech: in 1986, Scalia, then a Court of Appeals judge, joined Robert Bork to rule that the FCC's 1949 Fairness Doctrine, which mandated balanced coverage of public policy issues on the airwaves, was not binding. The policy, which media owners opposed, was rescinded by the Reagan administration the following year. By 2004, according to a study by Democracy Radio, conservative programming totaled more than thirteen times as many hours per week than liberal programming (see #13). Funny how ScaThomas's constitutional views *always* seem to end up protecting the interests of business over those of the public.

ScaThomas "are often called 'conservative,'" wrote Cohen, "but that does not begin to capture their philosophies. Both vehemently reject many of the core tenets of modern constitutional law." They reject a century-old stream of constitutional thought— one that runs through Justices Oliver Wendell Holmes and Felix Frankfurter to Stephen Breyer—which emphasizes that Supreme Court justices, who are unelected and serve for life, must safeguard democracy by striking down laws made by elected legislators *only* if it is beyond reasonable doubt that they were in error *or* when those laws threaten such essential democratic rights as the rights to vote and to speak—and, arguably, the personal and private choices made by women and gays and lesbians. The protection of democracy also implies, in Breyer's view, permitting affirmative action.

ScaThomas are, by contrast, "originalists" or "textualists" who believe the Constitution should be interpreted to mean exactly what it meant at the time that it was ratified—even though the Constitution itself doesn't specify such interpretation. Not only do originalists imply that they alone know the intentions of the Framers; they are unconcerned with the present-day *consequences* of their approach, which may be seriously harmful. In their view, as law professor Cass Sunstein noted, "If the Equal Protection Clause was originally understood to permit sex discrimination, then courts should permit sex discrimination. If the Second Amendment was originally understood to forbid gun control, then courts should forbid gun control."

ScaThomas meanwhile assert, with absolute certainty, certain principles that are clearly contrary to the letter and spirit of the Constitution. In 2005, on the issue of whether the Ten Commandments could be displayed in government buildings, ScaThomas declared, "we are a religious nation." As Leon Wieseltier observed in the *New Republic:*

> But what does the prevalence of a belief have to do with its veracity, or with its legitimacy? If every American but one were religious, we would still have to construct our moral and political order upon respect for that one. . . . [T]he proposition that "we are a religious nation" is like the proposition that "we are a white nation" or . . . that "we are a heterosexual nation," which is to say, it is a prescription for the tyranny of a majority. . . . The morning's disputations confirmed me in my view of Antonin Scalia's lack of intellectual distinction. . . . [H]e dripped certainties. "Government draws its authority from God." "Our laws are derived from God." . . . "Human affairs are directed by God." "God is the foundation of the state." These are dogmas, not proofs. . . . It is an insult to democratic discussion to

introduce these doctrines without an accompanying sense of the obligation to argue for them. But Scalia dispenses with argument. . . . Scalia's undisturbed experience of obvious truth is a kind of mental decadence.[74]

Addressing a synagogue audience in 2004, Scalia said that European government leaders don't invoke God in public, and asked: "Did it turn out that, by reason of the separation of church and state, the Jews were safer in Europe than they were in the [U.S.]? I don't think so." He must have been unfamiliar with *this* quote: "I say: my Christian feeling tells me that my lord and savior is a warrior [who] recognized the Jews for what they were, and called for a battle against them"—Adolf Hitler (who also said "secular schools can never be tolerated"). The Jews were safer in the U.S., blogger Sarah Posner noted, "because the U.S. has a secular government that protects the rights of all people to practice their own religion (or not practice one at all). Isn't *that* what the founders intended?"[75]

#10: CONDOLEEZZA ~~BU~~ RICE

As I was telling my husb—[pause]—as I was telling President Bush. . . .

—Condoleezza Rice (who has never been married), May 2004

Position sought: President of the United States
Experience: January 2005–Present: U.S. Secretary of State

74 Leon Wieseltier, "God Again," *The New Republic*, March 21, 2005.

75 Sarah Posner, "Scalia on the Separation of Church and State," *The Gadfly*, November 23, 2004.

- Promoted to the most important cabinet position because utterly devoted to "a boss whose sentences she can finish, and who trusts her totally to carry out his wishes," and "unlikely to have any agenda but Mr. **Bush**'s" (*New York Times*)—leaving "no doubt about where this administration is headed—full steam in the same perilous direction" (*The New Republic*).

2001–2004: Director of National Security

- Oversaw the worst national security failure in U.S. history, 9/11. Led in the administration's pre-9/11 neglect of terrorism—holding two sessions on terrorism out of nearly one hundred formal meetings of the national security leadership. Stayed fixated on the Reaganite dream of building a missile defense shield to prevail over the Soviets. Planned to give a speech on "the threats and problems of today and the day after, not the world of yesterday"—that is, missile defense—on 9/11.
- Led in the administration's *cover-up* of its pre-9/11 neglect of terrorism. Suffered severe amneezzia and made literally dozens of literally incredible statements under oath to the 9/11 Commission.
- Led in the administration's campaign to deceive America into war in Iraq. Member of the White House Iraq Group [see #17], set up for that express purpose. Leading purveyor of the administration's *continuing* claims, despite all reports and evidence to the contrary, that Iraq did have WMDs, was pursuing nuclear weapons, and was tied to Al Qaeda.
- Headed the Iraq Stabilization Group, with authority to manage postwar Iraq. Within seven months, the group had become "a metaphor for an Iraq policy that is adrift" (*Washington Post*) and was not publicly mentioned again by the White House.
- Was "one of the weakest National Security Advisers in recent history" (*Washington Post*)—but the most *partisan* adviser ever, as evidenced by stumping for Bush in the 2004 campaign

in defiance of the tradition and need for the national security advisor to remain objective.

- Called the earthquake and tsunamis that killed some 300,000 and left 1.1 million homeless in Southern Asia in December 2004 "a wonderful opportunity" for the U.S. to show its compassion, one that "has paid great dividends for us."

1991–2000: Board member of Chevron and chair of Chevron's Public Policy Committee—whose stated purpose was to monitor "domestic and foreign social, political and environmental issues"—while the company worked with Nigeria's "kill'n'go" Mobile Police and Nigerian troops, who used Chevron helicopters and boats to destroy villages and shoot peaceful protestors at a Chevron oil platform.

Languages: Russian, French, Spanish, BushSpeak (for disinformation and cover-ups).

Hobbies: Playing piano. Shopping for shoes during height of Hurricane Katrina disaster.

Favorite Sayings:

- "I don't think anybody could have predicted that they would try to use . . . a hijacked airplane as a missile." The CIA warned of such an attack twelve times in the seven years before 9/11.
- "No Al Qaeda threat was turned over to the new administration." "I don't remember the Al Qaeda cells as being something that we were told we needed to do something about." According to the 9/11 Commission Report, Richard Clarke in a January 2001 memo to Rice described the "urgent need" for a "principals-level review on the Al Qaeda network." Clarke told Rice "at least twice that Al Qaeda sleeper cells were likely in the United States."
- The Presidential Daily Brief Bush received on August 6, 2001, was merely "historical" and "analytic" in nature and contained "nothing about the threat of attack in the U.S," said Rice, under

oath, before admitting the brief was titled "Bin Laden Determined to Attack Inside the United States."

- "There was no recommendation that we do something about this . . . it was the FBI's responsibility," said the director of national security in Bush's "era of personal responsibility."
- "If we had known an attack was coming against the United States . . . we would have moved heaven and earth to stop it." Rice then admitted she was told an attack was coming and had read some of the chatter that was picked up that spring and summer: "Unbelievable news coming in weeks." "Big event—there will be a very, very, very, very big uproar." "There will be attacks in the near future." But, said the 9/11 Commission Report: "The domestic agencies never mobilized. . . . They did not have direction, and did not have a plan. . . . The borders were not hardened. Transportation systems were not fortified. . . . State and local law enforcement were not marshaled. . . . The public was not warned." And airport security was not beefed up.
- "We do know that [Saddam] is actively pursuing a nuclear weapon." The aluminum tubes Iraq purchased "are only really suited for nuclear weapons programs." Rice knew the government's foremost nuclear experts had declared the tubes "poorly suited" for that use, but she later denied having known "the nature of the dispute," which a former State Department intelligence analyst called "the mother of all intelligence disagreements," about the government's single best piece of evidence of Iraqi WMDs.
- "Not only did Saddam support terrorists, not only was he a weapons-of-mass-destruction threat and all those things"—but at that point (October 2004), the 9/11 Commission and the Duelfer Report had already contradicted both those claims.
- "We don't want the smoking gun to be a mushroom cloud." And *we* don't want the smoke-screening Condi to mushroom into president of the United States.

#9: PAUL WEYRICH:
GODAWFULFATHER OF THE RIGHT

"We are different from previous generations of conservatives. . . . We are radicals, working to overturn the present power structure of this country." "We are in an eternal battle. The battle is between right and wrong, between truth and lies, between life and death. . . . We are in a war." "The real enemy is the secular humanist mindset which seeks to destroy everything that is good in this society. . . . The secular humanist state is very similar to the Soviet state. . . . Remember, you have God. . . . They only have power. That's all that matters to them." "We are in the vanguard of those who understand the threat that true believing Moslems represent to both Christians and Jews and . . . all of us who believe in our Judeo-Christian civilization must fight together to preserve it." Muslims "should be encouraged to leave [America]. They are a 5th column in this country."

That kind of stuff *will* capture the imaginations of the faithful, fearful, fevered, and fatheaded more reliably than will, say, promises of expanded health care coverage. And that stuff is from Paul Weyrich, who has been called the father of the religious right or "New Right."

A phone call from Weyrich to **Karl Rove** is *taken*. A complaint from Weyrich to the Bush White House, and *action* is taken. A call from Weyrich to Domino's Pizza CEO and leading right-wing financier Tom Monaghan, and that pizza is *there* in less than thirty minutes.

Turn over any rock of the radical right and there, it seems, is Weyrich. He cofounded the **Heritage Foundation** (#8) in 1973 and, a year later, the Committee for the Survival of a Free Congress (CSFC), which was among the first grassroots organizations to recruit activists and root for support among evangelical Christian churches. In 1977, CSFC metastasized into the Free Congress Foundation (FCF), which lobbies, for example, for conservative judicial appointments and against gay rights initiatives and which remains the heart of Weyrich's evil empire. In 1979, Weyrich recruited a talented young pastor named Jerry Falwell (okay, he was forty-six), and together they founded the Moral Majority. Falwell went on to record such unforgettable hits as "AIDS is the wrath of a just God against homosexuals" and "Muhammad was a terrorist." Weyrich is also credited with convincing **Pat Robertson** (#55) to run for president in 1988. In 1978, Weyrich's political action committee helped sweep into Congress a new, radical breed of conservatives, including a young Georgian named Newt Gingrich, whom Weyrich had trained years earlier at a campaign seminar for newts.

In 1981—with funding from Texas billionaire Nelson Baker Hunt, a board member and leading financier of the ultra-rightist John Birch Society—Weyrich cofounded the Council for National Policy (CNP), a secretive, high-level, strategy-formulating organization or network or conspiracy whose membership is a Who's Who of the far right: it has included Falwell and Robertson; **Tim LaHaye** (#66), CNP's first president; **Grover Norquist** (#24); **James Dobson** (#15); **Phyllis Schlafly** (#20); **Tom DeLay** (#6); **Sun Myung Moon** (#54); Moral Majority cofounder and "direct-mail titan" or "guru" (your choice) Richard Viguerie; Rev. Donald Wildmon of the American Family Association; Brent Bozell, head of the Parents Television Council; **Discovery Institute** (#34) and Christian-right financier Howard Ahmanson; former attorney general Edwin Meese III; former Energy and Interior secretary and Christian Coalition president Donald Hodel; former **George W. Bush** cabinet members John Ashcroft and Tommy Thompson; senators Jon Kyl and Trent Lott; Oliver North; and Bob Jones III.

In the 1990s, Weyrich played a decisive role in the takeover of the House of Representatives by Gingrich and the right-wing Republicans. In 1999, the FCF bestowed its Liberty Award upon then–House Majority Whip Tom DeLay, Rep. Henry Hyde, and eleven other House managers for "their heroic efforts to try to

save America" by impeaching President Clinton in the wake of the
Monica Lewinsky affair.

In 2001, Weyrich led the lobbying effort for the nomination of
John Ashcroft as attorney general, which was payback for the
Christian right's help for Bush, first against John McCain in the
critical South Carolina primary, then during the Florida election
dispute. In 2004, Weyrich helped persuade the Bushies to change
the subject of the election campaign from Iraq to the culture war
and specifically to the "issue" of gay marriage—"or," he warned,
"we'll be talking about President Kerry."

Weyrich's "habit of flirting with racists and anti-Semites,"
wrote Joe Conason in *Salon*, dates back to his early involvement
with George Wallace's American Independent Party (AIP), which
embraced elements of the John Birch Society and the KKK. In
1976, Weyrich, who regarded the GOP as too moderate, tried to
make his Moral Majority cofounder Richard Viguerie the AIP's
presidential candidate.

"Among the many odious characters affiliated over the years
with Weyrich's [FCF]," Conason noted,

> is Laszlo Pastor, convicted of Nazi collaboration for his
> World War II role in the violently anti-Semitic and pro-
> Hitler Hungarian Arrow Cross party. . . . Another longtime
> Weyrich aide served on the editorial board of the
> *Ukrainian Quarterly*, an ethnic rightist publication
> strongly influenced by former Nazi collaborators. With
> encouragement from Pastor, Weyrich and Pat Buchanan,
> those same émigré extremists campaigned to shut down
> the Justice Department's ongoing pursuit of suspected Nazi
> war criminals. . . . [Another Weyrich associate] was
> revealed to have been an official of the Liberty Lobby, the
> nation's largest anti-Semitic propaganda outlet.

In an 2001 Easter essay, Weyrich—a Catholic and a professed

admirer of the pro-Nazi radio demagogue of the 1930s and forties, Father Coughlin[76]—wrote: "Christ was crucified by the Jews who had wanted a temporal ruler to rescue them from the oppressive Roman authorities. . . . He was not what the Jews expected. . . . Thus He was put to death." Conservatives, including Jewish ones, remained silent—with one exception: journalist Evan Gahr submitted a critique of Weyrich for circulating a "classical anti-Semitic lie" to **David Horowitz** (#31)'s FrontPage. Horowitz rejected the article and banned Gahr permanently from Front-Page.

Conservatives' "double standard on religious bigotry remains disgraceful," Conason noted:

> The Jews in the Nixon White House endured their president's coarse anti-Semitism without a peep, and even made excuses for him. . . . During the Reagan era, few on the right objected to the anti-Jewish bias of Patrick Buchanan, which had been painfully obvious for years. . . . If [Jesse] Jackson or [Al] Sharpton had delivered an Easter sermon dwelling on alleged Jewish responsibility for the death of Christ, the response from the right would have been explosive. . . . When Hillary Clinton was accused [in 2000] of having used an anti-Jewish expletive more than 20 years ago, her conservative enemies instantly went nuclear. But Weyrich . . . apparently merits not only a free pass but an impassioned defense.[77]

Today's conservatives aren't really as "different from previous generations" as Weyrich says—if you go back eight hundred years or so.

76 MediaTransparency.org, among other sources.
77 Joe Conason, "Blinded by the Right," *Salon*, April 24, 2001.

#8: ED FEULNER
AND THE HERITAGE FOUNDATION:
RIGHT-WING TALKING-POINTS . . .
IN MINUTES!

Along with the **American Enterprise Institute** (AEI, #7), the Heritage Foundation is the granddaddy and the most powerful of all the right-wing think tanks set up by corporate interests since the 1970s to sway political and public opinion toward pro-corporate positions.

When Heritage was "invented" in 1973 by two Capitol Hill political aides—**Paul Weyrich** (#9), the foundation's first president, and Edward Feulner, Jr., who has headed Heritage since 1974—this was a new idea. Unlike the "liberal" Brookings Institution, whose founder decreed it would be "free from any political or pecuniary interest," Heritage and AEI were, wrote John Judis, "expressions of [corporate] political and economic interests." At least Heritage was more open about this than AEI. "We're not here to be some kind of Ph.D. committee giving equal time," said its director of research. "Our role is to provide conservative public-policy makers with arguments to bolster our side." Heritage's aim was to influence Congress and the White House on a daily basis and provide Republicans with what Feulner called "quick response [research] capability," typically through article-length "backgrounders" that could be faxed to politicians and the media and read in an hour or less. It was no accident that while most other D.C.-based think tanks were in downtown Washington, Heritage set up its headquarters on Capitol Hill.

Heritage's initial funding came from brewing billionaire **Joseph Coors** (#53) and conspiracy-brewing billionaire **Richard Mellon Scaife** (#21). Since then, funding (around $30 million in 2004) has come from such sources as the Olin, Smith Richardson, and Bradley foundations, the founders of Amway Corp., and corporations such as General Motors, Chase Manhattan, Pfizer,

ExxonMobil, ChevronTexaco, and Shell (which *might* explain Heritage's claim that cars "clean our air"), as well from sources in Taiwan and South Korea, including the Korea Foundation, which conduits money from the South Korean government, **Sun Myung Moon** (#54)'s Unification Church, and, in the early 1980s, Korean intelligence, according to a document discovered by the South Korean National Assembly—an allegation Heritage denied.[78] Unlike most other think tanks, Heritage also raises millions from large numbers of smaller donors through direct-mail fund-raising—aided by the fact that, because it claims not to "lobby" (despite being located almost *in* the Capitol lobby), it retains tax-exempt status as a "charity." By 1985, Heritage's budget equaled those of AEI and Brookings combined.

Its influence on U.S. politics has been enormous ("1 *archaic*: exceedingly wicked; shocking"). The 1981 Heritage book *Mandate for Leadership* served as virtually an operating manual for the incoming Reagan administration. Heritage was "a key architect and advocate of the Reagan Doctrine, by which the U.S. government channeled overt and covert support to anti-Communist resistance movements and right-wing death squads in such places as Afghanistan, Angola, Cambodia and Nicaragua."[79] The foundation itself provided not just research but also direct political and military guidance to rebel/Contra forces. Heritage "also played a key role in building support for Reagan's "Star Wars" space- and faith-based missile defense initiative—a Cold War irrelevancy that diverts U.S. defense resources from real needs to this day (indeed, more than ever under **Rumsfeld** and **Bush**). The Reagan and Bush administrations have been lousy with former Heritage staff, including Reagan's national security advisor Richard Allen, Attorney General Edwin Meese, Navy Secretary John Lehman, and, under Bush II, Labor Secretary **Elaine Chao** (#47), Pentagon

78 "Heritage Foundation," Wikipedia.org.
79 Ibid.

spokesperson Lawrence Di Rita, and L. Paul Bremer, who (disastrously) headed the Coalition Provisional Authority in Iraq.

In partnership with the *Wall Street Journal* (#49), Heritage publishes the annual *Index of Economic Freedom*, which measures countries' freedom mainly in terms of *business's* freedom from taxes and government regulation. (*Labor's* economic freedom to organize and strike, of course, *lowers* a country's score.) After Paul Bremer liberated wealthy Iraqis by instituting a flat tax in their country, Heritage's top economist wrote that "come tax time next April [2004]," Americans "may begin to wonder who's better off," they or the Iraqis. (Seven percent of whom reported attempting suicide during the first year of occupation—a rate 437 times the global average. Taxes still too high, perhaps?)

Domestically, Heritage pushes supply-side economics—or as George Bush, Sr., once called it, "voodoo economics"—which holds that upper-income and corporate tax cuts, and *only* those, spur economic growth. In 2002, the foundation backed legislation that would make it even easier for U.S. companies to use offshore tax havens to evade taxes, and helped block Democrats' efforts to stop rich individuals from doing likewise.

In 2004, an administration-appointed panel stacked with Heritage lobbyists recommended that Congress not increase the federal minimum wage, which had been $5.15 since 1997. As always, the opponents of an increase claimed—despite abundant evidence to the contrary—that it would lead to layoffs. Their concern, you see, was for the *workers*. "Would it be so terrible if they confessed that what really bothers them is that higher labor costs mean less profit?" the *American Prospect* asked.

In December 2004, the Heritage-owned Web site Townhall.com offered a selection of "Politically Incorrect Christmas Gifts," such as:

- *The Politically Incorrect Guide to American History*, by Thomas Woods, which tells the *truth*: "The Puritans didn't steal Indian lands." "The Civil War was more about other issues than about slavery." "Joe McCarthy: a paranoid idiot? No." "How Bill Clinton abused power, abetted Islamists, lied, and wasted billions of taxpayer dollars for nothing" (No, "Bill Clinton" was *not* a typo for "George Bush").

- *The Sword of the Prophet*, by Serge Trifkovic: "What Muslims, multiculturalists, and the media *hope you never find out* about Islam"—namely, "its sanctioning of theft, deceit, lust and murder," and so forth.
- *A Concise History of the Crusades*, by Thomas F. Madden: "Misconceptions about the Crusades [as] a series of unprovoked holy wars against Islam" are "all too common."
- A wide selection of gifts for the **Ann Coulter** (#32) fetishist.
- An exact replica of the sword carried in the Civil War by General "Jo" Shelby, "the Confederate officer famed for never surrendering."

One begins to understand just which "heritage" the foundation stands for.

#7: CHRISTOPHER DEMUTH AND THE AMERICAN ENTERPRISE INSTITUTE

"Who runs the government? American Enterprise Institute for Public Policy Research" (AEI), ran some blogger's headline.

That is at least a 20 percent overstatement. These, however, are no exaggerations:

Right Web: The AEI "is today the single most influential think tank in America and the country's main bastion of neoconservatism." Ralph Nader: AEI "is loaded with corporate money, full of rich fellowships for Washington, D.C., influence peddlers . . . who wallow in plush offices figuring out how to assure that big corporations rule the U.S. and the rest of the world." Ronald Reagan in 1988: AEI "stands at the center of a revolution in ideas of which I, too, have been a part." AEI president Christopher DeMuth in the institute's 1994 Annual Report: "We are delighted to be members in good standing of the Washington Establishment, called upon many times each day for Congressional testimony, media commentary, and advice on all manner of current policy issues." Wikipedia, 2005: AEI "has emerged as one of the leading architects of the **Bush** administration's public policy; more than two dozen AEI alumni have served either in [the administration] or on one of the government's many panels and commissions." *Salon:* "In effect, the far-right AEI was running the [Bush] White House's Iraq policy—and the AEI's war-at-all-costs imperatives drove the Pentagon, too."

Not bad for a tax-exempt *charitable* organization that—legally, at least—is barred from political or lobbying activity and that says it "is strictly nonpartisan and takes no institutional positions" on policy questions. *And* which must make do on around $27 million a year from right-wing donors like the **Coors** (#53), **Scaife** (#21), Olin, and Harry Bradley foundations and from a couple of dozen giant corporations representing the oil, auto, insurance, food, tobacco, and telecom industries. Recent AEI trustees have included the CEOs of American Express, Cigna, Dow Chemical, Exelon, Forbes, Merck, Procter & Gamble, State Farm Insurance —and, until a few years ago, former Enron CEO Kenneth Lay. AEI's chairman is multibillionaire commodities king Bruce Kovner, manager of the world's largest hedge fund (he has been called "George Soros's right-wing twin"). AEI's vice chairman is **ExxonMobil** CEO **Lee Raymond** (#12).

Think tanks like AEI, said the *Washington Monthly*, "provide ideal cover for the advancement of a funder's economic or political agenda by shaping the intellectual atmosphere" in Washington —a process that has been called "deep lobbying." Think tank scholars "enjoy more credibility when quoted in newspapers, speaking on TV, or testifying on the Hill than do paid industry spokesmen," and they can "lobby" without registered lobbyists' legal restrictions—for example, on how much can be spent on meals and junkets for politicians.

DeMuth, who had been President Reagan's "deregulation czar," was brought in to head AEI in 1986 as a result of pressure from funders to push the group further to the right. It was the DeMuth administration that stocked AEI with right-wing ideologues and foreign-policy crazies.

Check out this "nonpartisan" list of AEI fellows, visiting scholars, and alumni: **Dick Cheney** (#2); his wife, Lynne Cheney, founder of a group that monitors American colleges to ensure conservative political correctness; **Antonin Scalia** (#11); Newt Gingrich; Reuel Marc Gerecht, director of the Middle East Initiative at the Project for the New American Century (PNAC; see #4); former Defense Policy Board chair and leading Iraq War promoter Richard Perle; leading *war* promoter **Michael Ledeen** (#26); leading torture defender **John Yoo** (#35); Bush hagiographer and former speechwriter David Frum; former UN ambassador Jeane Kirkpatrick, AEI's head of foreign and defense policy research; former President Gerald Ford; Nixon and Reagan cabinet secretary George Shultz; Bush I White House counsel C. Boyden Gray, who heads a group that pressures the Senate to rubber-stamp Bush II's judicial nominees (*in nominee patris et filii et spiritus* **Santorum**, #23) and is a major force in the **Federalist Society** (#25); neocon patriarch Irving Kristol; Reagan Supreme Court nominee Robert Bork; and conservative pundits Alan Keyes and Ben Wattenberg. AEI maintains close relations with and, hydra-like, generates and spins off other right-wing organizations and think tanks. AEI fellows routinely appear on the *Wall Street Journal* (#49)'s op-ed pages and in other leading right-wing venues.

Nonpartisan AEI is, to put it charitably and nonprofitably, the very crossroads of the vast right-wing conspiracy.

AEI lobbies—I mean, advocates—for deregulation of business, privatization of government services, "tort reform," and tax cuts for the rich, and against environmental regulations. At an AEI luncheon in January 2005, the keynote speaker was novelist Michael Crichton, who had for several years been attacking global warming as junk science and "environmentalism as a religion." Comparing believers in global warming to Nazi eugenicists, Crichton told the AEI audience, "Auschwitz exists because of politicized science." Funny, so does Bush environmental policy (see #18, #37, #38).

AEI's foreign policy positions are essentially those of the PNAC—which, as it happens, rents its office space from AEI. According to journalist George Packer, **Condoleezza Rice** (#10) rejected the help of less pro-war think tanks in planning for postwar Iraq and insisted on AEI because she knew that its attitude was—well, as DeMuth put it: "What's all this planning and thinking about postwar Iraq?" The Bush administration thought such planning "would get in the way of going to war," said Leslie Gelb of the Council on Foreign Relations, whose help was refused.

AEI fellow Laurie Mylroie lives for her theory that the 1993 World Trade Center bombing, along with everything else that has happened since around 1100 AD, was the work of Saddam Hussein. "Mylroie's explanation has found no support in the intelligence community," wrote Jay Bookman in the *Atlanta Journal Constitution*, "and in 2001, her credibility was strained further when she publicly suggested that Timothy McVeigh and Terry Nichols, convicted in the Oklahoma City bombing, might have been dupes acting at Saddam's behest." After 9/11, Mylroie naturally claimed *that* was Saddam's doing as well—*and* the anthrax-letter attacks a few weeks later, notwithstanding CIA and FBI analysis that the source was probably domestic.

Not only did AEI (and **Rupert Murdoch** [#14]'s HarperCollins) publish Mylroie's books; Cheney and the other chief architects of the Iraq War embraced her theory lovingly, nay, erotically. Richard Perle and former deputy defense secretary Paul Wolfowitz supplied cover blurbs for the 2002 reissue of Mylroie's book *The War against America*, to which **John Bolton** (#59) and Cheney aide Lewis "Scooter" Libby also lent assistance. Analysts at the Defense Intelligence Agency were instructed to study the book, "which they had already concluded was groundless." Nonetheless, "the message was, why can't we prove this is right?" a DIA official said.[80]

Four other examples of AEI scholarship demand your undivided revulsion:

- Jude Wanniski, the godfather of supply-side economics, used an AEI fellowship to write his 1978 book *The Way the World Works*, which promoted the idea that tax cuts lead to increased government revenue. (See, for example, the Bush deficit.) The voodoo economist has more recently become an adviser to Louis Farrakhan, and in 2002 wrote to George W. Bush: "I believe Min. Farrakhan is the most important Muslim leader in the world." (That's what *I* call a Laffer curve. . . .)

- AEI fellow Charles Murray is the coauthor of the 1994 book *The Bell Curve*, which argued that intelligence test score differences among the races were up to 80 percent genetically determined. Murray's book proposal said the book would make whites "who fear they are closet racists . . . feel better about things they already think but do not know how to say."

- In 1995, AEI published Dinesh D'Souza's best-selling book *The End of Racism*. D'Souza denies the existence of institutionalized racism in America, opposes affirmative action, and claims that the attitude of defiance bred under slavery has been self-destructive to African Americans in the long term. (You *might* suppose it had produced the civil rights movement.)

80 Jay Bookman, "[AEI] Scholar's Fallacy Fed Push for War," *Atlanta Journal Constitution*, September 21, 2003.

- Best of all is AEI fellow John Lott, whose 1998 book title *More Guns, Less Crime* sums up his main mission in life—and the quality of AEI scholarship. Lott produced data seeming to show that deaths from multiple-victim shootings dropped 90 percent in states that passed laws permitting concealed weapons. The gun lobby seized on his claims, and legislators in several states used his book to push through liberalization of gun laws. In 2003, Yale and Stanford economists published a paper charging Lott with falsifying his statistics. An expert panel set up by the National Academy of Sciences reviewed Lott's data and concluded: "There is no credible evidence that 'right-to-carry' laws . . . either decrease or increase violent crime." The editor-in-chief of *Science* called Lott a "fraud." And "Mary Rosh," a former student of Lott who defended him vigorously on various Web sites, turned out to be Lott himself, as he admitted. But "AEI did not fire Lott, or reprimand him, or even investigate him," the *Washington Monthly* noted. In fact, DeMuth had hired Lott after several AEI fellows warned him they suspected Lott of lack of scholarly honesty. Even after Roshgate, DeMuth defended Lott, questioned critics of his work, and bought him a lovely new skirt.

It's true what they say: guns don't kill people, right-wing think tanks do.

#6: TOM DELAY: I SAW THE BEST GOVERNMENT IN THE WORLD DESTROYED BY AVARICE . . . *WITH APOLOGIES TO ALAN GINSBERG AND HIS POEM* HOWL

By the time you read this, former House Majority Leader DeLay (R-TX) may be in prison for violating campaign finance laws and who knows what else. But what were we to do—simply omit DeLay, the font, origin, and symbol of modern Republican corruption?

DeLay, godfather of the GOP-corporate money-patronage-influence racket known as the K Street Project (see #24), which fills top lobbying positions with party loyalists, uses them to pressure Congress, ensures that corporate cash flows only to Republicans, and in turn delivers the legislation the lobbyists want?

DeLay, who warned corporations against employing or funding Democrats, declaring, "If you want to play in our revolution, you have to live by our rules,"

DeLay, purveyor of legislative favors to consumer-gouging energy companies and other corporate special interests,

DeLay, whose rise in politics was fueled by Enron and who, with Ken Lay, authored "the Enron bill," which would have completely deregulated the electricity industry,

DeLay, whose love is endless oil and stone! DeLay whose soul is electricity and banks!

DeLay, Congress's leading recipient of tobacco-industry hard money, who added a provision to *antiterrorism* legislation that would have prevented governments from recouping billions from tobacco companies in lost revenues and damages,

DeLay, who, after receiving more than $159,000 from the airline industry for his "leadership PAC," ordered mandatory security training for flight attendants changed to voluntary training, which flight attendants would have to pay for out of their own pockets,

Who used a newly set-up children's charity as a cover to collect banned "soft money" in the form of tax-deductible, "charitable" donations during the 2004 Republican National Convention,

Who took a $100,000 check for one of his "charities" from a private prison company that was lobbying for further privatization of Texas prisons and had a history "fraught with malfeasance, mismanagement, and abuse,"

Who fought for years against a campaign reform bill, boasting, "The DeLay strategy worked. Delay, delay, delay,"

Who, asked whether he would *ever* require public disclosure of political donors' names—whether he believed "the citizens of this country have the right to know who pays for a campaign ad"—replied: "Absolutely not,"

DeLay, whose mind is pure machinery! DeLay, whose blood is running money! DeLay, whose fingers are ten armies! DeLay, whose breast is a cannibal dynamo!

DeLay, former employer of indicted lobbyist Michael Scanlon and receiver of favors from Scanlon and his indicted partner Jack Abramoff, "one of my closest and dearest friends,"

DeLay, architect of the infamous, apartheid-style congressional redistricting in Texas in 2003, whose way was paved by illegal funding of state races with corporate money raised by "DeLay Inc.," according to DeLay's and his henchmen's grand jury indictments,

Who, violating House rules, sicked the Department of Homeland Security on a group of domestic terrorists known as Texas Democratic legislators, who had left the state to prevent a vote on DeLay's redistricting plan,

Who used his legal defense fund "as another avenue to raise significant special interest money and contributions from elected officials" who wished to curry favor,

Who offered a political endorsement to the son of Rep. Nick Smith (R-MI) in exchange for Smith's "yea" vote on **Bush's** Medicare bill (Smith said he was also offered $100,000),

DeLay, who "has taken every norm the Legislature has operated on and shredded it," said Norm Ornstein of the conservative **American Enterprise Institute** (#7), adding: "On a scale of 1 to 10, Democrats abused their majority status at about a level 5 or 6. . . . Republicans today have moved it to about an 11",

DeLay, who—while telling his evangelical brethren that God was

using him to promote "a biblical worldview" in U.S. politics—
earned four rebukes from the House Ethics Committee over a
six-year period during which only five other members of Congress received even one,

DeLay, who, when reminded by a waiter about the laws against
smoking in a federal building, said, "I *am* the federal government,"

DeLay! DeLay! Nightmare of DeLay! DeLay the loveless! Mental
DeLay! DeLay the heavy judger of men!

Yes, it *is* enough to make you howl.

#5: OSAMA BIN LADEN: DEAD OR ALIVE

The ruling to kill the Americans and their allies is an
individual duty for every Muslim who can do it. . . .
This is in accordance with the words of Almighty God.
                                    —Osama bin Laden, February, 1998

What more need be said? He preaches that mass murder is a religious duty. Millions admire him, and who knows how many are
willing to kill and die and win a place in paradise in the service of
the jihad he preaches. They think in literally millennial terms, in
which short-term setbacks mean nothing. They may not quit any-
time soon. And if they do, bin Laden may be the hero in whose
name, far in the future, the movement and organization will recon-
stitute themselves.

I would only add that, in bringing us 9/11—with all its loss of
life and the resulting constant strain on the nation's and world's
political, economic, and nervous systems—bin Laden and company also reversed the falling political fortunes of the president
who failed to prevent the attack, sending his approval ratings up

to more than 90 percent. Bin Laden gave **George W. Bush** a huge stock of political capital to pursue his plutocratic and theocratic agenda, pretexts to attack everything from environmental protections to Iraq, and Republican victories in 2002 and 2004. In turn, bin Laden's stock was raised in the Muslim world by the Bushites' Iraq misadventure.

But without Osama bin Laden and 9/11, we would still have had Bush's first term, at least, with all that implies—including, probably, the Iraq War, for which some other rationale would surely have been found. Without Bush—*with* an administration in office that was more focused on real threats and less on ideological and personal obsessions—the 9/11 plot might have been foiled. That is why bin Laden is at #5 and not at #1.

#4: DONALD RUMSFELD: WEAKENING AMERICA'S DEFENSES

That is the slogan that should be wallpapered all over the set when Rummy (or his boss) gives public speeches. How has our defense secretary weakened national security in the course of his long career? Through harebrained personal and ideological fixations, astounding arrogance and hubris, habitual dishonesty, and sheer, bumbling incompetence. Rummy:

- Made nice with Saddam in Baghdad as Reagan's special envoy during two visits in 1983 and 1984. That was the *good* Saddam—when he was using chemical weapons against the Iranians and when Bechtel, the construction giant run by Reagan-Bush pals, wanted to build an oil pipeline across Iraq. Rummy was dispatched to Baghdad by Secretary of State George Schultz, who had headed Bechtel until just the year before. On Rummy's second visit, despite official U.S. policy barring the export of military equipment to Iraq, some was evidently provided on a "don't-ask-don't-tell" basis.

- Became a card-carrying member of the Project for the New American Century (PNAC), a group formed in 1997 that included **Cheney**, Lewis Libby, Richard Perle, Paul Wolfowitz, and **John Bolton** (#59)—most of the future architects of **Bush** foreign policy and the Iraq debacle. The group advocated unchallenged global hegemony by the United States, huge military spending increases, repudiation of the Anti-Ballistic Missile Treaty, the development of a missile defense system and of nuclear weapons for actual battlefield use, "preemption" rather than containment of rivals, and "a more permanent [U.S.] role" in the Persian Gulf region, for which "the unresolved conflict with Iraq provides the immediate justification," according to a PNAC report that became the blueprint for the "Bush Doctrine." Or rather, the Cheney-Rumsfeld doctrine. Rumsfeld and Cheney were hell-bent on curing America of the "Vietnam syndrome"—its post-'Nam aversion to war; on exorcising, as Maureen Dowd put it, "all the ghosts of the 60's . . . and the feeling that America is in decline or in the wrong"; and on restoring the war-making powers, secrecy, and unaccountability of the pre-Watergate "imperial presidency." In the summer of 2001, Rumsfeld's office sponsored a study of ancient empires—Alexander the Great's, the Romans, the Mongols—to determine how they had maintained their dominance.

- Threatened a Bush veto when Congress tried to fill gaps in Bush's counterterrorism budget with $600 million diverted from missile defense, Rummy's pet project. That was on September 9, 2001.

- *Five hours* after the 9/11 attacks, told his aides to come up with plans for striking Iraq. Argued that Afghanistan, home to Al Qaeda's training camps, did not offer "enough good targets. . . . We should do Iraq." (Why not Mexico or Canada? Even more convenient.)

- Within a month of 9/11, had created "a boutique CIA in the bowels of the Pentagon," as the *New York Times* put it, because the other CIA wasn't giving the Bushies the "intelligence" they wanted connecting Saddam to terrorists. Was soon claiming there was "bullet-proof" evidence of close ties. No evidence was ever put forward, making its bullet-resistance impossible to test. Told America: "No terrorist state poses a greater or more immediate threat" than Iraq.
- Said "everything humanly possible" was done to avoid war. More like, to *ensure* war. UN weapons inspectors were not given a chance; every possible fabrication about the Iraqi "threat" was put forward; and a last-minute, back-channel offer by Saddam to let U.S. troops and experts search suspected weapons sites, to turn over a suspect in the 1993 World Trade Center bombing, to give U.S. energy companies preferential rights to Iraqi oil, and to hold UN-supervised elections—an offer Richard Perle, to whom it was relayed, called "astonishing"—was rebuffed. Dick and Donald and George *had* to have this war, or else what fun would life be?
- Rebuked, then sacked Army chief of staff General Eric Shinseki for predicting a prolonged occupation requiring hundreds of thousands of troops.
- Permitted Coalition Provisional Authority head Paul Bremer to disarm and dismantle the Iraqi military—an error the U.S. has been struggling unsuccessfully to reverse ever since.
- Said of the looting of Iraq's museums of antiquities following the invasion: "It is the same picture of some person walking out of some building with a vase and you see it 20 times. And you think, my goodness. . . . Is it possible that there were that many vases in the whole country?" Moron.
- Permitted 380 tons of high explosives to be looted from a bunker in Iraq. Iraq's nuclear repositories were likewise left unguarded and looted.
- Used a preposterous statistical sleight to suggest that U.S. troops in Iraq were safer than residents of Washington, D.C.

- Failed to provide the troops with necessary body and vehicle armor; opposed a law passed by Congress requiring the Pentagon to reimburse soldiers and their families who paid for such equipment themselves; then failed to implement the law. In September 2005, a year after Congress demanded action, the Associated Press reported: "Soldiers and their parents are still spending hundreds and sometimes thousands of dollars for armor they say the military won't provide." (But billions for experimental and unworkable defense against missiles none of our enemies possess? Sure.) Rumsfeld dismissed the criticisms by saying, "you go to war with the army you have." "You go to war prepared," suggested a father and ex-Marine who had just spent $1,000 for armor for his son, a Marine serving in Fallujah.

- Banned photographs of returning coffins of U.S. troops, and kept as many as thirty thousand serious U.S. casualties— so-called "nonbattle" injuries and diseases—out of official published casualty reports.

- Paved the way for torture at Abu Ghraib, Guantánamo, and who knows how many secret military prisons by (a) designating "unlawful combatants" as a category of people who merit no legal rights; (b) conspiring with Cheney to ignore the Constitution by deciding that domestic and international prohibitions against torture were "inapplicable"; and (c) secretly approving "exceptional interrogations" and twenty-four specific "techniques" such as keeping prisoners stripped naked, threatening them with dogs, and depriving them of sleep. Then said he "cannot conceive" that the Abu Ghraib guards thought their actions were condoned or encouraged. And: "What was going on in the midnight shift in Abu Ghraib prison halfway across the world is something that clearly someone in Washington, D.C., can't manage or deal with. And so I have no regrets."

- Lied that the Abu Ghraib "abuses" were "an exceptional, isolated" case. Maj. Gen. Antonio Taguba's report cited "numerous incidents of sadistic, blatant and wanton criminal abuses" at Abu Ghraib. Abuses at Guantánamo proved to be even worse. Moreover, as Jonathan Schell wrote in *The Nation*, "An unexpected problem arose. The prisoners neither possessed the desired information nor had committed the offenses." Taguba estimated that more than 60 percent of Abu Ghraib detainees were civilians "of no intelligence value." By November 2005, not a single Guantánamo inmate had even been brought before a tribunal.

- *Was* appalled by the *photos* from Abu Ghraib: "People are running around with digital cameras and taking these unbelievable photographs and then passing them off, against the law, to the media, to our surprise." As comedian Jon Stewart put it: "If I've said it once, I've said it a thousand times—we've got to find these weapons of mass documentation."
- Promoted Lt. Gen. Ricardo Sanchez, who authorized the presence of attack dogs during interrogations, among other harsh measures, to four-star general. Made Maj. Gen. Geoffrey Miller, who was "credited" with bringing Guantánamo's methods to Abu Ghraib, senior commander in charge of detention operations in Iraq. Put Maj. Gen. Barbara Fast, the highest-ranking intelligence officer tied to the Abu Ghraib scandal, in charge of the U.S. Army's main interrogation training facility at Fort Huachuca, Arizona.
- Warned that criticism of U.S. policy in Iraq might embolden terrorists. Republican Senator and Vietnam veteran Chuck Hagel: "I find that offensive. I heard that same argument in Vietnam for 11 years: 'Don't dare question. Don't dare probe.' "
- Defended Deputy Undersecretary of Defense Lt. Gen. William Boykin after he told Christian groups in 2003 that Muslims worship "an idol," Islamists hate the U.S. "because we're a Christian nation," terrorists "will only be defeated if we come against them in the name of Jesus," and—referring to a Muslim Somali warlord—"I knew my God was bigger than his." Rumsfeld:

Boykin "has an outstanding record" and "[t]here are a lot of things that are said . . . we are free people and that's the wonderful thing about our country." Congress shall make no law preventing imbeciles and bigots from achieving high official rank.

- Declined to comment after Marine Lt. Gen. James N. Mattis said in February 2005 about serving in Iraq: "Actually, it's a lot of fun to fight. . . . It's fun to shoot some people."

- Opposed the 9/11 Commission's chief recommendation, the creation of a Director of National Intelligence, because he did not want to diminish the Pentagon's overwhelming control over intelligence agencies and budgets.

- Named top executives from military contractors as heads of the three services, including first-term Secretary of the Army Thomas White from Enron, where he ran one of the shadiest of Enron's businesses, Enron Energy Services, which lost upward of $500 million. (Private-sector expertise and efficiency—that's what government needs.) Altogether, named at least thirty-two former executives, consultants, or major shareholders of top military contractors to top policy-making positions.

- Proposed legislation that would allow the Department of Defense (DOD) to award major contracts without congressional review or public accountability; strip DOD employees of union rights, annual pay raises, and whistle-blower protections; and exempt the DOD from environmental rules on 23 million acres of public land and from numerous congressional oversight rules, such as the need to notify Congress of the leasing of major equipment. At the time, the DOD was arranging for the Air Force to lease one hundred fuel-tanker aircraft from Boeing at a cost to taxpayers of billions of dollars more than buying the planes outright.

- More than four years after 9/11, *where in Allah's name is **Osama bin Laden**?* Well, as Rumsfeld answered helpfully in

October 2002: "He's either alive and well, or alive and not too well, or not alive."

- "[T]he leader of the opposition Northern Alliance, Masoud, lay dead, his murder ordered by Saddam Hussein. . . . Saddam Hussein, if he's alive, is spending a whale of a lot of time trying to not get caught. And we've not seen him on a video since 2001"—Rumsfeld, September 2004, once again confusing bin Laden with Saddam.

The cynicism Rumsfeld has done so much to induce in Americans—principally by crying "wolfowitz" over Iraq, then bumbling so badly and squandering so much in lives, treasure, and credibility there—could prove disastrous when it comes to winning public support for action on *real* national security threats. "But he's so studly!" Remember all that? "He's a rock star!" Hm. I'm thinking "grateful dead." I don't know why.

#3: KARL ROVE: WHERE "ALL LOW ROADS LEAD"

Republicans say he is unfairly maligned. So do I. Even though he has literally become a cartoon villain (the animated TV series *American Dad* depicted him as a vampire), and the documentary *Bush's Brain* calls him "the most powerful political consultant in American history . . . in essence, a co-president," I say Karl Christian Rove doesn't get all the credit he deserves, because even his critics are reluctant to believe the White House harbors *so* vile a boil on the body politic, so foul a canker or (where's my thesaurus) pustule of base trickery, corruption, and partisan extremism.

In 2000, **George W. Bush** promised to change the tone in Washington. No one has done more to accomplish that—or to *get*

Bush to Washington and keep him there—than "the boy genius," or "Turd Blossom" (a flower that grows from cow shit), as Bush likes to call Rove. (Apt enough, give or take a blossom.) The "Mayberry Machiavelli," as a former Bush official called him, is said to reread his Machiavelli "the way the devout study their Bibles." Former Nixon White House counsel John Dean, referring to Nixon's two "heavies," called Rove "Haldeman and Ehrlichman all in one." Rove, he added, makes Nixon aide Charles Colson, who once said he would run over his grandmother to get Nixon reelected, "look like a novice."

No doubt there are fascinating examples of Rove's political chicanery starting in nursery school; but let's fast-forward to college, when, in 1970, he used a false identity to gain entry to Illinois Democrat Alan Dixon's campaign offices, stole some letterhead stationery, and sent out a thousand fake campaign rally fliers promising "free beer, free food, girls and a good time for nothing." Speaking of breaking into Democrats' offices, during the 1972 presidential campaign, Rove—a protégé of Watergate conspirator Donald Segretti—toured the country as head of the College Republican National Committee, giving young Republicans "dirty tricks" training and boasting about the Dixon caper. Later, according to John Dean, "the Watergate prosecutors were interested in Rove's activities . . . but because they had bigger fish to fry they did not aggressively investigate him."

Rove worked on the 1980 vice-presidential campaign of George H. W. Bush and introduced him to his friend and mentor, Lee Atwater, who was, in the words of admirers, "notorious as the very definition of smashmouth politics, in which every effort is made to destroy the reputations, careers and lives of political opponents"; "the Darth Vader of the Republican Party," "the guy who went negative for the sheer joy of it." During the 1980s, Rove's Austin, Texas, consulting firm worked on the campaigns of such statesmen as then-Congressman Phil "We're going to keep on until we're hunting Democrats with dogs" Gramm. While working for the 1986 Texas gubernatorial campaign of Republican Bill Clements, Rove claimed his office had been bugged by the Democrats. A police and FBI investigation raised suspicions that Rove had planted the bug himself.

In 2003, Rove, perhaps criminally, revealed to columnist Robert Novak and *Time* reporter Matt Cooper the identity of CIA operative Valerie Plame Wilson, allegedly in revenge against and/or to discredit her husband, former ambassador Joseph Wilson, who had contradicted administration claims about Iraqi efforts to purchase nuclear weapons fuel. Immediately after Novak's column appeared, Rove called MSNBC's Chris Matthews and told him Wilson's wife was "fair game." Well, oddly enough, back in 1992, Rove was fired from George H. W. Bush's presidential campaign after he planted a story with, hello, Robert Novak about dissatisfaction with Bush's fund-raising chief Robert Mosbacher, Jr. (who, Novak wrote, had "shoved [Rove] aside").

Rove wasn't exactly out on the street: His other clients included John Ashcroft in his successful 1994 Senate campaign; cigarette pusher Philip Morris; and, by 1993, George W. Bush's first Texas gubernatorial campaign. Rove made "tort reform"— that is, making it harder to sue corporations like, say, tobacco companies—the campaign's centerpiece. And as Rove boasted, "business groups flocked to us."

Wrote one blogger, "Somehow, when Rove's candidate needs a boost, an opponent is attacked with a whisper campaign; rumors and innuendos emerge that have nothing to do with the issues . . . yet have a strong, visceral influence on voters."[81] During Bush's 1994 gubernatorial campaign, a rumor began that incumbent Ann Richards might be a lesbian. During Bush's crucial South Carolina primary campaign against John McCain in 2000, McCain's military service was attacked and his mental stability, after being a POW for more than five years, was questioned. Rove was allegedly

81 "Bush's Brain," Blogcritics.org, September 4, 2004.

behind a "push poll" that asked potential voters, "Would you be more likely or less likely to vote for John McCain for president if you knew he had fathered an illegitimate black child?" ~~Rove~~ The mother, it was rumored, was a prostitute. Actually, McCain had adopted a dark-skinned Bangladeshi daughter from Mother Theresa's organization.

To Rove, who gave an enthusiastic endorsement to right-wing guru **David Horowitz** (#31)'s book *The Art of Political War*, politics was, as Rove said, "a gigantic war"—against gay rights, abortion rights, all opponents of the Robin-Hood-in-reverse Bush economic agenda, all remnants of moderation and bipartisanship:

- In December 2000, Rove masterminded the emergency airlift of Republican supporters and thugs to Florida to intimidate local election officials during the recount fight.
- In his first five months in the White House, Rove refused to divest stocks he held in drug companies, energy companies (including Enron), and Intel. During that time, he met with drug industry lobbyists, was involved in administration energy policy meetings, and successfully advocated a merger between a Dutch company and an Intel supplier. Ethics? Trifling details. We're at war!
- When the Senate Judiciary Committee rejected Bush's Fifth Circuit Court nominee Charles Pickering, who had a long record of opposition to racial integration, civil rights, and voting rights and possible links with a segregationist organization in his native Mississippi, Rove called the rejection a "judicial lynching"—yet paid no fines for indecency!
- The day before a commencement speech in 2002 in which Bush called on students to embrace "some cause larger than his or her own profit," Rove told a conference of business leaders: "This is war, and we need to make an ongoing commitment to winning the effort to repeal the death tax"—that is, the estate tax, which affected only the richest two percent

of Americans—people like those in his audience and his administration.

- In 2002, as Bush was promising he had "no ambition whatsoever to use the war as a political issue," Rove advised GOP operatives to tell the American people they could "trust the Republican Party to do a better job of . . . protecting America" and to focus on Iraq as the key to maintaining "a positive issue environment" for the 2002 midterm elections.

- Eight months before the invasion of Iraq, Rove chaired meetings of the secretive White House Iraq Group (WHIG), which managed the White House's disinformation campaign about the threat from Saddam Hussein. Rove helped write and coordinate speeches by Bush officials emphasizing Iraq's nuclear threat.

- Rove was an old friend of Bob Perry, the chief financier of the so-called Swift Boat Veterans for Truth ad campaign that lyingly smeared John Kerry's Vietnam record in the months before the 2004 election. According to political analyst and recovering Republican Marshall Wittmann, "Anyone who was involved in the 2000 McCain campaign, as I was, knows exactly who is responsible for the 'Swift boat' slime attack on Senator Kerry—in Bush World, all low roads lead to Rove." Bush called Rove "the architect" of his victory.

- In June 2005, Rove declared: "Conservatives saw the savagery of the 9/11 attacks and prepared for war; liberals . . . wanted to prepare indictments and offer therapy and understanding for our attackers." Now, in actual fact, what Rove and his crew saw in 9/11 was a domestic political opportunity. And what every Democratic senator voted for was military force against Al Qaeda. (The White House called Rove's comments "very accurate" and said the calls for an apology were "somewhat puzzling.")

"What Mr. Rove understood, long before the rest of us," wrote columnist Paul Krugman, is that . . . we're living in a country in which there is no longer such a thing as nonpolitical truth [and] there are few, if any, limits to what conservative politicians can get away with: the faithful will follow the twists and turns of the party line with a loyalty that would have pleased the Comintern. . . . Mr. Rove also understands, better than anyone else in American politics, the power of smear tactics. Attacks . . . don't have to be true, or even plausible, to undermine that person's effectiveness. All they have to do is get a lot of media play.

(You can believe Krugman: he's **Goldberg**'s #8.)

After the outing of Valerie Plame, the White House repeatedly denied that Rove had any involvement. "Totally ridiculous," said spokesman Scott McClellan. "I didn't know her name and didn't leak her name," Rove told CNN in 2004. Rove "did not tell any reporter that Valerie Plame worked for the CIA," Rove's lawyer insisted in July 2005. Right—Rove only told Matt Cooper that "Wilson's wife" "apparently" worked at "the agency," and that she had authorized her husband's trip to Niger (false). His wording also suggested that, contrary to his later denials, he knew he was outing an *undercover* operative, which can be a federal felony. As for Novak, Rove only *confirmed* it when Novak told *him* that he'd heard Plame was a CIA operative. Rove later admitted to violating his signed White House agreement not to disclose classified information to unauthorized persons. Straight-shootin' Dubya had said he would fire anyone who did that or who was involved in leaking Plame's identity.

Whether or not Rove broke laws, there's no question that by leaking the identity of a WMD expert at a time when the United States had gone to war based on the supposed threat from such weapons, he damaged national security for partisan advantage. "If a Democrat had done that," Krugman remarked, "Republicans would call it treason."

But, two and a half years after the act, Rove remained Bush's senior adviser, indeed had been "promoted" to deputy chief of staff in charge of policy. (As if Rove hadn't been in charge of policy all along.) And "none of the 306 Republican members of Congress had expressed public concern about Rove's continued role in the Bush Administration."[82]

#2: GEORGE W. BUSH: "WHERE WINGS TAKE DREAM"

Strong. Steady. Staunch. Steady, strong, staunch, and steadfast. Steadfast in his "resolve" to reward his corporate backers and cronies. To cut taxes for the richest and shift the tax burden to the middle class and poor. Put tax cuts for the rich ahead of everything, even national security. Conquer Iraq—kick some fuckin' ass—threat or no threat, casualties or (as he told **Pat Robertson** [#55] there would be) "no casualties." Strut like the great war leader. Own the U.S. flag. Own the "war on terrorism" while *blowing* the war on terrorism.

Steadfast in his "resolve" to expand presidential power and secrecy. Keep his employers, the public, in the dark. Turn Congress and the courts into handmaidens of the president. Stack the courts with radical reactionaries. Spy on citizens. Weaken or eliminate laws protecting workers and consumers from corporate greed and negligence. Turn everything from the public schools to the armed forces to natural disasters into profit-makers for well-connected companies. Destroy the most successful and vital government social programs, Social Security and Medicare, to enrich Wall Street financial services firms, his biggest funders. Destroy the most critical environmental protections to repay his energy,

82 "Karl Rove," Wikipedia.org.

mining, logging, and real estate industry backers. Deny the hell out of global warming and keep us addicted to oil. Fill every top regulatory post with executives and lobbyists from the very industries they are supposed to oversee in the *public* interest. Not rest until every American corporation that helped fund his campaigns is safe from the threat of social responsibility—while preaching "personal responsibility" and "moral values" to everyone else. "Solve" every social problem with "faith" and privatization. Destroy the separation of church and state and replace the teaching of science with religion to accommodate supporters who want to make America a Christian Iran where abortion is a crime, gays are forced backed into closets, Muslims are despised, Jews' function is to help bring about an Apocalypse in which they themselves will perish, and Zoroastrians don't stand a chance in Hell.

Stem cells. Phony AIDS initiative. Assault weapons. Bankruptcy "reform." Tort "reform." "PATRIOT Act." Abu Ghraib. New Orleans. *My Pet Goat.* Indefinite detention without charges at the president's whim. **Alberto Gonzales.** John Ashcroft. **Karl Rove. Dick Cheney. Halliburton.** "Scooter" Libby. **Donald Rumsfeld.** Paul Wolfowitz. Douglas Feith. **John Bolton. Condi** "I don't remember, I was not told" **Rice.** General William "Muslims worship an idol" Boykin. Code Yellow. Code Orange. Code Yellow. Michael "Brownie" Brown. Bernard Kerik. "Kennie Boy" Lay. Armstrong Williams and Maggie Gallagher and "Karen Ryan" and "Jeff Gannon" and Jessica Lynch and Pat Tillman and John Poindexter and the Office of Strategic Influence and the Swift Boat Veterans for Truth and the Ministry of Truth and the Department of Good and Evil.

The "Grecians." The "Kosovians." "So what state is Wales in?" "Is our children learning?" "More and more of our imports are coming from overseas." "I know how hard it is to for you to put food on your family." "Families is where our nation finds hope, where wings take dream." "Fool me once, shame—shame on—you. . . . Fool me—can't get fooled again."

Shame on *you*, #57: You got fooled again.

#1: DICK HEAD-OF-GOVERNMENT CHENEY

Bush can't dump Cheney, for it is Cheney, not Rove, who is Bush's backroom brain. . . . Cheney knows how to play Bush so that Cheney is absolutely no threat to him, makes him feel he is president, but Bush can't function without a script, or without Cheney. Bush is head of state; Cheney is head of government.

> —Former Nixon White House counsel John Dean, interview in *Salon*,
> March 31, 2004

The Cheney-Bush administration—and that's the accurate order—has simply become more than I can stand. . . . I am more fearful for the state of this nation than I have ever been—because this country is in the hands of an evil man: Dick Cheney.

> —Republican former Minnesota governor Elmer Andersen, *Minneapolis*
> *Star-Tribune*, October 13, 2004

[Cheney has] come to stand for special interests, secrecy and political coercion.

> —Sidney Blumenthal, *Salon*, July 1, 2004

Cheney [as CEO of Halliburton] was willing first to do business with countries on the U.S. government's terror list, then to travel abroad and condemn U.S. counter-terrorism policy when it got in his way. In the process, Cheney proved repeatedly he could be trusted to put Halliburton's bottom line ahead of his country's national security. . . . Far from embodying lofty ideals of "freedom" and "democracy," Cheney's record depicts a man governed by greed.

> —David Sirota and Jonathan Baskin,
> *American Prospect*, September 1, 2004

Criticizing—and violating—U.S. trade sanctions against Iran and Libya while CEO of **Halliburton** (#72). Doing business with Indonesia's Suharto (named "the most corrupt leader in modern history" by Transparency International) and Nigeria's rulers ($180 million in Halliburton bribes) and death squads. Violating U.S. trade sanctions against Saddam Hussein's Iraq and against Burma, where Halliburton built a gas pipeline involving forced labor, forced "depopulation" of whole towns, "and even murder, torture and rape."[83] "You've got to go where the oil is." Knowing Halliburton was using accounting gimmicks to inflate profits on paper by $120 million. Selling most of his shares shortly before news of an SEC investigation of the accounting practices wiped out most of the stock's value.

Refusing to name energy industry insiders who met with his White House "task force" to shape national energy policy to their liking (after writing in 1999 to Vice President Al Gore opposing more stringent air pollution standards and calling on Gore to address any new rules in "full and open debate"). Delivering an "energy policy" that was little more than a series of multibillion-dollar tax breaks for oil and gas companies.

"Taking charge" of a new terrorism task force in May 2001 that never met once before 9/11. Doing "a tremendous job," as **Bush** would say, in hampering inquiries into the 9/11 "intelligence failures" (read, White House leadership failures and lack of interest in Al Qaeda). Leading the drive to war in Iraq and the fabrication of phony intelligence to justify it. (Cheney, who had five draft deferments during the 1960s, was the "steamroller" for the war, wrote Bob Woodward.) Repeatedly suggesting Saddam-Al Qaeda links but refusing to provide any evidence. Trying to shut down the Senate Select Committee on Intelligence inquiry into prewar intelligence on Iraq. Pressuring the committee to put all the blame on the CIA and ignore the White House's role entirely. Plamegate.

83 EarthRights International.

(Was Valerie Plame preparing a sting operation involving Cheney-connected businesses selling WMD components in the Middle East?) "Coordinating" no-bid Iraq contracts for Halliburton (from which he continued to receive about $150,000 a year in deferred pay). Defending Halliburton as "unfairly maligned" after it over-charged the U.S. government by around $165 million *and* failed to deliver vital goods and services to the troops.

Making deep cuts in active-duty troop strength, the Reserves, and the National Guard and boasting of setting "an all-time record" for killing weapons programs as defense secretary under Bush I—leaving the U.S. military stretched thin even fifteen years later—then attacking John Kerry in 2004 for having "voted against weapons systems for the military." Saying that if Americans "make the wrong choice" on Election Day, 2004, "then the danger is that we'll get hit again" by terrorists "in a way that will be devastating." "I think **Donald Rumsfeld** (#4) is the best Secretary of Defense the United States has ever had." **Wal-Mart** (#44) "exemplifies some of the very best qualities in our country—hard work, the spirit of enterprise, fair dealing, and integrity." **Fox News** (#28) is "more accurate" than other media. To a senator who questioned Halliburton contracts: "Fuck off."

To the "second" in command but first in our hearts: I second that motion.

ACKNOWLEDGMENTS

Thanks to Renée Sicalides, Shelley Hopkins, Gill Kent, Ruth Baldwin, and Carl Bromley for their editing help; Anna Sussman and Emily Lodish for their research assistance; William Clark, Elliot Majerczyk, and Brenda Chabon for their advice and encouragement; everyone who suggested names or suffered my going on about the whole thing all the time; and my mother, Ruth Huberman, for asking constantly if I was eating and sleeping properly. (I wasn't, by the way, as though the rest of you care.) And thanks, of course, to Bernard Goldberg (#73), the inspirer and *necessitator* of this book—the *sine qua non, reductio ad absurdum*, and *podex perfectus* of "100 People" books.